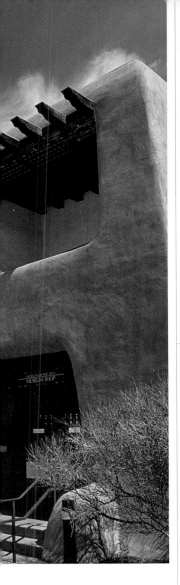

2 Dining

A rising national culinary destination, the city has superb restaurants that offer both traditional New Mexican fare and more eclectic global cuisine. *(Ch. 3)*

3 Railyard District

The popular indoor-outdoor farmers' market, a fun urban park, and hip restaurants, galleries, and indie shops keep things bustling in this redeveloped area. *(Ch. 2)*

W9-BWJ-368

4 Scenic Drives

Santa Fe is a nexus of road trips through jaw-dropping scenery. Musts include the Turquoise Trail, south toward Albuquerque, and the High Road to Taos. *(Ch. 8)*

5 Santa Fe Opera

Simply stunning, the opera's indoor-outdoor amphitheater is carved into a hillside. A noted summer festival presents five works every June through August. *(Ch. 5)*

6 Galleries

Gallery hopping is a prime activity in Santa Fe, including First Friday night Art Walks. The city's nearly 200 galleries tempt with ceramics, paintings, photography, and sculptures for all budgets. *(Ch. 6)*

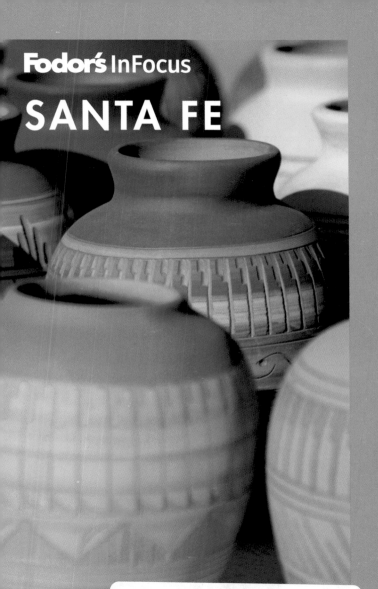

Fodor's InFocus

SANTA FE

15
TOP EXPERIENCES

Santa Fe offers terrific experiences that should be on every traveler's list. Here are Fodor's top picks for a memorable trip.

1 Museums

Learn about local and regional culture at the excellent institutions on Santa Fe's Museum Hill. The Museum of Indian Arts and Culture (pictured) presents interactive exhibits in its adobe-style building. *(Ch. 2)*

7 Meow Wolf

Spend a few hours wandering through this wildly imaginative and completely immersive 30,000-square-foot collaborative art installation. It's a wild ride that's great fun for kids and adults. *(Ch. 2)*

8 Intimate Inns

Unwind in a southwestern-style abode like the captivating Rosewood Inn of the Anasazi. Traditional artwork, handcrafted furnishings, and authentic woven rugs capture the city's unique ambience. *(Ch. 4)*

9 Georgia O'Keeffe

Connect with the work of this prominent American Modernist artist, who drew inspiration from the area's landscape, at the exceptional Georgia O'Keeffe Museum. You can also visit her house in Abiquiú. *(Ch. 2, 8)*

10 Holiday Season

Ancient buildings aglow in lights, Christmas Eve strolls, and elaborate celebrations make the city's most festive season a truly magical experience. *(Ch. 2)*

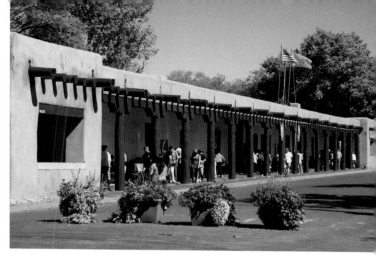

11 Santa Fe Plaza

Join the fun in this lively square, the city's historic heart and gathering spot. Events such as September's Fiestas de Santa Fe are good times to explore galleries and restaurants or browse the shops. *(Ch. 2)*

12 Kasha Katuwe Tent Rocks National Monument

Known for bizarre sandstone rock formations that look like stacked tepees, this box canyon is a memorable hiking getaway about 40 miles west of Santa Fe. *(Ch. 8)*

13 Bandelier National Monument

See the cave dwellings and ceremonial kivas of ancestral Puebloans in this 33,000-acre natural wonder with abundant wildlife, waterfalls, cliffs, and mesas. *(Ch. 8)*

14 Spas

Indulge yourself in a day (or two) of relaxation at a tranquil retreat such as Bishop's Lodge's ShaNah Spa, set against the striking Sangre de Cristo Mountains. *(Ch. 4)*

15 Native American Culture

Santa Fe celebrates Native culture at historic monuments and museums throughout the city. During the summer, Museum Hill's Milner Plaza hosts Native American dances and jewelry-making demonstrations. *(Ch. 2)*

CONTENTS

ABOUT THIS GUIDE

Fodor's Recommendations
Everything in this guide is worth doing—we don't cover what isn't—but exceptional sights, hotels, and restaurants are recognized with additional accolades. Fodor'sChoice★ indicates our top recommendations. Care to nominate a new place? Visit Fodors.com/contact-us.

Trip Costs
We list prices wherever possible to help you budget well. Hotel and restaurant price categories from $ to $$$$ are noted alongside each recommendation. For hotels, we include the lowest cost of a standard double room in high season. For restaurants, we cite the average price of a main course at dinner or, if dinner isn't served, at lunch. For attractions, we always list adult admission fees; discounts are usually available for children, students, and senior citizens.

Hotels
Our local writers vet every hotel to recommend the best overnights in each price category, from budget to expensive. Unless otherwise specified, you can expect private bath, phone, and TV in your room. For expanded hotel reviews,visit Fodors.com.

Restaurants
Unless we state otherwise, restaurants are open for lunch and dinner daily. We mention dress code only when there's a specific requirement and reservations only when they're essential or not accepted. For expanded restaurant reviews, visit Fodors.com.

Credit Cards
The hotels and restaurants in this guide typically accept credit cards. If not, we'll say so.

Top Picks
★ Fodor'sChoice

Listings
⊠ Address
⊠ Branch address
☏ Mailing address
☎ Telephone
🖷 Fax
⊕ Website
✉ E-mail

🎫 Admission fee
🕑 Open/closed times
Ⓜ Subway
✛ Directions or Map coordinates

Hotels & Restaurants
🏨 Hotel
🛏 Number of rooms
🍽 Meal plans

✕ Restaurant
⌂ Reservations
🏛 Dress code
🚫 No credit cards
$ Price

Other
⇨ See also
☞ Take note
🏌 Golf facilities

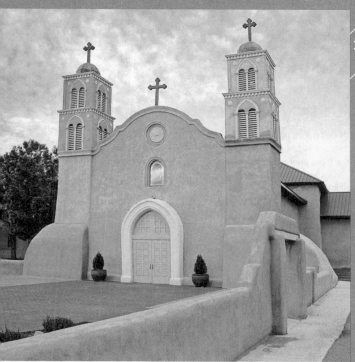

EXPERIENCE
SANTA FE

WHAT'S WHERE

1 The Plaza. The heart of historic Santa Fe.

2 Old Santa Fe Trail and South Capitol. A historic section that joins the Plaza after passing the state capitol and some of the area's oldest neighborhoods.

3 East Side and Canyon Road. One of the city's oldest streets, lined with galleries, shops, and restaurants housed in adobe compounds.

4 Museum Hill. Four excellent museums, the Santa Fe Botanical Garden, a café, and superb views of the Jémz and Sangre de Cristo mountains.

5 The Railyard District. A model for urban green space; the vibrant farmers' market, hip restaurants, shops, art galleries, and SITE Santa Fe contemporary art museum.

6 West of the Plaza. This historic, mostly residential, neighborhood has several notable restaurants and shops on Guadalupe Street and in a popular shopping mall, DeVargas Center.

7 North Side. This scenic expanse of Sangre de Cristo foothills is home to the charming village of Tesuque, the Santa Fe Opera House, and some high-profile resorts (Ten Thousand Waves, the Four Seasons).

8 South Side. Affordable chain lodgings, good restaurants and craft breweries, and the city's hottest arts attraction, Meow Wolf.

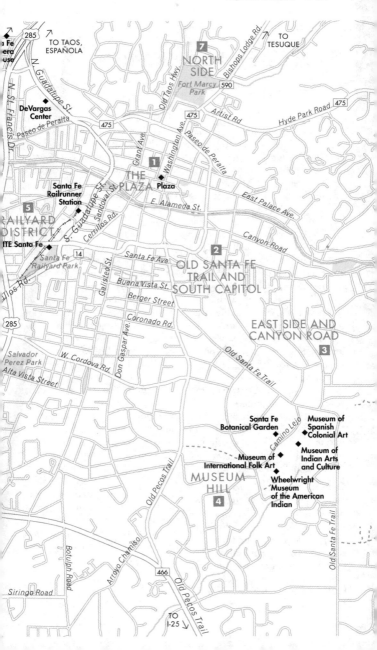

TO TAOS,
ESPAÑOLA

TO
TESUQUE

7

**NORTH
SIDE**

Fort Marcy
Park

285

a Fe
era
use

N. St. Francis Dr.

N. Guadalupe St.

DeVargas
Center

Paseo de Peralta

475

Grant Ave.

Old Taos Hwy.

Washington Ave.

Bishops Lodge Rd.

590

Artist Rd.

475

Paseo de Peralta

Hyde Park Road   475

1

**THE
PLAZA**

Plaza

Santa Fe
Railrunner
Station

S. Guadalupe St.

Sandoval St.

Cerrillos Rd.

E. Alameda St.

East Palace Ave.

RAILYARD
DISTRICT

5

ITE Santa Fe

14

Santa Fe
Railyard Park

llos Rd.

285

Galisteo St.

Santa Fe Ave.

Buena Vista St.

Berger Street

Coronado Rd.

Canyon Road

2

**OLD SANTA FE
TRAIL AND
SOUTH CAPITOL**

**EAST SIDE AND
CANYON ROAD**

3

Salvador
Perez Park

Alta Vista Street

W. Cordova Rd.

Don Gaspar Ave.

Old Santa Fe Trail

Old Santa Fe Trail

Santa Fe
Botanical Garden

Camino Lejo

Museum of
Spanish
Colonial Art

Museum of
International Folk Art

Museum of
Indian Arts
and Culture

Wheelwright
Museum
of the American
Indian

**MUSEUM
HILL**

4

Old Pecos Trail

Botulph Road

Arroyo Chamiso

466

Old Pecos Trail

Siringo Road

TO
I-25

SANTA FE PLANNER

When to Go

Hotel rates are highest in summer. Between September and November and in April and May they're lower, and (except for the major holidays) from December to March they're the lowest. Santa Fe has four distinct seasons, and the sun shines brightly during all of them (about 320 days a year). June through August—when most of the city's famous arts festivals take place—temperatures typically hit the high 80s to low 90s during the day and the low 50s at night, with afternoon rain showers usually cooling the air. The often sudden rain showers can come unexpectedly and quickly drench you. September and October bring beautiful weather and a marked reduction in crowds. Temperatures—and prices—drop significantly after Halloween. December through March is ski season. Spring comes late at this elevation. April and May are blustery, with warmer weather finally arriving in May.

Getting Here and Around

Santa Fe is easy to reach by plane but a full day's drive from major metro areas in the neighboring states. Unless you're up for a long road trip (the scenery en route is spectacular, especially coming from Arizona, Utah, and Colorado), it generally makes the most sense to fly here.

Most visitors to Santa Fe and north-central New Mexico fly into the state's main air gateway, Albuquerque International Sunport (ABQ), which is served by all of the nation's major domestic airlines as well as some smaller regional ones; there are direct flights from all major West Coast and Midwest cities and a few big East Coast cities. From here it's an easy 60-minute drive to Santa Fe, or a 2½-hour drive to Taos (shuttle services are available). Santa Fe Municipal Airport (SAF) has ramped up commercial service in recent years and is an increasingly viable option with direct flights on American Airlines from Dallas and Phoenix and United Airlines from Denver. A car is your best way to get around the region. You can see much of Downtown Santa Fe and Taos on foot, but a car is handy for exploring farther afield. In Albuquerque a car is really a necessity for any serious touring and exploring. Note that it's easy to get from Albuquerque to Santa Fe either by regularly scheduled shuttle bus or on the scenic Rail Runner commuter train. *For more flight information and ground transportation options, see the Travel Smart section at the back of this book.*

WHAT'S NEW IN NORTHERN NEW MEXICO

Art on the Edge

These days you'll find a growing crop of galleries in the area specializing in abstract, contemporary, and often international works. One of the first major forces in the city's artistic evolution, the acclaimed SITE Santa Fe museum, opened in 1995 but underwent a dramatic redesign and expansion in fall 2017. The surrounding Railyard District has seen an emergence of provocative, modern galleries in recent years, as have Downtown and Canyon Road. But the biggest artistic development in Santa Fe has been the opening of a permanent multimillion-dollar art complex by Santa Fe's edgy Meow Wolf art collective.

Hotel Happenings

Several spa-oriented resorts in the region have recently upped their game, including the historic and tranquil Ojo Caliente Mineral Springs Resort & Spa, about an hour north of Santa Fe, which took over and completely redesigned the beautiful Sunrise Springs Spa Resort on Santa Fe's South Side. On the horizon, with an anticipated opening of summer 2018, the historic and storied Bishop's Lodge Resort has undergone an ambitious renovation and expansion following its acquisition by the posh Auberge Resorts group. Guests will be able to enjoy a new restaurant, lounge, and spa facilities while soaking up dazzling views of the Sangre de Cristo Mountains. In 2017 in Albuquerque, the city's newest upscale accommodation, Hotel Chaco, opened in Old Town, and one of the state's most enchanting hideaways, Los Poblanos Inn, completed a $10-million expansion that added additional guest rooms, a new lobby, and a stunning farm-to-table restaurant, Campo.

Craft Beverages on Tap

Sure, craft breweries are popping up like daisies in every zip code in the nation. But the beer scenes in Santa Fe, Taos, and especially Albuquerque—which has more beer producers per capita than Portland, Oregon—are especially impressive and innovative. Among the up-and-coming standouts, consider Duel Brewing—which specializes in Belgian-style farmhouse ales—in Santa Fe, Taos Mesa Brewing in Taos, and La Cumbre, Bosque, Bow & Arrow, Drafty Kilt, and Tractor breweries in Albuquerque, all of which are earning raves, and awards, for their distinctive creations. New Mexico has a surprisingly robust wine-making culture, too. The most celebrated winery in the state, Gruet, opened a stylish tasting room in Santa Fe in 2017 just off the lobby of the historic St. Francis.

IF YOU LIKE

Historic Sites

There's no state in the Union with a richer historical heritage than New Mexico, which contains not only buildings constructed by Europeans well before the Pilgrims set foot in Massachusetts but also still-inhabited pueblos that date back more than a millennium. Santa Fe and the surrounding region are particularly rife with ancient sites, including mystical Native American ruins and weathered adobe buildings. Stately plazas laid out as fortifications by the Spanish in the 17th century still anchor many communities in this part of the state, including Albuquerque, Las Vegas, Santa Fe, and Taos. Side trips from these cities lead to ghost towns and deserted pueblos that have been carefully preserved by historians. Here are some of the top draws for history buffs.

Santa Fe's **San Miguel Mission** is a simple, earth-hue adobe structure built in about 1625—it's the oldest church still in use in the continental United States.

A United Nations World Heritage Site, the 1,000-year-old **Taos Pueblo** has the largest collection of multistory pueblo dwellings in the United States.

The oldest public building in the United States, the Pueblo-style **Palace of the Governors** anchors Santa Fe's historic Plaza and has served as the residence for 100 Spanish, Native American, Mexican, and American governors; it's now the state history museum.

A scenic hour-long side trip from Santa Fe, the small town of Las Vegas, which was developed as a major stop on the Old Santa Fe Trail, has one of the most picturesque plazas in New Mexico and is also home to several historic districts and more than 900 buildings on the National Register of Historic Places.

Hiking Adventures

At just about every turn in northern New Mexico, whether you're high in the mountains or low in a dramatic river canyon, hiking opportunities abound. Five national forests cover many thousands of acres around New Mexico, as do 40 state parks and a number of other national and state monuments and recreation areas. Ski areas from Albuquerque north to Taos make for great mountaineering during the warmer months, and the state's many Native American ruins are also laced with trails.

Hiking is a year-round activity in Santa Fe and the surrounding area, as you can virtually always find temperate weather somewhere in the state. Consider the following areas for an engaging ramble.

1

About midway between Santa Fe and Albuquerque, **Kasha-Katuwe Tent Rocks National Monument** is so named because its bizarre rock formations look like tepees rising over a narrow box canyon. The hike here is relatively short and only moderately challenging, offering plenty of bang for the buck.

On the main road to Santa Fe's ski area, the **Aspen Vista Trail** takes in breathtaking fall-foliage scenery but makes for an enjoyable trek in spring and summer, too—in winter, it's a popular spot for snowshoeing.

One of the more strenuous hiking challenges in the state is **Wheeler Peak**. The 8-mile round-trip trek to New Mexico's highest point (elevation 13,161 feet) rewards visitors with stunning views of the Taos Ski Valley.

From the northeastern fringes of Albuquerque, **La Luz Trail** winds 9 miles (with an elevation gain of more than 3,000 feet) to Sandia Crest.

Dramatic Photo Ops
Northern New Mexico's spectacular landscapes and crystal-clear atmosphere can help just about any amateur with a decent camera—or even phone—produce professional-looking photos. Many of the common scenes around the state seem tailor-made for photography

sessions: terra-cotta-hued adobe buildings against azure blue skies, souped-up lowrider cars cruising along wide-open highways, and rustic fruit and chile stands by the sides of rural roads. In summer, dramatic rain clouds contrast with vermilion sunsets to create memorable images. Come fall, shoot the foliage of cottonwood and aspen trees, and in winter, snap the state's snowcapped mountains.

The **High Road to Taos,** a stunning drive from Santa Fe with a rugged alpine backdrop, encompasses rolling hillsides studded with orchards and tiny villages.

More than 500 balloons lift off from the **Albuquerque International Balloon Fiesta,** affording shutterbugs countless opportunities for great photos—whether from the ground or the air. And there are year-round opportunities to soar above the city.

The dizzyingly high **Rio Grande Gorge Bridge,** near Taos, stands 650 feet above the Rio Grande—the reddish rocks dotted with green scrub contrast brilliantly against the blue sky.

GREAT ITINERARIES

ALBUQUERQUE TO TAOS: NEW MEXICO MOUNTAIN HIGH

Day 1: Albuquerque

Start out by strolling through the shops of Old Town Plaza, then visit the New Mexico Museum of Natural History and Science and Albuquerque Museum of Art and History. For lunch, stop by the Indian Pueblo Cultural Center to sample the hearty indigenous-inspired fare at Pueblo Harvest Cafe.

In the afternoon, drive east a couple of miles along Central to reach the University of New Mexico's main campus—with its gracious adobe buildings and outstanding Maxwell Museum of Anthropology—and the nearby Nob Hill District, a hip bastion of offbeat shops and noteworthy restaurants. If it's summer, meaning that you still have some time before the sun sets, it's worth detouring from Old Town to Far Northeast Heights (a 15-minute drive), where you can take the Sandia Peak Aerial Tramway 2.7 miles up to Sandia Peak for spectacular sunset views of the city. Either way, plan to have dinner back in Nob Hill, perhaps at Frenchish or Bistronomy B2B. If you're still up for more fun, check out one of the neighborhood's lively lounges and craft-beer bars.

Days 2 and 3: Santa Fe

On Day 2, head to Santa Fe early in the morning by driving up the scenic Turquoise Trail; once you arrive in town, explore the adobe charms of the Downtown central Plaza. Visit the Palace of the Governors and check out the adjacent New Mexico History Museum. A short drive away at the nearby Museum of Indian Arts and Culture you can see works by talented members of the state's pueblos, and across the courtyard at the Museum of International Folk Art, you can see how different cultures in New Mexico and elsewhere in the world have expressed themselves artistically. Return Downtown and give yourself time to stroll its narrow, adobe-lined streets, and treat yourself to some authentic New Mexican cuisine in the evening, perhaps with a meal at The Shed or Cafe Pasqual's.

On your second day in town, plan to walk a bit. Head east from the Plaza up to Canyon Road and peruse the galleries. Have lunch at one of the restaurants midway uphill, such as the Teahouse or El Farol. If you're up for some exercise, hike the foothills—there are trails beginning at the Randall Davey Audubon Center and also from the free parking area (off Cerro Gordo Road) leading into the Dale Ball Trail Network, both a short drive from the Plaza.

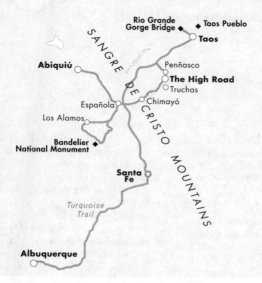

You might want to try one of Santa Fe's truly stellar, upscale restaurants your final night in town, either La Boca or Sazón.

Day 4: Abiquiú

From Santa Fe, drive north up U.S. 285/84 through Española, and then take U.S. 84 from Española up to Abiquiú, the fabled community where Georgia O'Keeffe lived and painted for much of the final five decades of her life. On your way up, make the detour toward Los Alamos and spend the morning visiting Bandelier National Monument. In Abiquiú, plan to tour Georgia O'Keeffe's home (open early March–late November).

Days 5 and 6: Taos

Begin by strolling around Taos Plaza, taking in the galleries and crafts shops. Head south two blocks to visit the Harwood Museum. Then walk north on Paseo del Pueblo to the Taos Art Museum at Fechin House. In the afternoon,

drive out to the Rio Grande Gorge Bridge. Return the way you came to see the Millicent Rogers Museum on your way back to town. In the evening, stop in at the Adobe Bar at the Taos Inn and plan for dinner at Love Apple or Byzantium. On the second day, drive out to Taos Pueblo in the morning and tour the ancient village while the day is fresh. Return to town and go to the Blumenschein Home and Museum, lunching afterward at El Gamal. After lunch drive out to La Hacienda de los Martinez for a look at early life in Taos and then to Ranchos de Taos to see the San Francisco de Asís Church.

Day 7: The High Road

On your final day, drive back down toward Albuquerque and Santa Fe via the famed High Road, which twists through a series of tiny, historic villages—including Peñasco, Truchas, and Chimayó. In the latter village, be sure to stop by El Santuario de Chimayó. Have lunch at

Rancho de Chimayó, and do a little shopping at Centinela Traditional Arts. From here, it's a 30-minute drive to Santa Fe.

SANTA FE SIGHTS

It's best to explore Santa Fe one neighborhood at a time and arrange your activities within each. If you've got more than two days, be sure to explore the northern Rio Grande Valley. ■ TIP→ **For the best tour, combine your adventures in Santa Fe with some from the Day Trips section, which highlights several trips within a 30- to 90-minute drive of town.**

Plan on spending a full day wandering around Santa Fe Plaza, strolling down narrow lanes, under portals, and across ancient cobbled streets. Sip coffee on the Plaza, take in a museum or two (or three) and marvel at the cathedral. The **New Mexico History Museum** and **Palace of the Governors** are great places to start to gain a sense of the history and cultures that influence this area. ■ TIP→ **Take one of the docent-led tours offered by the museums.** Almost without exception the docents are engaging and passionate about their subjects. You gain invaluable insight into the collections and their context by taking these free tours. Inquire at the front desk of the museums for more information.

A few miles south of the Plaza on Museum Hill, you'll find four world-class museums, all quite different and all highly relevant to the culture of Santa Fe and northern New Mexico, plus the Santa Fe Botanical Garden. Start at the intimate gem, the **Museum of Spanish Colonial Art,** where you'll gain a real sense of the Spanish empire's influence on the world beyond Spain. The **Museum of International Folk Art** is thoroughly engaging for both young and old. If you have the stamina to keep going, have a tasty lunch at the Museum Hill Café and then visit the **Museum of Indian Arts and Culture** before moving on to the **Wheelwright Museum of the American Indian.** There is a path linking all these museums together, and the walk is easy. The museum shops are all outstanding—if you're a shopper, you could easily spend an entire day in the shops alone.

A short walk from any of the Downtown lodgings, Canyon Road should definitely be explored on foot. Take any of the side streets and stroll among historical homes and ancient *acequias* (irrigation ditches). If you really enjoy walking, keep going up the road past Cristo Rey Church, where the street gets even narrower and is lined with residential compounds. At the top is the **Randall Davey Audubon Center,** which draws bird-watchers.

GLOSSARY OF TERMS

Perhaps more than any other region in the United States, New Mexico has its own distinctive cuisine and architectural style, both heavily influenced by Native American, Spanish-colonial, Mexican, and American frontier traditions. The brief glossary that follows explains terms used frequently in this book.

Menu Guide

Aguacate: Spanish for avocado, the key ingredient of guacamole.

Albóndigas: Meatballs, usually cooked with rice in a meat broth.

Bizcochitos: Buttery cookies flavored with cinnamon and anise seeds and served typically at Christmas but available throughout the year.

Burrito: A warm flour tortilla wrapped around meat, beans, and vegetables and smothered in chiles and cheese; many New Mexicans also love breakfast burritos (filled with any combination of the above, along with eggs and, typically, bacon or sausage and potatoes).

Calabacitas: Summer squash, usually served with corn, chiles, and other vegetables.

Carne adovada: Red-chile-marinated pork (or, occasionally, chicken).

Chalupa: A corn tortilla deep-fried in the shape of a bowl, filled with pinto beans (sometimes meat), and topped with cheese, guacamole, sour cream, lettuce, tomatoes, and salsa.

Chicharrones: Fried pork rinds.

Chilaquiles: Often served at breakfast, this casserole-like dish consists of small pieces of fried tortillas baked with red or green chiles, bits of chicken or cheese, and sometimes eggs.

Chile: A stewlike dish with Texas origins that typically contains beans, beef, and red chile.

Chile relleno: A poblano pepper peeled, stuffed with cheese or a special mixture of spicy ingredients, dipped in batter, and fried.

Chiles: New Mexico's famous hot peppers, which come in an endless variety of sizes and in various degrees of hotness, from the thumb-size jalapeño to the smaller and often hotter serrano. They can be canned or fresh, dried or cut up into salsa. Most traditional New Mexican dishes are served either with green, red, or both types of chiles (ask for "Christmas" when indicating to your server that you'd like both red and green). Famous regional uses for green chile include green-chile stew (usually made with shredded pork), green-chile cheeseburgers, and green-chile-and-cheese tamales.

Chimichanga: The same as a burrito, only deep-fried and topped with a dab of sour cream or salsa. (The chimichanga was allegedly invented in Tucson, Arizona.)

Chipotle: A dried smoked jalapeño with a smoky, almost sweet, chocolaty flavor.

Chorizo: Well-spiced Spanish sausage, made with pork and red chiles.

Enchilada: A rolled or flat corn tortilla filled with meat, chicken, seafood, or cheese, an enchilada is covered with chile and baked. The ultimate enchilada is made with blue Native American corn tortillas. New Mexicans order them flat, sometimes topped with a fried egg.

Fajitas: A Tex-Mex dish of grilled beef, chicken, fish, or roasted vegetables topped with peppers, onions, and pico de gallo, served with tortillas; traditionally known as *arracheras*.

Flauta: A tortilla filled with cheese or meat and rolled into a flutelike shape ("flauta" means flute) and lightly fried.

Frijoles refritos: Refried beans, often seasoned with lard or cheese.

Frito Pie: Originally from Texas but extremely popular in New Mexican diners and short-order restaurants, this savory, humble casserole consists of Fritos snack chips layered with chile, cheese, green onions, and pinto beans.

Guacamole: Mashed avocado, mixed with tomatoes, garlic, onions, lemon juice, and chiles, used as a dip, a side dish, or a topping.

Hatch: A small southern New Mexico town in the Mesilla Valley, known for its outstanding production and quality of both green and red chiles. The "Hatch" name often is found on canned chile food products.

Huevos rancheros: New Mexico's answer to eggs Benedict—eggs doused with chile and sometimes melted cheese, served on top of a corn tortilla (they're best with a side order of chorizo).

Nopalitos: The pads of the prickly pear cactus, typically cut up and served uncooked in salads or baked or stir-fried as a vegetable side dish. (The tangy-sweet, purplish-red fruit of the prickly pear is often used to make juice drinks and margaritas.)

Posole: Resembling popcorn soup, this is a sublime marriage of lime, hominy, pork, chiles, garlic, and spices.

Quesadilla: A folded flour tortilla filled with cheese and meat or vegetables and warmed or lightly fried so the cheese melts.

Queso: Cheese; an ingredient in many Mexican and Southwestern recipes (cheddar or Jack is used most commonly in New Mexican dishes).

Ristra: String of dried red chile peppers, often used as decoration.

Salsa: Finely chopped concoction of green and red chile peppers, mixed with onion, garlic, and other spices.

Sopaipilla: Puffy deep-fried bread that's similar to Navajo fry bread (found in Arizona and western New Mexico); it's served either as a dessert with honey drizzled over it or savory as a meal stuffed with pinto beans or meat.

Taco: A corn or flour tortilla served either soft, or baked or fried and served in a hard shell; it's then stuffed with vegetables or spicy meat and garnished with shredded lettuce, chopped tomatoes, onions, and grated cheese.

Tacos al carbón: Shredded pork cooked in a mole sauce and folded into corn tortillas.

Tamale: Ground corn made into a dough, often filled with finely ground pork and red chiles; it's steamed in a corn husk.

Tortilla: A thin pancake made of corn or wheat flour, a tortilla is used as bread, as an edible "spoon," and as a container for other foods. Locals place butter in the center of a hot tortilla, roll it up, and eat it as a scroll.

Trucha en terra-cotta: Fresh trout wrapped in corn husks and baked in clay.

Verde: Spanish for "green," as in chile verde (a green chile sauce).

Art and Architecture

Adobe: A brick of sun-dried earth and clay, usually stabilized with straw; a structure made of adobe.

Banco: A small bench, or banquette, often upholstered with handwoven textiles, that gracefully emerges from adobe walls.

Bulto: Folk-art figures of a santo (saint), usually carved from wood.

Camposanto: A graveyard.

Capilla: A chapel.

Casita: Literally "small house," this term is generally used to describe a separate guesthouse.

Cerquita: A spiked, wrought-iron, rectangular fence, often marking grave sites.

Coyote fence: A type of wooden fence that surrounds many New Mexico homes; it comprises branches, usually from cedar or aspen trees, arranged vertically and wired tightly together.

Farolito: Small votive candles set in paper-bag lanterns, farolitos are popular at Christmastime. The term is used in northern New Mexico only. People in Albuquerque and points south call the lanterns *luminarias,* which in the north is the term for the bonfires of Christmas Eve.

Heishi: Technically the word means "shell necklace," but the common usage refers to necklaces made with rounded, thin, disc-shaped beads in various materials, such as turquoise or jet.

Hornos: Domed outdoor ovens made of plastered adobe or concrete blocks.

Kiva: A circular ceremonial room, built at least partially underground, used by Pueblo Indians of the Southwest. Entrance is gained from the roof.

Kiva fireplace: A corner fireplace whose round form resembles that of a kiva.

Nicho: A built-in shelf cut into an adobe or stucco wall.

Placita: A small plaza.

Portal: A porch or large covered area adjacent to a house.

Pueblo Revival (also informally called Pueblo style): Most homes in this style, modeled after the traditional dwellings of the Southwest Pueblo Indians, are cube or rectangle shaped. Other characteristics are flat roofs, thick adobe or stucco walls, small windows, rounded corners, and viga beams.

Retablo: Holy image painted on wood or tin.

Santero: Maker of religious images.

Terrones adobes: Adobe cut from the ground rather than formed from mud.

Viga: Horizontal roof beam made of logs, usually protruding from the side of the house.

EXPLORING
SANTA FE

Updated
by Andrew
Collins

ON A PLATEAU AT THE base of the Sangre de Cristo Mountains—at an elevation of 7,000 feet—Santa Fe brims with reminders of four centuries of Spanish and Mexican rule, and of the Pueblo cultures that have been here for hundreds of years more.

The town's placid central Plaza has been the site of bull-fights, gunfights, political rallies, promenades, and public markets since the early 17th century. A one-of-a-kind destination, Santa Fe is fabled for its chic art galleries, superb restaurants, and diverse shops selling everything from Southwestern furnishings and cowboy gear to Tibetan textiles and Moroccan jewelry. If Santa Fe had a somewhat provincial, regional vibe at one time, the scene has changed considerably of late, with more and more retail and dining mixing local with international, often cutting-edge, styles.

La Villa Real de la Santa Fe de San Francisco de Asísi (the Royal City of the Holy Faith of St. Francis of Assisi) was founded in the early 1600s by Don Pedro de Peralta, who planted his banner in the name of Spain. During its formative years, Santa Fe was maintained primarily for the purpose of bringing the Catholic faith to New Mexico's Pueblo Indians. In 1680, however, the Indians rose in revolt and the Spanish colonists were driven out of New Mexico. The tide turned 12 years later, when General Don Diego de Vargas returned with a new army from El Paso and recaptured Santa Fe. To commemorate de Vargas's recapture of the town in 1692, Las Fiestas de Santa Fe celebration—which includes the infamous burning of Zozóbra—has been held annually since 1712.

Following de Vargas's defeat of the Pueblos, the then-grand Camino Real (Royal Road), stretching from Mexico City to Santa Fe, brought an army of conquistadors, clergymen, and settlers to the northernmost reaches of Spain's New World conquests. In 1820 the Santa Fe Trail—a prime artery of U.S. westward expansion—spilled a flood of covered wagons from Missouri onto the Plaza. After Mexico achieved independence from Spain in 1821, its subsequent rule of New Mexico further increased this commerce. The Santa Fe Trail's heyday ended with the arrival of the Atchison, Topeka & Santa Fe Railway in 1880. The trains, and later the nation's first highways, brought a new type of settler to Santa Fe—artists who fell in love with its cultural diversity, history, and magical color and light. Their presence attracted tourists, who quickly became a primary local source of income.

Santa Fe is renowned for its arts scene, vibrant tricultural (Native American, Hispanic, and Anglo) heritage, and adobe architecture. The Pueblo people built their homes using a "puddled-mud" method (liquid mud poured between upright wooden frames), which melded well with the adobe brick construction introduced to the Spanish by the Moors. The Hispanic culture, still deeply rooted in its ancient ties to Spain and Catholicism, remains a strong influence on the easier pace of this city. Cosmopolitan visitors from around the world are consistently surprised by the city's rich and varied cultural offerings despite its relatively small size. Often referred to as the "City Different," Santa Fe became the first American city to be designated a UNESCO Creative City, acknowledging its place in the global community as a leader in art, crafts, design, and lifestyle.

ORIENTATION AND PLANNING

Humorist Will Rogers said on his first visit to Santa Fe, "Whoever designed this town did so while riding on a jackass, backwards, and drunk." The maze of narrow streets and alleyways confounds motorists; however, pedestrians delight in the vast array of shops, restaurants, flowered courtyards, and eye-catching galleries at nearly every turn. Park your car, grab a map, and explore the town on foot.

THE PLAZA

Much of the history of Santa Fe, New Mexico, the Southwest, and even the West has some association with Santa Fe's central Plaza, which New Mexico governor Don Pedro de Peralta laid out in 1610. The Plaza was already well established by the time of the Pueblo revolt in 1680. Freight wagons unloaded here after completing their arduous journey across the Santa Fe Trail. The American flag was raised over the Plaza in 1846, during the Mexican War, which resulted in Mexico's loss of all its territories in the present Southwestern United States. For a time the Plaza was a tree-shaded park with a white picket fence. In the 1890s it was an expanse of lawn where uniformed bands played in an ornate gazebo. Particularly festive times on the Plaza are the weekend after Labor Day, during Las Fiestas de Santa Fe,

TOP REASONS TO GO

A winter stroll on Canyon Road: There are few experiences to match walking this ancient street on Christmas Eve when it's covered with snow, scented by piñon fires burning in luminaries along the road, and echoing with the voices of carolers and happy families.

A culinary adventure: Start with blue-corn pancakes for breakfast and try Spanish tapas or farm-to-table regional fare for dinner. Enjoy some strawberry-habanero gelato at Ecco or sip an Aztec Warrior Elixir at Kakawa Chocolate. Take a cooking lesson. Santa Fe is an exceptional dining town, the perfect place to push the frontiers of your palate.

Into the wild: Follow the lead of locals and take any one of the many easy-access points into the incredible, and surprisingly lush, mountains that rise out of Santa Fe. Raft the Rio Grande, snowboard, snowshoe, or try mountain biking.

Market mashup: Summer offers the phenomenal International Folk Art Market, the famed Indian Market, and the two-for-one weekend of Traditional Spanish Market and Contemporary Hispanic Market. Plus there's an outstanding farmers' market on Saturday and Tuesday mornings. The offerings are breathtaking and the community involvement is yet another aspect of Santa Fe to fall in love with.

and at Christmas, when all the trees are filled with lights, and rooftops are outlined with *farolitos,* votive candles lit within paper-bag lanterns.

TOP ATTRACTIONS

Georgia O'Keeffe Museum. One of many East Coast artists who visited New Mexico in the first half of the 20th century, O'Keeffe returned to live and paint here, eventually emerging as the demigoddess of Southwestern art. O'Keeffe's innovative view of the landscape is captured in *From the Plains,* inspired by her memory of the Texas plains, and *Jimson Weed,* a study of one of her favorite plants. Special exhibitions with O'Keeffe's modernist peers are on view throughout the year—many of these are exceptional, sometimes even more interesting than the permanent collection, which numbers some 3,000 works. The museum is also your point of contact for booking guided tours of O'Keeffe's historic home and studio an hour north in

Abiquiú. ✉ *217 Johnson St., The Plaza* ☎ *505/946–1000* ⊕ *www.okeeffemuseum.org* 🎟 *$13.*

★ Fodor'sChoice **The New Mexico History Museum.** This impressive,
FAMILY modern museum anchors a campus that encompasses the
Palace of the Governors, the **Palace Print Shop & Bind-
ery,** the **Fray Angélico Chávez History Library,** and **Photo
Archives** (an assemblage of more than 1 million images
dating from the 1850s). Behind the palace on Lincoln
Avenue, the museum thoroughly explores the early history
of indigenous people, Spanish colonization, the Mexican
Period, and travel and commerce on the legendary Santa
Fe Trail. Inside are changing and permanent exhibits. By
appointment, visitors can tour the comprehensive Fray
Angélico Chávez Library and its rare maps, manuscripts,
and photographs (more than 120,000 prints and negatives).
The Palace Print Shop & Bindery, which prints books, pam-
phlets, and cards on antique presses, also hosts bookbinding
demonstrations, lectures, and slide shows. The Palace of
the Governors is a humble one-story neo-Pueblo adobe on
the north side of the Plaza, and is the oldest public building
in the United States. Its rooms contain period furnishings
and exhibits illustrating the building's many functions
over the past four centuries. Built at the same time as the
Plaza, circa 1610, it was the seat of four regional gov-
ernments—those of Spain, Mexico, the Confederacy, and
the U.S. territory that preceded New Mexico's statehood,
which was achieved in 1912. It served as the residence for
100 Spanish, Mexican, and American governors, including
Governor Lew Wallace, who wrote his epic *Ben Hur* in its
then drafty rooms, all the while complaining of the dust
and mud that fell from its earthen ceiling.

Dozens of Native American vendors gather daily under
the portal of the Palace of the Governors to sell pottery,
jewelry, bread, and other goods. With few exceptions, the
more than 500 artists and craftspeople registered to sell here
are Pueblo or Navajo Indians. The merchandise for sale is
required to meet strict standards. Prices tend to reflect the
high quality of the merchandise but are often significantly
less than what you'd pay in a shop. Please remember not
to take photographs without permission. ✉ *Palace Ave.,
north side of Plaza, 113 Lincoln Ave., west of the Palace,
The Plaza* ☎ *505/476–5100* ⊕ *www.nmhistorymuseum.org*
🎟 *$12* ☽ *Nov.–Apr., closed Mon.*

★ FodorsChoice **New Mexico Museum of Art.** Designed by Isaac Hamilton Rapp in 1917, the museum contains one of America's finest regional collections. It's also one of Santa Fe's earliest Pueblo Revival structures, inspired by the adobe structures at Acoma Pueblo. Split-cedar *latillas* (branches set in a crosshatch pattern) and hand-hewn vigas form the ceilings. The 20,000-piece permanent collection, of which only a fraction is exhibited at any given time, emphasizes the work of regional and nationally renowned artists, including the early modernist Georgia O'Keeffe; realist Robert Henri; the Cinco Pintores (five painters) of Santa Fe (including Fremont Elis and Will Shuster, the creative mind behind Zozóbra); members of the Taos Society of Artists (Ernest L. Blumenschein, Bert G. Phillips, Joseph H. Sharp, and E. Irving Couse, among others); and the works of noted 20th-century photographers of the Southwest, including Laura Gilpin, Ansel Adams, and Dorothea Lange. Rotating exhibits are staged throughout the year. Many excellent examples of Spanish-colonial-style furniture are on display. Other highlights include an interior *placita* (small plaza) with fountains, WPA murals, and sculpture, and the St. Francis Auditorium, where concerts and lectures are often held. ✉ *107 W. Palace Ave., The Plaza* ☎ *505/476–5072* ⊕ *www.nmartmuseum.org* 🎫 *$12* ⊗ *Nov.–Apr., closed Mon.*

St. Francis Cathedral Basilica. The iconic cathedral, a block east of the Plaza, is one of the rare significant departures from the city's nearly ubiquitous Pueblo architecture. Construction was begun in 1869 by Jean Baptiste Lamy, Santa Fe's first archbishop, who worked with French architects and Italian stonemasons. The Romanesque style was popular in Lamy's native home in southwest France. The circuit-riding cleric was sent by the Catholic Church to the Southwest to change the religious practices of its native population (to "civilize" them, as one period document puts it) and is buried in the crypt beneath the church's high altar. He was the inspiration behind Willa Cather's novel *Death Comes for the Archbishop* (1927). In 2005 Pope Benedict XVI declared St. Francis the "cradle of Catholicism" in the Southwestern United States, and upgraded the status of the building from mere cathedral to cathedral basilica—one of just 36 in the country.

A small adobe chapel on the northeast side of the cathedral, the remnant of an earlier church, embodies the Hispanic architectural influence so conspicuously absent from the cathedral itself. The chapel's *Nuestra Señora de la Paz* (Our

NEW MEXICO CULTURE PASS

With a New Mexico Culture Pass (⊕ www.newmexico-culture.org), which you can purchase for $30 online or at any participating museum, you gain admission to each of the 15 state museums and monuments once over a 12-month period. These include a number of attractions elsewhere in the state (Albuquerque's National Hispanic Center and New Mexico Museum of Natural History and Science, the state monuments in Jémez, Coronado, and several other places) as well as the following Santa Fe museums: New Mexico History Museum/Palace of the Governors, New Mexico Museum of Art, Museum of Indian Arts & Culture, and Museum of International Folk Art. Note that the first Sunday of each month, these four museums offer free admission.

Lady of Peace), popularly known as *La Conquistadora,* the oldest Madonna statue in the United States, accompanied Don Diego de Vargas on his reconquest of Santa Fe in 1692, a feat attributed to the statue's spiritual intervention. Every Friday the faithful adorn the statue with a new dress. Take a close look at the keystone in the main doorway arch: it has a Hebrew tetragrammaton on it. It's widely speculated that Bishop Lamy had this carved and placed to honor the Jewish merchants of Santa Fe who helped provide necessary funds for the construction of the church. ✉ *131 Cathedral Pl., The Plaza* ☎ *505/982–5619* ⊕ *www.cbsfa.org.*

WORTH NOTING

La Fonda. A *fonda* (inn) has stood on this site, southeast of the Plaza, for centuries. Architect Isaac Hamilton Rapp, who put Santa Fe style on the map, built this area landmark in 1922. Remodeled in the early 20th century by architects John Gaw Meem and Mary Elizabeth Jane Colter, the hotel was sold to the Santa Fe Railway in 1926 and remained a Harvey House hotel until 1968. The property completed its latest major renovation in 2013, its guest rooms receiving a smart but still classic makeover, but the historic public areas retain their original design elements. Because of its proximity to the Plaza and its history as a gathering place for everyone from cowboys to movie stars (Errol Flynn stayed here), it's referred to as "The Inn at the End of the Trail." Free guided tours, which touch on the hotel's rich history and detail key pieces in the astounding public art collection, are offered Wednesday–Saturday mornings at 10:30. Step inside to browse the shops on the main floor or to eat at one of the restaurants (La Plazuela or the French Bakery). The dark, cozy bar draws both locals and tourists and has live music many nights. For a real treat: Have a drink at the fifth-floor Bell Tower Bar (open late spring–late fall), which offers tremendous sunset views. ✉ *100 E. San Francisco St., at Old Santa Fe Trail, The Plaza* ☎ *505/982–5511* ⊕ *www.lafondasantafe.com.*

Museum of Contemporary Native Arts (MoCNA). This fascinating museum that's part of the esteemed Institute of American Indian Arts (IAIA) is just a block from the Plaza and contains the largest collection—some 7,500 works—of contemporary Native American art in the United States. The collection of paintings, photography, sculptures, prints, and traditional crafts was created by past and present students and teachers. In the 1960s and 1970s it blossomed into the nation's premier center for Native American arts and its alumni represent almost 600 tribes around the country. The museum continues to showcase the cultural and artistic vibrancy of indigenous people and expands what is still an often limited public perception of what "Indian" art is and can be. Be sure to step out back to the beautiful sculpture garden. Artist Fritz Scholder taught here, as did sculptor Allan Houser. Among their disciples were the painter T. C. Cannon and sculptor and painter Dan Namingha. ✉ *108 Cathedral Pl., The Plaza* ☎ *505/983–1777, 888/922–4242* ⊕ *www.iaia.edu* ▧ *$10* ☉ *Closed Tues.*

NEED A BREAK? **Ecco Gelato and Espresso. Café.** This airy, contemporary café across from the Downtown public library has large plate-glass windows, and brushed-metal tables inside and out on the sidewalk under the portal. Try the delicious and creative gelato flavors (strawberry-habanero, brandied cherry, fig-and-walnut, chocolate-banana) or some of the espressos and coffees, pastries, and sandwiches (roast beef and blue cheese, tuna with dill, cucumber, and sprouts). ✉ *128 E. Marcy St., The Plaza* ☎ *505/986–9778* ⊕ *www. eccogelato.com.*

Sena Plaza. Two-story buildings enclose this courtyard, which can be entered only through two small doorways on Palace Avenue or the shops facing Palace Avenue. Surrounding the oasis of flowering fruit trees, a fountain,

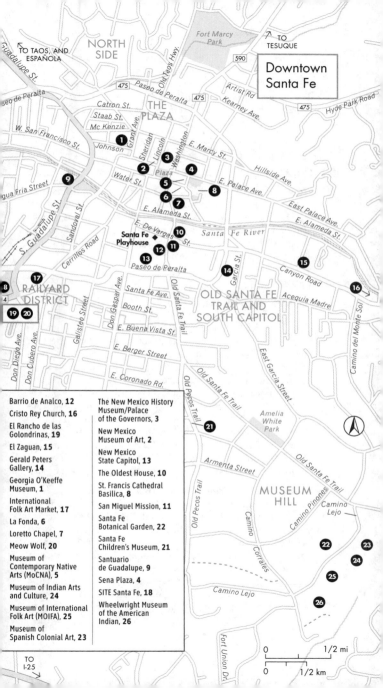

Downtown Santa Fe

TO TAOS, AND ESPAÑOLA

NORTH SIDE

Fort Marcy Park

TO TESUQUE

THE PLAZA

RAILROAD DISTRICT

OLD SANTA FE TRAIL AND SOUTH CAPITOL

Santa Fe Playhouse

Santa Fe River

MUSEUM HILL

Amelia White Park

TO I-25

Barrio de Analco, **12**

Cristo Rey Church, **16**

El Rancho de las Golondrinas, **19**

El Zaguan, **15**

Gerald Peters Gallery, **14**

Georgia O'Keeffe Museum, **1**

International Folk Art Market, **17**

La Fonda, **6**

Loretto Chapel, **7**

Meow Wolf, **20**

Museum of Contemporary Native Arts (MoCNA), **5**

Museum of Indian Arts and Culture, **24**

Museum of International Folk Art (MOIFA), **25**

Museum of Spanish Colonial Art, **23**

The New Mexico History Museum/Palace of the Governors, **3**

New Mexico Museum of Art, **2**

New Mexico State Capitol, **13**

The Oldest House, **10**

St. Francis Cathedral Basilica, **8**

San Miguel Mission, **11**

Santa Fe Botanical Garden, **22**

Santa Fe Children's Museum, **21**

Santuario de Guadalupe, **9**

Sena Plaza, **4**

SITE Santa Fe, **18**

Wheelwright Museum of the American Indian, **26**

0   1/2 mi

0   1/2 km

and inviting benches are a variety of locally owned shops. The quiet courtyard is a good place for repose or to have lunch at La Casa Sena. The buildings, erected in the 1700s as a single-family residence, had quarters for blacksmiths, bakers, farmers, and all manner of help. ✉ *125 E. Palace Ave., The Plaza.*

OLD SANTA FE TRAIL AND SOUTH CAPITOL

It was along the Old Santa Fe Trail that wagon trains from Missouri rolled into town in the 1820s, forever changing Santa Fe's destiny. This street, off the south corner of the Plaza, is one of Santa Fe's most historic and is dotted with houses, shops, markets and the (relatively modern) state capitol several blocks down.

TOP ATTRACTIONS

New Mexico State Capitol. The symbol of the Zía Pueblo, which represents the Circle of Life, was the inspiration for the capitol, also known as the Roundhouse. Doorways at opposing sides of this 1966 structure symbolize the four winds, the four directions, and the four seasons. Throughout the building are artworks from the outstanding 600-work collection of the Capitol Art Foundation, historical and cultural displays, and handcrafted furniture—it's a superb and somewhat overlooked array of fine art. The **Governor's Gallery** hosts temporary exhibits. Six acres of imaginatively landscaped gardens shelter outstanding sculptures. ✉ *Old Santa Fe Trail at Paseo de Peralta, Old Santa Fe Trail and South Capitol* ☎ *505/986–4589* ⊕ *www.nmlegis.gov/lcs/visitors.aspx* ◲ *Free* ⊙ *Closed Sun., also Sat. Sept.–late May.*

★ **Fodor'sChoice San Miguel Mission.** Believed to be the oldest church still in use in the United States, this simple earth-hue adobe structure was built around 1610 by the Tlaxcalan Indians of Mexico, who came to New Mexico as servants of the Spanish. Badly damaged in the 1680 Pueblo Revolt, the structure was restored and enlarged in 1710. On display in the chapel are priceless statues and paintings and the San José Bell, weighing nearly 800 pounds, which is believed to have been cast in Spain in 1356. In winter the church sometimes closes before its official closing hour. Latin mass is held daily at 2, and new mass is on Sundays at 5 pm. ✉ *401*

Old Santa Fe Trail, Old Santa Fe Trail and South Capitol
☏ *505/983–3974* ⊕ *www.sanmiguelchapel.org.*

WORTH NOTING

Barrio de Analco. Along the south bank of the Santa Fe River, the barrio—its name means "District on the Other Side of the Water"—is one of America's oldest neighborhoods, settled in the early 1600s by the Tlaxcalan Indians (who were forbidden to live with the Spanish near the Plaza) and in the 1690s by soldiers who had helped recapture New Mexico after the Pueblo Revolt. Plaques on houses on East De Vargas Street will help you locate some of the important structures. Check the performance schedule at the **Santa Fe Playhouse** on De Vargas Street, founded by writer Mary Austin and other Santa Feans in 1922. ✉ *Old Santa Fe Trail at E. De Vargas St., Old Santa Fe Trail and South Capitol.*

Loretto Chapel. A delicate Gothic church modeled after Sainte-Chapelle in Paris, Loretto was built in 1878 by the same French architects and Italian stonemasons who built St. Francis Cathedral, and is known for the "Miraculous Staircase" that leads to the choir loft. Legend has it that the chapel was almost complete when it became obvious that there wasn't room to build a staircase to the choir loft. In answer to the prayers of the cathedral's nuns, a mysterious carpenter arrived on a donkey, built a 20-foot staircase—using only a square, a saw, and a tub of water to season the wood—and then disappeared as quickly as he came. Many of the faithful believed it was St. Joseph himself. The staircase contains two complete 360-degree turns with no central support; no nails were used in its construction. The chapel closes for services and special events. Adjoining the chapel are a small museum and gift shop. ✉ *207 Old Santa Fe Trail, Old Santa Fe Trail and South Capitol* ☏ *505/982–0092* ⊕ *www.lorettochapel.com* ▤ *Free* ☉ *May close without advance notice for special events.*

The Oldest House. This house is said to be the oldest in the United States—a sign on the exterior puts the date at 1646. Some say it's much older, but historians currently can verify only that it dates back to the mid-1700s. ✉ *215 E. De Vargas St., Old Santa Fe Trail and South Capitol.*

EAST SIDE AND CANYON ROAD

Once a trail used by indigenous people to access water and the lush forest in the foothills east of town, then a route for Hispanic woodcutters and their burros, and for most of the 20th century a prosaic residential street with only a gas station and a general store, Canyon Road today is lined with nearly 100 mostly upscale art galleries along with a handful of shops and restaurants. The narrow road begins at the eastern curve of Paseo de Peralta and stretches for about 2 miles uphill at a moderate incline. Upper Canyon Road (past East Alameda) is narrow and residential, with access to hiking and biking trails along the way, and the Randall Davey Audubon Center at the far east end. Elsewhere on neighboring streets in the East Side, you'll find a few bed-and-breakfasts as well as the beautifully situated campus of St. John's College, but this part of town is mostly residential.

There are few places as festive as Canyon Road on Christmas Eve, when thousands of farolitos illuminate walkways, walls, roofs, and even trees. In May the scent of lilacs wafts over the adobe walls, and in August red hollyhocks enhance the surreal color of the blue sky on a dry summer day.

WORTH NOTING

Cristo Rey Church. Built in 1940 and designed by legendary Santa Fe architect John Gaw Meem to commemorate the 400th anniversary of Francisco Vásquez de Coronado's exploration of the Southwest, this church is the largest Spanish adobe structure in the United States and is considered by many the finest example of Pueblo-style architecture anywhere. The church was constructed in the old-fashioned way by parishioners, who mixed the more than 200,000 mud-and-straw adobe bricks and hauled them into place. The 225-ton stone reredos (altar screen) is magnificent. ⊠ *1120 Canyon Rd., East Side and Canyon Road* ☎ *505/983–8528* ⊕ *www.cristoreyparish.org* ▭ *Free.*

El Zaguan. Headquarters of the **Historic Santa Fe Foundation (HSFF)**, this 19th-century Territorial-style house has a small exhibit on Santa Fe architecture and preservation, but the real draw is the small but stunning garden abundant with lavender, roses, and mid-19th-century trees. You can relax on a wrought-iron bench and take in the fine views of the hills northeast of town. Tours are available of many of the foundation's properties on Mother's Day. ⊠ *545 Canyon*

Rd., East Side and Canyon Road ☎ *505/983–2567* ⊕ *www. historicsantafe.org* 🎫 *Free* ⊙ *Office closed weekends, garden closed Sun.*

Gerald Peters Gallery. While under construction, this 32,000-square-foot building was dubbed the "ninth northern pueblo," its scale supposedly rivaling that of the eight northern pueblos around Santa Fe. The suavely designed Pueblo-style gallery is Santa Fe's premier showcase for American and European art from the 19th century to the present. It feels like a museum, but all the works are for sale. Pablo Picasso, Georgia O'Keeffe, Charles M. Russell, Winslow Homer, Grant Wood, and members of the Taos Society are among the artists represented, along with nationally renowned contemporary ones. ✉ *1011 Paseo de Peralta, East Side and Canyon Road* ☎ *505/954–5700* ⊕ *www.gpgallery.com* 🎫 *Free* ⊙ *Closed Sun.*

NEED A BREAK? **Downtown Subscription.** Café. Locals congregate in the courtyard or on the front portal of Downtown Subscription, a block east of Canyon Road. A great, friendly spot to people-watch, this café-newsstand sells coffees, snacks, and pastries, plus one of the largest assortments of newspapers and magazines in town. It has lovely outdoor spaces to sit and sip during warm weather. ✉ *376 Garcia St., East Side and Canyon Road* ☎ *505/983–3085.*

MUSEUM HILL

What used to be the outskirts of town became the site of gracious, neo-Pueblo style homes in the mid-20th century, many of them designed by the famed architect John Gaw Meem. Old Santa Fe Trail takes you to Camino Lejo, aka Museum Hill, where you'll find four excellent museums, a botanical garden, and a café.

TOP ATTRACTIONS

Museum of Indian Arts and Culture. An interactive, multimedia exhibition tells the story of Native American history in the Southwest, merging contemporary Native American experience with historical accounts and artifacts. The collection includes some of New Mexico's oldest works of art: pottery vessels, fine stone and silver jewelry, intricate textiles, and other arts and crafts created by Pueblo, Navajo, and Apache artisans. Changing exhibitions feature arts and traditions of historic and contemporary Native Americans. You can also see art demonstrations and a video about the life and work of Pueblo potter Maria Martinez. ⊠ *710 Camino Lejo, Museum Hill* ☎ *505/476–1250* ⊕ *www.indianartsandculture.org* ⊠ *$12* ☉ *Closed Mon.*

★ Fodor'sChoice **Museum of International Folk Art (MOIFA).** A delight
FAMILY for adults and children alike, this museum is the premier institution of its kind in the world, with a permanent collection of more than 130,000 objects from about 100 countries. In the Girard Wing you'll find thousands of amazingly inventive handmade objects—a tin Madonna, a devil made from bread dough, dolls from around the world, and miniature village scenes galore. The Hispanic Heritage Wing contains art dating from the Spanish-colonial period (in New Mexico, 1598–1821) to the present. The 3,000-piece exhibit includes religious works—particularly *bultos* (carved wooden statues of saints) and *retablos* (holy images painted on wood or tin), as well as textiles and furniture. The exhibits in the Neutrogena Wing rotate, showing subjects ranging from outsider art to the magnificent quilts of Gee's Bend. Lloyd's Treasure Chest, the wing's innovative basement section, provides a behind-the-scenes look at this collection. You can rummage through storage drawers, peer into microscopes, and, on occasion, speak with conservators and other museum personnel. Allow time to visit the outstanding gift shop and bookstore. ⊠ *706 Camino Lejo, Museum Hill* ☎ *505/476–1200* ⊕ *www.internationalfolkart.org* ⊠ *$12* ☉ *Nov.–Apr., closed Mon.*

★ Fodor'sChoice **Museum of Spanish Colonial Art.** This 5,000-square-foot adobe museum occupies a classically Southwestern former home designed in 1930 by acclaimed regional architect John Gaw Meem. The Spanish Colonial Art Society formed in Santa Fe in 1925 to preserve traditional Spanish-colonial art and culture, and the museum, which sits next to the Museum of International Folk Art and the Museum of Indian Arts and Culture complex, displays the fruits of the society's labor—one of the most comprehensive collections of Spanish-colonial art in the world. The more than 3,700 objects here, dating from the 16th century to the present, include retablos, elaborate santos, tinwork, straw appliqué, furniture, ceramics, and ironwork. The contemporary collection of works by New Mexico Hispanic artists helps put all this history into regional context. On the grounds outside, you can also view the exterior of a 1780s Mexican-colonial house and visit the small but colorful Artist's Garden. ✉ *750 Camino Lejo, Museum Hill* ☏ *505/982–2226* ⊕ *www.spanishcolonial.org* 🖃 *$10* ⊘ *Late Oct.–Apr., closed Mon..*

Santa Fe Botanical Garden. This 14-acre garden across the street from Milner Plaza's parking lot provides another great reason for exploring the Museum Hill neighborhood outside of the collections in its four world-class museums. Situated on a bluff with fantastic views of the surrounding mountains, the facility is divided into four sections that emphasize distinct elements of New Mexico's flora and terrain: the Orchard Gardens, Ojos y Manos: Eyes and Hands, the Courtyard Gardens, and the Arroyo Trails. You can gain a much fuller sense of what's planted and why by embarking on one of the free guided tours, offered daily (call for hours). The organization also operates 35-acre Leonora Curtin Wetland Preserve on 27283 I–25 West Frontage Road (next to El Rancho de las Golondrinas), which is open spring through fall—check the SFBG website for more information. ✉ *725 Camino Lejo, Museum Hill* ☏ *505/471–9103* ⊕ *www. santafebotanicalgarden.org* 🖃 *Apr.–Oct. $10; Nov.–Mar. $7* ⊘ *Closed Nov.–Mar., Mon.–Wed.*

WORTH NOTING

International Folk Art Market. Held the second full weekend in July on Milner Plaza, this market is a truly remarkable art gathering. Master folk artists from every corner of the planet come together to sell their work amidst a festive array of huge tents, colorful banners, music, food, and delighted crowds. The feeling of fellowship and celebration here enhances the satisfaction of buying wonderful folk art. ✉ *706 Camino Lejo, Museum Hill* ☏ *505/992–7600* ⊕ *www.folkartalliance.org.*

FAMILY **Santa Fe Children's Museum.** Stimulating hands-on exhibits, a solar greenhouse, oversize geometric forms, and an 18-foot indoor rock-climbing wall all contribute to this museum's popularity with kids. Outdoor gardens with climbing structures, forts, and hands-on activities are great for whiling away the time in the shade of big trees. Puppeteers and storytellers perform often. ✉ *1050 Old Pecos Trail, Old Santa Fe Trail and South Capitol* ☏ *505/989–8359* ⊕ *www.santafechildrensmuseum.org* 🖃 *$7.50* ⊘ *Closed Mon.; Sept.–May, closed Mon. and Tues.*

Wheelwright Museum of the American Indian. A private institution in a building shaped like a traditional octagonal Navajo hogan, the Wheelwright opened in 1937. Founded by Boston scholar Mary Cabot Wheelwright and Navajo medicine man Hastiin Klah, the museum originated as a place to house ceremonial materials. Those items were returned to the Navajo in 1977, but what remains is an incredible collection of 19th- and 20th-century baskets, pottery, sculpture, weavings, metalwork, photography, paintings, including contemporary works by Native American artists, and typically fascinating changing exhibits. The Case Trading Post on the lower level is modeled after the trading posts that dotted the Southwestern frontier more than 100 years ago. It carries an outstanding selection of books and contemporary Native American jewelry, kachina dolls, weaving, and pottery. ⊠ *704 Camino Lejo, Museum Hill* ☎ *505/982–4636* ⊕ *www.wheelwright.org* ⊒ *$8.*

RAILYARD DISTRICT

The most significant development in Santa Fe in recent years has taken place in the Railyard District, a neighborhood just south of the Plaza that was for years called the Guadalupe District (and is occasionally still known by that name). Comprising a few easily walked blocks along Guadalupe Street between Agua Fria and Paseo de Peralta, the district has been revitalized with a snazzy park and outdoor performance space, a permanent indoor-outdoor home for the farmers' market, and quite a few notable restaurants, shops, and galleries.

This historic warehouse and rail district endured several decades of neglect after the demise of the train route through town. But rather than tearing the buildings down (this is a city where 200-year-old mud-brick buildings sell at a premium, after all), the city, with extensive input from residents, worked with developers to gradually convert the low-lying warehouses into artists' studios, antiques shops, bookstores, indie shops, and restaurants. The Rail Runner commuter train to Albuquerque has put the rail tracks as well as the vintage mission-style depot back into use.

A central feature of the district's redevelopment is Railyard Park, at the corner of Cerrillos Road and Guadalupe Street, which was designed to highlight native plants and provide citizens with a lush, urban space. The buildings just north, in the direction of the Plaza, contain the vibrant Santa Fe Farmers' Market, the teen-oriented community art center Warehouse21, the stunningly redesigned and expanded SITE Santa Fe museum, art galleries, shops, restaurants, and live-work spaces for artists. This dramatic development reveals the fascinating way Santa Feans have worked to meet the needs of an expanding city while paying strict attention to the city's historic relevance.

TOP ATTRACTIONS

SITE Santa Fe. The events at this nexus of international contemporary art include lectures, concerts, author readings, films, performance art, and gallery shows. The facility hosts a biennial exhibition, SITElines, staged every even-numbered year. Exhibitions are often provocative, and the immense, open space, which underwent a massive expansion and redesign in 2017, provides an ideal setting for the many larger-than-life installations. ✉ *1606 Paseo de Peralta, Railyard District* ☎ *505/989–1199* ⊕ *sitesantafe.org* 🎫 *$10.*

WORTH NOTING

Santuario de Guadalupe. A massive-walled adobe structure built by Franciscan missionaries between 1776 and 1795, this is the oldest shrine in the United States to Our Lady of Guadalupe, Mexico's patron saint. The church's adobe walls are nearly 3 feet thick, and among the sanctuary's religious art and artifacts is a beloved image of Nuestra Virgen de Guadalupe, painted by Mexican master Jose de Alzibar in 1783. Highlights are the traditional New Mexican carved and painted altar screen called a reredo, an authentic 19th-century sacristy, a pictorial-history archive, a library devoted to Archbishop Jean Baptiste Lamy that is furnished with many of his belongings, and a garden with plants from the Holy Land. ✉ *100 Guadalupe St., Railyard District* ☎ *505/988–2027* 🎫 *Donations accepted* ⊙ *May–Oct., closed Sun.; Nov.–Apr., closed weekends.*

NEED A BREAK? Whoo's Donuts. Café. Begun by Jeff and Kari Keenan, the talents behind the terrific artisan shop ChocolateSmith, which is next door and also well worth investigating for a sweet snack, Whoo's has developed a near-fanatical following for its traditional as well as creative doughnuts (maple-bacon with dark-chocolate glaze and chile-brown sugar, blueberry-jelly with cherry glaze, white-chocolate pistachio), which are prepared daily from scratch, sourcing organically as much as possible. Get here early—Whoo's is open daily from 7 until 3 (or until that day's doughnuts have sold out). ⊠ *851 Cerrillos Rd., Railyard District* ☏ *505/629–1678* ⊕ *www. whoosdonuts.com.*

WEST OF THE PLAZA

Although most of Downtown's commercial activity beyond the Plaza extends south and east, a handful of notable restaurants, shops, and inns do lie to the west, especially along Guadalupe Street between Alameda Street and Paseo de Peralta and the historic blocks just west. At the intersection of Paseo de Peralta and Guadalupe, you'll find the expansive DeVargas shopping center, which has a few notable shops and eateries, a movie theater, and some larger grocery and big-box stores—handy if you just need basic supplies (and still within walking distance of the Plaza).

NORTH SIDE

You'll find some of Santa Fe's prettiest scenery on the hilly north side of town, which extends from the Sangre de Cristo foothills (home to some distinctive accommodations, including Ten Thousand Waves and the Four Seasons) west through the historic and artsy village of Tesuque, and then across rolling, sagebrush-dotted mesas that contain the city's famed opera house and one of the popular Marty Sanchez golf courses.

SOUTH SIDE

The majority of Santa Feans live on the South Side, which encompasses a vast stretch of relatively level mesa land. What this largely middle-class and in some places sprawly part of town lacks in scenic beauty—especially along traffic-choked and strip-mall-lined Cerrillos Road—it makes up for in convenient services. It's also where you're going to find most of the area's mid-range and budget chain accommodations and fast-food restaurants, along with an increasing number of genuinely notable eateries, from down-home neighborhood favorites like Horseman's

Haven and Tecolote Café to inspired contemporary spots like Harry's Roadhouse, Midtown Bistro, and Dr. Field Goods Kitchen. One burgeoning sub-neighborhood on the South Side, the Midtown Innovation District, has sprung up along Siler Road—just off Cerrillos Road— and is anchored by the spectacular new Meow Wolf art complex as well as a growing number of hip breweries, eateries, galleries, and art studios.

TOP ATTRACTIONS

El Rancho de las Golondrinas. Sometimes dubbed the "Colonial Williamsburg of the Southwest," El Rancho de las Golondrinas ("Ranch of the Swallows") is a reconstruction of a small agricultural village with buildings from the 17th to 19th century. Travelers on El Camino Real would stop at the ranch before making the final leg of the journey north, a half-day ride from Santa Fe in horse-and-wagon time. By car, the ranch is only a 25-minute drive from the Plaza. It's also a 10-minute drive from where the Turquoise Trail (NM 14) intersects with Interstate 25, making it a fun stop—especially for kids—on your way to or from Albuquerque. Self-guided tours interpret the lives of locals from the mid-17th through late 19th century. Farm animals roam through the barnyards on the 200-acre complex. During the ranch's many festivals—Spring & Fiber Fest, the Herb & Lavender Festival, Viva México, La Panza Llena New Mexico Food Fest, Santa Fe Wine Festival, and others—music, dance, food, and crafts are offered. In April, May, and October, the museum is open weekdays only, by advance reservation. ⊠ *334 Los Pinos Rd., South Side* ☎ *505/471–2261* ⊕ *www.golondrinas.org* 🎫 *$6* ⊘ *Closed Nov.–Mar. and Mon. and Tues.*

★ **Fodor's**Choice **Meow Wolf.** Meow Wolf is both an ambitious
FAMILY visual and musical arts collective and the name of the dazzling multimillion-dollar arts complex the group created out of a former bowling alley in 2016, with much of the funding coming from Santa Fe–based *Game of Thrones* author George R.R. Martin. Visitors now flock to the arts complex's first permanent exhibition, the self-billed "immersive art installation" *House of Eternal Return*, which has become one of the city's leading attractions. Give yourself at least a couple of hours to tour this sci-fi-inspired 20,000-square-foot interactive exhibit in which you'll encounter hidden doorways, mysterious corridors, ambient music, and clever, surrealistic, and often slyly humor-

ous artistic renderings. It's a strange, almost impossible to describe, experience, but it is absolutely family-friendly, and although wildly imaginative and occasionally eerie, the subject matter isn't at all frightening. Tickets are good throughout the day—you can leave and reenter the installation, and perhaps break up the experience by enjoying a light bite and craft beer from Duel Brewing in the bar-café in the lobby. Meow Wolf is open until 8 most evenings and 10 on Fridays and Saturdays. The collective has also produced notable temporary installations in a number of cities around the country (plans were announced to open a second complex in Denver, CO in 2020), and organizers continue to present concerts and other events both at the Meow Wolf arts complex and at other venues around the city. ⊠ *1352 Rufina Cir., South Side* ☎ *505/395–6369* ⊕ *www.meowwolf.com* ✉ *$20* ☉ *Closed Tues.*

WHERE TO EAT

Updated
by Andrew
Collins

EATING OUT IS A MAJOR pastime in Santa Fe and it's well worth coming here with a mind to join in on the fun. Restaurants with high-profile chefs stand beside low-key joints, many offering unique and intriguing variations on regional and international cuisine. You'll find restaurants full of locals and tourists alike all over the Downtown and surrounding areas. Although Santa Fe does have some high-end restaurants where dinner for two can exceed $200, the city also has plenty of reasonably priced dining options.

Waits for tables are very common during the busy summer season, so it's a good idea to call ahead even when reservations aren't accepted, if only to get a sense of the waiting time. Reservations for dinner at the better restaurants are a must in summer and on weekends the rest of the year.

So-called Santa Fe–style cuisine has so many influences that the term has become virtually meaningless, especially with many of the city's top eateries embracing a more international approach to cuisine, albeit all the while sourcing more and more from local farms and ranches. At many top spots in town, you'll detect Latin American, Mediterranean, and East Asian influences. Yet plenty of traditional, old-style Santa Fe restaurants still serve authentic New Mexican fare, which combines both Native American and Hispanic traditions and is quite different from Americanized as well as regional Mexican cooking.

Santa Fe's culinary reputation continues to grow not just in terms of restaurants but also in businesses that produce or sell specialty foods and beverages, from fine chocolates and local honeys and jams to increasingly acclaimed New Mexico wines, beers, and spirits. *See Chapter 6, Shops and Spas, for a list of these purveyors.* Don't miss Santa Fe Farmers' Market, one of the best in the Southwest.

WHAT IT COSTS			
$	$$	$$$	$$$$
Restaurants under $18	$18–$24	$25–$30	over $30

Prices in the restaurant reviews are the average cost of a main course at dinner or, if dinner is not served, at lunch.

Restaurant reviews have been shortened. For full information, visit Fodors.com.

THE PLAZA

★ Fodor'sChoice ✕ **Cafe Pasqual's.** *Southwestern.* A perennial
$$$ favorite, this cheerful cubbyhole dishes up Nuevo Latino and occasional Asian specialties for breakfast, lunch, and dinner. The culinary muse behind Pasqual's is James Beard Award–winning chef and cookbook author Katharine Kagel, who champions organic, local ingredients, and whose expert kitchen staff produces mouthwatering breakfast and lunch specialties like huevos motuleños (eggs in a tangy tomatillo salsa with black beans and fried bananas), and the sublime grilled free-range chicken sandwich on toasted-chile corn bread. **Known for:** smoked-trout hash with tomatillo salsa; mole enchiladas; dining room filled with colorful folk art and murals. [$] *Average main: $30* ✉ *121 Don Gaspar Ave., The Plaza* ☎ *505/983–9340* 🌐 *www.pasquals.com.*

3

$$$$ ✕ **Coyote Cafe.** *Southwestern.* A Santa Fe hot spot since it opened in 1987, this pioneer of contemporary Southwestern cuisine has experienced some ups and downs over the years but is currently enjoying a bit of a renaissance, having completed a handsome renovation in early 2018 and serving some of the most extravagant and delicious cuisine in the city. Prices are also among Santa Fe's highest, although you can enjoy terrific, lighter bites in the adjacent Coyote Cantina, a fun rooftop space with a loud and lively social scene serving drinks and flavorful under-$20 fare like burgers and pork carnitas tacos with pineapple-habanero salsa. **Known for:** tellicherry peppered elk tenderloin; Frito pie in Coyote Cantina; creative agave and tequila cocktails. [$] *Average main: $39* ✉ *132 W. Water St., The Plaza* ☎ *505/983–1615* 🌐 *www.coyotecafe.com* ⏲ *No lunch at Coyote Cafe (Rooftop Cantina only).*

$$$ ✕ **El Mesón & Chispa Tapas Bar.** *Spanish.* This place is as fun for having drinks and late-night tapas or catching live music (from tango nights to Sephardic music) as for enjoying a full meal. The dining room has an old-world feel with simple dark-wood tables and chairs, creamy plastered walls, and a wood-beam ceiling—unpretentious yet elegant. **Known for:** live jazz and tango; paella à la Valenciana with seafood, chorizo, and chicken; nice selection of Spanish wines, including Jerez sherries. [$] *Average main: $25* ✉ *213 Washington Ave., The Plaza* ☎ *505/983–6756* 🌐 *www.elmeson-santafe.com* ⏲ *Closed Sun. and Mon. No lunch.*

$$$ ✕ **Il Piatto.** *Italian.* This chef-owned neighborhood spot near the Plaza charms its legions of fans with creative

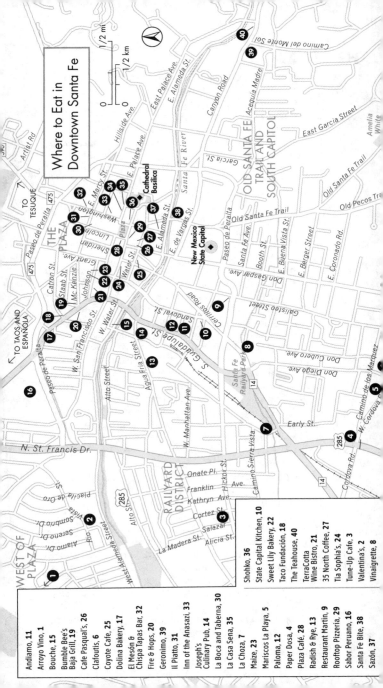

Where to Eat in Downtown Santa Fe

0   1/2 mi

0   1/2 km

TO TESUQUE

TO TAOS AND ESPAÑOLA

THE PLAZA

Cathedral Basilica

New Mexico State Capitol

OLD SANTA FE TRAIL AND SOUTH CAPITOL

RAILYARD DISTRICT

WEST OF PLAZA

Andiamo, 11
Arroyo Vino, 1
Bouche, 15
Bumble Bee's Baja Grill, 19
Cafe Pasqual's, 26
Clafoutis, 6
Coyote Cafe, 25
Dolina Bakery, 17
El Mesón & Chispa Tapas Bar, 32
Fire & Hops, 20
Geronimo, 39
Il Piatto, 31
Inn of the Anasazi, 33
Joseph's Culinary Pub, 14
La Boca and Taberna, 30
La Casa Sena, 35
La Choza, 7
Maize, 23
Mariscos La Playa, 5
Paloma, 12
Paper Dosa, 4
Plaza Café, 28
Radish & Rye, 13
Restaurant Martín, 9
Rooftop Pizzeria, 29
Sabor Peruano, 16
Santa Fe Bite, 38
Sazón, 37

Shohko, 36
State Capital Kitchen, 10
Sweet Lily Bakery, 22
Taco Fundación, 18
The Teahouse, 40
TerraCotta Wine Bistro, 21
35 North Coffee, 27
Tia Sophia's, 24
Tune-Up Cafe, 3
Valentina's, 2
Vinaigrette, 8

pasta dishes like *pappardelle* with braised duckling ragù and homemade pumpkin ravioli with pine nuts and sage brown butter. The menu, which usually features several creative specials, emphasizes locally sourced ingredients. **Known for:** local-beef carpaccio; "medium plates" option on pastas and entrées; great early-evening and late-afternoon happy hour. $ *Average main: $27* ✉ *95 W. Marcy St., The Plaza* ☎ *505/984–1091* 🌐 *www.ilpiattosantafe.com* 🕓 *No lunch Sun.–Tues.*

3

★ Fodor's Choice 🍴 **Inn of the Anasazi.** *Modern American.* The
$$$$ expert culinary team at this romantic, intimate 38-seat restaurant with hardwood floors, soft lighting, and Chaco Valley stone–inspired walls balances a Latin and European sensibility in its approach to the menu. If you're wanting a less formal vibe, dine in the more spacious, convivial bar or on the lively streetside patio, which features lighter but no less accomplished cuisine, such as carne asada street tacos and green-chile buffalo sliders. **Known for:** gracious and knowledgeable service; exceptional craft cocktails; Sunday brunch. $ *Average main: $36* ✉ *113 Washington Ave., The Plaza* ☎ *505/988–3030* 🌐 *www.innoftheanasazi.com.*

★ Fodor's Choice 🍴 **La Boca and Taberna.** *Spanish.* A beacon of
$$$ superbly crafted, authentic yet creatively updated Mediterranean—and especially Spanish—cuisine, La Boca comprises two distinct spaces: an intimate and quieter storefront dining room that's better for a leisurely romantic repast, and in back, spilling out into a cloistered courtyard, Taberna, a bustling tavern with live music, ample seating indoor and out, and late hours. Both spaces feature the delectable small-plates cooking of celebrated chef James Cambpell Caruso, and a full meal in either spot is similarly priced though just a tad more expensive in the main restaurant, where the food also tends more toward contemporary. **Known for:** fine Spanish meats and cheeses; extensive selection of authentic Spanish tapas; a nice variety of Spanish sherries. $ *Average main: $26* ✉ *72 W. Marcy St., The Plaza* ☎ *505/982–3433* 🌐 *www.labocasantafe.com.*

$$$ 🍴 **La Casa Sena.** *Modern American.* The Southwestern-accented and Continental fare served at La Casa Sena is beautifully presented, and the scenery, especially during the warmer months, is part of the charm. Get a table on the patio surrounded by hollyhocks, flowering shrubs, and centuries-old adobe walls, or for a musical meal (evenings only), sit in the restaurant's adjacent, less-pricey Cantina, where the talented and perky staff belt out Broadway show tunes. **Known for:** grilled Colorado rack of lamb; gorgeous

patio; singing waitstaff in the cantina. [$] *Average main: $30* ✉ *Sena Plaza, 125 E. Palace Ave., The Plaza* ☎ *505/988–9232* 🌐 *www.lacasasena.com.*

$$$ ✕ **Maize.** *Modern American.* Opened in fall 2017 in a historic redbrick house beside the O'Keeffe Museum, this atmospheric space with warm lighting, beamed ceilings, and an inviting tree-shaded slate patio has quickly earned raves for its well-conceived blend of Spanish, French, and indigenous cuisine. As the restaurant's name suggests, corn plays a key role in many dishes, as do other local staples like chayote, trout, elk, and pinto beans. **Known for:** wagyu green-chile cheeseburger with yucca fries; good selection of shareable small plates; tranquil patio. [$] *Average main: $28* ✉ *225 Johnson St., The Plaza* ☎ *505/780–5125* 🌐 *www.maizesantafe.com* ⏲ *Closed Sun. and Mon. No lunch.*

$ ✕ **Plaza Café.** *American.* Run with homespun care by the Razatos family since 1947, this café has been a fixture on the Plaza since 1905. The decor—red leather banquettes, black Formica tables, tile floors, a coffered tin ceiling, and a 1940s-style service counter—hasn't changed much in the past half century. **Known for:** chicken-fried steak; retro diner charm; breakfast all day. [$] *Average main: $17* ✉ *54 Lincoln Ave., The Plaza* ☎ *505/982–1664* 🌐 *www.plazacafesantafe.com.*

$ ✕ **Rooftop Pizzeria.** *Pizza.* For sophisticated pizza, head to this slick indoor-outdoor restaurant on the upper level of Santa Fe Arcade. The kitchen here scores high marks for its rich and imaginative pizza toppings: consider the one topped with lobster, shrimp, mushrooms, apple-smoked bacon, caramelized leeks, truffle oil, Alfredo sauce, and four cheeses on a blue-corn crust. **Known for:** unusual pizza toppings; great salads; well-chosen wine and microbrew beer list. [$] *Average main: $16* ✉ *60 E. San Francisco St., The Plaza* ☎ *505/984–0008* 🌐 *www.rooftoppizzeria.com.*

★ $$$$ Fodor's Choice ✕ **Sazón.** *Modern Mexican.* The realm of Mexico City–born chef Fernando Olea, who's been working his culinary magic at different Santa Fe restaurants since 1991, Sazón offers an upscale take on regional Mexican fare, complete with an exhaustive list of artisan tequilas and mezcals. The food focus in this handsome dining room warmed by a kiva fireplace and filled with Frida Kahlo and Day of the Dead–inspired artwork is one of Mexico's greatest dishes, mole. **Known for:** house-made mole sauces; chapulines (baby grasshoppers) on corn taquitos; encyclopedic selection of artisan mezcals. [$] *Average main:*

$37 ✉ 221 Shelby St., The Plaza ☎ 505/983–8604 🌐 www.sazonsantafe.com ⊗ Closed Sun. No lunch.

★ Fodor'sChoice ✕ **The Shed.** *Southwestern.* The lines at lunch attest to the status of this Downtown eatery that's been family operated since 1953 and that serves some of the most flavorful New Mexican food, and margaritas, around. The rambling, low-doored, and atmospheric adobe dating from 1692 is decorated with folk art, and service is downright neighborly. **Known for:** red-chile enchiladas; posole; potent margaritas. [$] *Average main: $14 ✉ 113½ E. Palace Ave., The Plaza ☎ 505/982–9030 🌐 www.sfshed.com ⊗ Closed Sun.*
$

$$$ ✕ **Shohko.** *Japanese.* Shohko and her family run this first-rate Japanese restaurant that's known for the freshest, best-prepared sushi and sashimi in town, along with an extensive selection of seafood and veggie tempura, teriyaki grills, udon and buckwheat bonito broths, and izakaya-style starters. On any given night there are two dozen or more varieties of fresh fish available. **Known for:** sushi and sashimi; ramen-style noodle broths; fine selection of premium sakes. [$] *Average main: $26 ✉ 321 Johnson St., The Plaza ☎ 505/982–9708 🌐 www.shohkocafe.com ⊗ Closed Sun. and Mon. No lunch Sat.*

$ ✕ **Sweet Lily Bakery.** *Bakery.* Feathery cakes and luscious pies, along with an impressive selection of gluten-free scones, cupcakes, and other sweet treats, are what this casual bakery/café is best known for, but it's also a great spot for savory breakfast and lunch fare. You'll always find a couple of meat and veggie quiches of the day, along with puff pies (the beef burgundy one is delicious) and panini sandwiches. **Known for:** savory puff pies; gluten-free baked goods; fresh-baked cakes and pies. [$] *Average main: $8 ✉ 229 Johnson St., The Plaza ☎ 505/982–0455 🌐 www.sweetlilybakerysf.com ⊗ Closed weekends. No dinner.*

$$ ✕ **TerraCotta Wine Bistro.** *Wine Bar.* This reasonably priced, warmly decorated bistro and wine bar occupies a cozy late-19th-century Territorial-style house near the O'Keeffe Museum. The menu favors snacking and sharing—salmon salad with pomegranate vinaigrette, bruschetta with Brie and fig-port jam, flatbread pizzas, panini, grilled flank steak. **Known for:** bruschetta with a variety of toppings; panini sandwiches; terrific wine list. [$] *Average main: $21 ✉ 304 Johnson St., The Plaza ☎ 505/989–1166 🌐 www.terracottawinebistro.com ⊗ No lunch Sun.*

$ ✕ **35 North Coffee.** *Café.* There are plenty of spots near the Plaza for grabbing a latte, but this coffeehouse stands out for brewing exceptional house-roasted, single-origin coffees from Guatamala, Kenya, Sumatra, and other java hot spots around the world. You can order a pour-over made with beans of your choosing, or sample the house-made chai, nitro cold brew, and "latitude adjustment" (coffee blended with organic grass-fed butter, MCT oil, and coconut oil). **Known for:** high-grade single-origin coffees; house-made chai; breakfast croissants. [$] *Average main: $6* ✉ *60 E. San Francisco St., The Plaza* ☎ *505/983–6138* 🌐 *www.35north-coffee.com* ⏲ *No dinner.*

$ ✕ **Tia Sophia's.** *Southwestern.* This Downtown joint serves strictly New Mexican breakfasts and lunches (open until 2 pm most days and 1 on Sundays). You're as likely to be seated next to a family from a remote village in the mountains as you are to a legislator or lobbyist from the nearby state capitol. **Known for:** breakfast burritos; popular with locals; traditional New Mexican, down to the fiery chiles. [$] *Average main: $9* ✉ *210 W. San Francisco St., The Plaza* ☎ *505/983–9880* 🌐 *tiasophias.com* ⏲ *No dinner.*

OLD SANTA FE TRAIL AND SOUTH CAPITOL

$ ✕ **Clafoutis.** *Café.* Undeniably French, this bustling café serves authentic, delicious food. Walk through the door of this bright, open space and you'll almost certainly be greeted with a cheery "*bonjour*" from Anne-Laure, who owns it with her husband, Philippe. **Known for:** bounteous salads; French omelets; clafoutis dessert. [$] *Average main: $11* ✉ *333 W. Cordova Rd., Old Santa Fe Trail and South Capitol* ☎ *505/988–1809* ⏲ *Closed Sun. No dinner.*

$ ✕ **Mariscos la Playa.** *Mexican.* Yes, even in landlocked Santa Fe it's possible to find incredibly fresh and well-prepared seafood served in big portions. This cheery, colorful Mexican restaurant surrounded by strip malls is just a short hop south of Downtown. **Known for:** delightfully friendly staff; ceviche tostadas; trout grilled with butter and paprika. [$] *Average main: $15* ✉ *537 W. Cordova Rd., Old Santa Fe Trail and South Capitol* ☎ *505/982–2790* 🌐 *www.mariscoslaplayarestaurant.com.*

★ $ Fodor's Choice ✕ **Paper Dosa.** *Modern Indian.* Begun as a catering business that threw occasional pop-up dinners, Paper Dosa became so beloved for its boldly flavored southern Indian cuisine that the owners opened what has become a tremendously popular brick-and-mortar restaurant. Dosas (thin, rolled-crepes made with fermented rice and lentils and stuffed with different fillings) are the specialty here and come in about 10 varieties, from paneer and peas to a locally inspired version with green chile and three cheeses. **Known for:** dosas with interesting fillings; chile-dusted mango salad; a thoughtful world-beat wine list. [$] *Average main: $17* ✉ *551 W. Cordova Rd., Old Santa Fe Trail and South Capitol* ☎ *505/930–5521* 🌐 *www.paper-dosa.com* 🕒 *Closed Mon. No lunch.*

★ Fodor's Choice ✕ **Restaurant Martin.** *Modern American.* Having
$$$$ cooked at some of the best restaurants in town (Geronimo, the Old House, Anasazi), acclaimed James Beard–nominated chef Martin Rios now flexes his culinary muscles in his own place, a simple, elegant restaurant with a gorgeous patio. Rios prepares progressive American cuisine, which is heavily influenced by his French culinary training. **Known for:** daily-changing vegetarian tasting plate; Sunday brunch; attractively landscaped patio. [$] *Average main: $32* ✉ *526 Galisteo St., Old Santa Fe Trail and South Capitol* ☎ *505/820–0919* 🌐 *www.restaurantmartinsantafe.com* 🕒 *Closed Mon. No lunch Sat.*

$ ✕ **Santa Fe Bite.** *Burger.* John and Bonnie Eckre, the former
FAMILY owners of the legendary but now defunct Bobcat Bite burger joint, now serve their juicy green-chile cheeseburgers and humongous 16-ounce "Big Bite" burgers—along with hefty steaks—to a much bigger audience in this kitsch-filled space off the lobby of Garrett's Desert Inn. There's breakfast and weekend brunch, too—morning highlights include brioche French toast with strawberries and maple-caramel sauce, and traditional steak-and-eggs. **Known for:** green-chile cheeseburgers; hearty breakfast fare; malted milk shakes. [$] *Average main: $14* ✉ *Garrett's Desert Inn, 311 Old Santa Fe Trail, Old Santa Fe Trail and South Capitol* ☎ *505/982–0544* 🌐 *www.santafebite.com* 🕒 *Closed Mon.*

$$ ✕ **Vinaigrette.** *American.* A novel and noble alternative to the many Santa Fe restaurants that favor filling (and often fattening) dishes, Vinaigrette is all about the greens, which are sourced organically, with the majority of produce raised on owner Erin Wade's 10-acre farm in nearby Nambé. This isn't mere rabbit food, however—the hearty salads make a satisfying meal, especially when you add toppings like grilled flank steak, hibiscus-cured duck confit, or seared sea scallops. **Known for:** hearty salads; daily house-made fruit pies; baked panko-crusted goat cheese (which can be added to any salad). [$] *Average main: $18* ✉ *709 Don Cubero Alley, Old Santa Fe Trail and South Capitol* ☎ *505/820–9205* 🌐 *www.vinaigretteonline.com* 🕒 *Closed Sun.*

EAST SIDE AND CANYON ROAD

★ Fodor's Choice 🍴 **Geronimo.** *Modern American.* This bastion of
$$$$ dazzling, sophisticated contemporary cuisine occupies the Borrego House, a massive-walled Canyon Road adobe dating from 1756 with intimate white dining rooms, beamed ceilings, wood floors, fireplaces, and cushioned *bancos* (banquettes). It's one of the loveliest venues in New Mexico for a special meal, perhaps local rack of lamb with roasted leeks and a Merlot–natural jus reduction, or Hawaiian ahi sashimi and tartare with buttermilk scallion cakes. **Known for:** complex and sophisticated contemporary fare; setting in beautiful 18th-setting Canyon Road adobe; sublime service. [$] *Average main: $42* ✉ *724 Canyon Rd., East Side and Canyon Road* ☎ *505/982–1500* 🌐 *www.geronimorestaurant.com* ⊗ *No lunch.*

$ 🍴 **The Teahouse.** *Café.* A delightful spot toward the end of gallery row at the intersection of Canyon Road and East Palace Avenue, The Teahouse has several bright dining rooms throughout the converted adobe home, and a tranquil outdoor seating area in a rock garden. In addition to fine teas from all over the world, you can find extremely well-prepared breakfast, lunch, and dinner options, including baked polenta with poached eggs and romesco sauce, bagels and lox, and wild-mushroom panini. **Known for:** fine teas and coffees; serene rock garden seating; delicious breakfasts. [$] *Average main: $15* ✉ *821 Canyon Rd., East Side and Canyon Road* ☎ *505/992–0972* 🌐 *www.teahousesantafe.com.*

RAILYARD DISTRICT

$ 🍴 **Andiamo.** *Italian.* A longtime locals' favorite, Andiamo scores high marks for its friendly staff, consistently good northern Italian food, and comfortable dining room. Produce from the farmers' market down the street adds to the seasonal surprises of this intimate restaurant set inside a sweet cottage in the Railyard District. **Known for:** crispy duck leg confit with polenta; great pizzas; charming cottage setting. [$] *Average main: $17* ✉ *322 Garfield St., Railyard District* ☎ *505/995–9595* 🌐 *www.andiamoonline.com* ⊗ *No lunch weekends.*

★ Fodor's Choice 🍴 **Joseph's Culinary Pub.** *Modern American.*
$$$ Chef-restauranteur Joseph Wrede has garnered countless accolades since the 1990s at various restaurants in Taos and then Santa Fe, and his current eatery—a stylish gastropub set in a vintage adobe with low beamed ceilings, slate

floors, and a cozy patio—continues to showcase his considerable talents, featuring a menu of deliciously updated comfort fare. Dishes you're already familiar with receive novel twists, including lasagna with ricotta, mascarpone, pecorino Romano, and a hearty rabbit Bolognese sauce, and chicken posole with a farm egg, tomatillos, and avocado. **Known for:** rabbit Bolognese lasagna; lamb burger; stellar beer and wine selection. $ *Average main: $25* ✉ *428 Agua Fria St., Railyard District* ☎ *505/982–1272* 🌐 *www.josephsofsantafe.com* 🕒 *No lunch.*

★ Fodor's Choice ✕ **La Choza.** *Southwestern.* The off-the-beaten-path and less expensive sister to the Shed, La Choza (which means "the shed" in Spanish), serves supertasty, supertraditional New Mexican fare. It's hard to go wrong here: chicken or pork *carne adovada* (marinated in red chile and slow-cooked until tender) burritos, white clam chowder spiced with green chiles, and the classic huevos rancheros are exceptional. **Known for:** clam chowder with green chiles; bean-stuffed sopaipillas; outstanding and extensive margarita and premium-tequila list. $ *Average main: $14* ✉ *905 Alarid St., Railyard District* ☎ *505/982–0909* 🌐 *www.lachozasf.com* 🕒 *Closed Sun.*

$ FAMILY

$$ ✕ **Paloma.** *Modern Mexican.* A fun go-to for happy hour, weekend brunch, or dinner with a few friends, this bright and bustling modern take on a Mexican cantina offers plenty of shareable small plates as well as a few bigger dishes, including a perfectly roasted half chicken with Swiss chard, squash, and a classic mole poblano sauce. Street tacos—crispy Baja-style sea bass, cauliflower with marcona almonds, lamb barbacoa with smoky adobo sauce—are another specialty, as is the remolacha salad of hibiscus beets, citrus, seasonal fruits, and frisee. **Known for:** roast half-chicken with mole poblano; street-food-style tacos; weekend brunch. $ *Average main: $21* ✉ *401 S. Guadalupe St., Railyard District* ☎ *505/467–8624* 🌐 *www.palomasantafe.com* 🕒 *No dinner Sun. No lunch.*

★ Fodor's Choice ✕ **Radish & Rye.** *Modern American.* Set in an intimate old house on the edge of the Railyard District with both a large and lively bar area and a more formal dining room, this darkly lighted space decorated with vintage bourbon barrels stands out both for its deftly crafted modern American food and one of the best small-batch bourbon selections in the Southwest. The kitchen focuses on farm-to-table victuals—seasonally rotating dishes like roasted beets and labneh cheese with pinon vinaigrette, and grilled local pork chops with bacon, polenta, and wild

$$$

mushrooms. **Known for:** farm-to-table grills and local vegetables; bourbon pecan pie; an encyclopedic list of small-batch bourbons. [$] *Average main: $29* ✉ *548 Agua Fria St., Railyard District* ☎ *505/930–5325* 🌐 *www.radishandrye.com* ⏲ *Closed Mon. No lunch.*

$$$$ ✕ **State Capital Kitchen.** *Modern American.* The dangling Edison bulbs, abstract art, brick walls, and decided lack of Southwestern trappings are an immediate clue that this intimate, high-end farm-to-table bistro strives for an urbane, worldly ambience—indeed, it wouldn't look at all out of place in Brooklyn or San Francisco. Chef-owner Mark Connell sources ingredients predominantly from sustainable ranches and fisheries and local farmers and foragers, and his plates burst with flavor and color. **Known for:** charcuterie and cheese plates; beautifully plated farm-to-table cuisine; five-course tasting menu. [$] *Average main: $34* ✉ *500 Sandoval St., Railyard District* ☎ *505/467–8237* 🌐 *www.statecapitalkitchen.com* ⏲ *Closed Sun. and Mon. No lunch.*

WEST OF THE PLAZA

★ Fodor's Choice ✕ **Arroyo Vino.** *Modern American.* It's worth
$$$ making the 15-minute trek out to Santa Fe's western mesa to dine at this outstanding bistro–cum–wineshop that's quickly developed a devout following among locals. At the store, stock up on often hard-to-find vintages from all over the world—for a $30 corkage fee, you can also enjoy your new Bordeaux or Albariño in the airy dining room, where tables are set around a central wine bar and the night's specials are handwritten on a chalkboard. **Known for:** butter-poached Maine lobster; rich and beautifully plated desserts; stellar wine selection. [$] *Average main: $29* ✉ *218 Camino la Tierra, off NM 599, 4 miles west of U.S. 285/84, West of the Plaza* ☎ *505/983–2100* 🌐 *www.arroyovino.com* ⏲ *Closed Sun. and Mon. No lunch.*

$$$ ✕ **Bouche.** *French.* Talented chef-owner Charles Dale (who previously cooked at Rancho Encantado's Terra, Daniel Boulud's Le Cirque, and at his own James Beard–lauded Renaissance restaurant in Aspen) operates this lively, modern take on a traditional French neighborhood bistro. Choose a cozy table by the fireplace and try the consistently stellar renditions of calf's liver Dijonnaise, tenderloin steak tartare with a fresh farm egg, sautéed sweetbreads with local mushrooms, and truffle frites—prices are more than fair compared with similarly upscale eateries around town. **Known for:** sautéed sweetbreads; calf's liver Dijon-

naise; tiramisu. [$] *Average main: $30* ✉ *451 W. Alameda St., West of the Plaza* ☎ *505/982–6297* 🌐 *www.bouchebistro.com* ⏲ *Closed Sun. and Mon. No lunch.*

$ ✕ **Bumble Bee's Baja Grill.** *Mexican.* A bright, vibrantly colored restaurant with closely spaced tables, piñatas, and ceiling fans whirling overhead, Bumble Bee's (the nickname of the ebullient owner, Bob) delights locals with its superfresh Cal Mex–style food. If you like fish tacos, the mahimahi ones with creamy, nondairy slaw are outstanding; try them with a side of salad instead of beans and rice. **Known for:** Baja-style mahimahi tacos; variety of fresh-made salsas; Mexican chocolate brownie. [$] *Average main: $10* ✉ *301 Jefferson St., West of the Plaza* ☎ *505/820–2862* 🌐 *www.bumblebeesbajagrill.com.*

FAMILY

3

$ ✕ **Dolina Bakery.** *Café.* Slovakian transplant Annamaria O'Brien opened this bustling bakery and brunch spot with whitewashed beamed ceilings, tile floors, and angular polished-wood tables in 2017, and her menu borrows a bit from Eastern Europe but also features regional U.S. dishes, like cornmeal waffles with buttermilk fried chicken and ham-mushroom omelets with red or green chile. The quiche of the day is always delicious. **Known for:** Eastern European pastries; eclectic and hearty breakfast-brunch fare; Mexican mochas. [$] *Average main: $11* ✉ *402 N. Guadalupe St., West of the Plaza* ☎ *505/982–9394* 🌐 *www.dolinasantafe.com* ⏲ *No dinner.*

★ Fodor's Choice ✕ **Fire & Hops.** *Eclectic.* Tucked inside a cozy
$ and modest house on busy Guadalupe Street, Fire & Hops turns out some of the most flavorful and affordable food in Santa Fe while also offering a stellar list of craft beers from some of the best producers in the West, including such regional notables as Bosque, Bow & Arrow, and Le Cumbre. Among the food choices, you can't go wrong with the house-made lamb sausage with green papaya and red curry, or the Cubano sandwich with beer-brined pork. **Known for:** lamb sausage with green papaya and red curry; a fantastic list of beers on tap and in bottles; house-made ice cream in unusual flavors. [$] *Average main: $17* ✉ *222 N. Guadalupe St., West of the Plaza* ☎ *505/954–1635* 🌐 *www.fireandhopsgastropub.com* ⏲ *No lunch.*

$ ✕ **Sabor Peruano.** *Peruvian.* Among the more unlikely locales for a exceptionally good Peruvian lunch or early dinner, this lively eatery decorated with colorful Andes textiles, paintings, and crafts occupies a windowless (but well-lighted) space inside humdrum DeVargas shopping center. The authentic food here relies heavily on organic ingredients, and many vegetarian and vegan options are offered, including avocados stuffed with olives, peppers, cherry tomatoes, and other vegetables. **Known for:** causa rellena limena; several vegan options; an on-site boutique selling Peruvian arts and crafts. ⓢ *Average main: $14* ✉ *DeVargas Center, 163 Paseo de Peralta, West of the Plaza* ☎ *505/358–3829* ⊕ *www.saborperuanosf.com* ☉ *Closed Sun.*

$ ✕**Taco Fundación.** *Mexican.* Tasty and affordable regional Mexican-style tacos, with soft corn tortillas, are the name of the game at this hip fast-food joint where you order at the counter and enjoy your meal in the tiny no-frills dining area or outside at a wooden picnic table or covered bench (or, as many locals do, in your car). You'll find nearly 20 taco fillings—fried squash blossom, goat, bison, al pastor (roasted marinated pork with pineapple), and shrimp are among the best—plus rice bowls, burritos, and sides of guacamole and pinto beans. **Known for:** huge variety of taco fillings; Mexican soft drinks; Mexican soft-serve ice cream. ⓢ *Average main: $9* ✉ *235 N. Guadalupe St., West of the Plaza* ☎ *505/982–8286* ⊕ *tacofundación.com* ☉ *Closed Sun.*

★ **Fodor'sChoice** ✕**Tune-Up Cafe.** *Southwestern.* This cozy locals'
$ favorite has colorful walls and wood details, booths, a few tables, and a community table. The shaded patio out front is a great summertime spot to enjoy the toothsome Southwest-inspired cooking, from breakfast through dinner. **Known for:** breakfast rellenos; buffalo burgers; homemade cakes and pies. ⓢ *Average main: $11* ✉ *1115 Hickox St., West of the Plaza* ☎ *505/983–7060* ⊕ *www. tuneupsantafe.com.*

$ ✕**Valentina's.** *Southwestern.* This colorfully decorated locals' spot in a shopping center on the West Side doesn't look like anything special from the outside, but it's one of Santa Fe's most consistently excellent purveyors of Mexican and New Mexican fare. If you're at a loss to make a decision after perusing the leviathan menu, consider one of the combo platters piled high with enchiladas, burritos, stuffed sopaipillas, tacos, and the like. **Known for:** New Mexican combo platters; carne asada with eggs; live mariachi music. ⓢ *Average main: $10* ✉ *New Solana Shopping Center, 945 W. Alameda St., West of the Plaza* ☎ *505/988–7165.*

NORTH SIDE

$$$ ✕ **El Nido.** *Italian.* For decades a handsome adobe steak house in the cottonwood-shaded heart of little Tesuque village, El Nido shuttered in 2010 but has been brought back to life as a stylish, upscale Italian restaurant specializing in wood-fired grills and pizzas and handmade pastas. Among the latter, few dishes more effectively warm the soul on a New Mexico winter evening than chianti-infused pappardelle pasta with wild boar ragu, rosemary, and Parmesan. **Known for:** popular for pre-opera dinners; pappardelle pasta with wild boar ragu; flamenco dancing and music on certain evenings. [$] *Average main: $27* ✉ *1577 Bishop's Lodge Rd., Tesuque* ☎ *505/954–1272* 🌐 *www.elnidosantafe.com* ⏲ *No lunch.*

$$$ ✕ **Izanami.** *Japanese.* Set in the pine-scented foothills northeast of town, the ethereal boutique resort and spa Ten Thousand Waves has always cultivated a tranquil East Asian aesthetic, so it made perfect sense when it opened a long-awaited restaurant in 2014 that the look and culinary approach would be Japanese. Paper lanterns hang from the lofty, pitched ceiling, and a traditional tatami room is available for patrons seeking a completely authentic vibe. **Known for:** the omakase chef's choice tasting menu; the foie gras burger; an outstanding selection of first-rate sakes. [$] *Average main: $26* ✉ *Ten Thousand Waves, 21 Ten Thousand Waves Way, North Side* ✣ *Off NM 475, 4 miles northeast of the Plaza* ☎ *505/982–9304* 🌐 *www.tenthousandwaves.com/food* ⏲ *No lunch Tues.*

$$$$ ✕ **Terra.** *Modern American.* Among the many reasons guests of the Four Seasons Rancho Encantado often find it difficult to ever leave the gloriously situated property is this handsome yet down-to-earth restaurant that serves tantalizingly delicious and creative contemporary American and Southwestern cuisine. A specialty here is the exquisitely plated seafood, from ahi tuna and beef carpaccio to grilled prawns with cucumber "spaghetti," wild mushrooms, prickly pear pesto, macadamia crumbs, and bacon. **Known for:** creatively prepared seafood; Monday and Tuesday afternoon high tea; stunning mountain views. [$] *Average main: $39* ✉ *Four Seasons Rancho Encantado, 198 NM 592, North Side* ☎ *505/946–5700* 🌐 *www.fourseasons.com/santafe.*

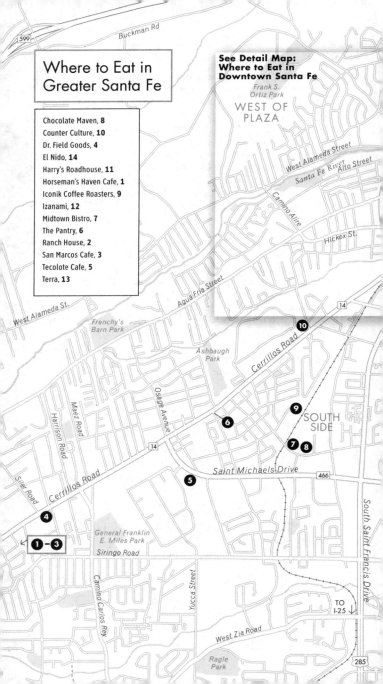

Where to Eat in Greater Santa Fe

See Detail Map: Where to Eat in Downtown Santa Fe

Chocolate Maven, **8**
Counter Culture, **10**
Dr. Field Goods, **4**
El Nido, **14**
Harry's Roadhouse, **11**
Horseman's Haven Cafe, **1**
Iconik Coffee Roasters, **9**
Izanami, **12**
Midtown Bistro, **7**
The Pantry, **6**
Ranch House, **2**
San Marcos Cafe, **3**
Tecolote Cafe, **5**
Terra, **13**

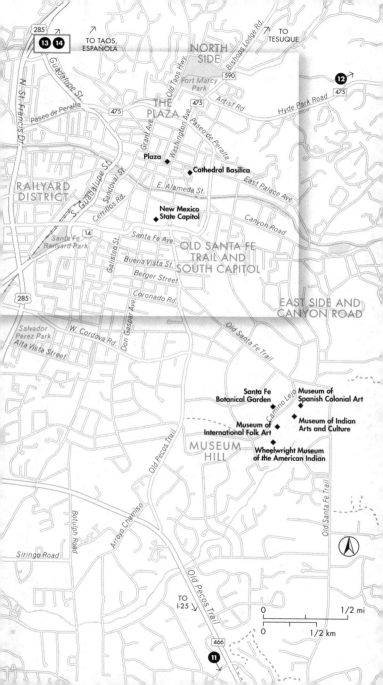

SOUTH SIDE

$ 🍴 **Chocolate Maven.** *Café.* Although the name of this cheery bakery suggests sweets, and it does sweets especially well, Chocolate Maven produces impressive savory breakfast and lunch fare. Meals are "farmers' market–inspired" and feature seasonal dishes, including wild-mushroom-and-goat-cheese focaccia sandwiches, eggs ménage à trois (one each of eggs Benedict, Florentine, and Madison—the latter consisting of smoked salmon and poached egg), and Caprese salad of fresh mozzarella, basil, and tomatoes. **Known for:** breakfast burritos; Roman-style thin-crust pizzas; local, seasonal ingredients. [$] *Average main: $13* ✉ *821 W. San Mateo St., South Side* ☎ *505/984–1980* 🌐 *www.chocolatemaven.com* ⏲ *No dinner.*

$ 🍴 **Counter Culture.** *Café.* It's taken a few years for this low-key, slightly off-the-beaten-path café that's well regarded by locals to catch on with tourists, but Counter Culture is worth finding for its delicious breakfasts, lunches, dinners, or even just afternoon coffee breaks—there's a spacious covered patio beyond the dining room with long communal tables and a few smaller, more private ones. Inside this hip industrial space, tuck into plates of huevos rancheros and other eggy fare in the morning, and a mix of Southwestern and Asian dishes later in the day. **Known for:** smothered breakfast burritos; well-prepared espresso drinks; cash only. [$] *Average main: $13* ✉ *930 Baca St., South Side* ☎ *505/995–1105* 🌐 *www.counterculturesantafe.com* 💳 *No credit cards* ⏲ *No dinner Sun. and Mon.*

$ 🍴 **Dr. Field Goods.** *Eclectic.* Ardent foodies regularly trek 4 miles south along traffic-choked Cerrillos Road to experience one of the more memorable farm-to-table dining adventures in Santa Fe. Chef Josh Gerwin ran this operation out of a wildly popular food truck before opening the airy and attractive brick-and-mortar restaurant in 2013, situated in a nondescript shopping center beside Jackalope. **Known for:** the "Bad Ass BLT"; queso dip; kimchi patatas bravas. [$] *Average main: $16* ✉ *2860 Cerrillos Rd., South Side* ☎ *505/471–0043* 🌐 *www.drfieldgoods.com.*

★ Fodor's Choice 🍴 **Harry's Roadhouse.** *Eclectic.* This busy, friendly,
$ art-filled compound 6 miles southeast of Downtown con-
FAMILY sists of several inviting rooms, from a diner-style space with counter seating to a cozier nook with a fireplace, and an enchanting courtyard out back with juniper trees and flower gardens. The varied menu of contemporary diner favorites, pizzas, New Mexican fare, and bountiful salads

is supplemented by a long list of daily specials, which often include delicious ethnic dishes and an array of scrumptious homemade desserts. **Known for:** friendly neighborhood hangout; stellar margaritas; house-made desserts. Ⓢ *Average main: $13* ✉ *96-B Old Las Vegas Hwy., 1 mile east of Old Pecos Trail exit off I–25, South Side* ☎ *505/989–4629* ⊕ *www.harrysroadhousesantafe.com.*

$ ✕**Horseman's Haven Cafe.** *Southwestern.* Tucked behind the Giant gas station, this no-frills diner-style restaurant close to the many chain hotels along lower Cerrillos Road has long been a standout for some of the spiciest and tastiest northern New Mexican fare in town, including superb green chile-bacon-cheeseburgers, blue-corn tacos packed with beef or chicken, huevos rancheros, and the hearty *plato sabroso* (a 12-ounce rib steak with rolled enchilada, beans, posole, rice, and hot sopaipillas with honey). Grab one of the comfy red-leatherette corner booths or a stool at the counter, and enjoy the people-watching. **Known for:** blue corn tacos with beef or chicken; green-chile bacon cheeseburgers; hearty New Mexican breakfasts. Ⓢ *Average main: $10* ✉ *4354 Cerrillos Rd., South Side* ☎ *505/471–5420* ⊘ *No dinner Sun.*

$ ✕**Iconik Coffee Roasters.** *Café.* First and foremost a lively coffeehouse that turns out expertly prepared pour-overs, lattes, cold brews, and other delicious espresso drinks using house-roasted beans, this funky, inviting space with vintage chandeliers, comfy armchairs, and sturdy wooden communal tables also serves tasty and eclectic salads, sandwiches, and tapas. The menu spans the globe, featuring breakfast tacos, Korean steak bowls, ramen, and poached-egg salads. **Known for:** pour-over single-origin coffees; chocolate milk stout on tap; ramen with miso-coconut broth. Ⓢ *Average main: $10* ✉ *1600 Lena St., Suite A2, South Side* ☎ *505/428–0996* ⊕ *www.iconikcoffee.com.*

$$ ✕**Midtown Bistro.** *Modern American.* A couple of miles south of Downtown in a spacious adobe building with pitched ceilings and a charming patio, Midtown Bistro presents creative modern American cuisine at prices a couple of notches below what the upscale heavy hitters near the Plaza and Canyon Road charge. In every sense, from the service to the excellent food, this somewhat under-the-radar eatery succeeds. **Known for:** filet mignon with truffle oil butter; classic Cobb salad; weekend brunch. Ⓢ *Average main: $24* ✉ *901 W. San Mateo St., South Side* ☎ *505/820–3121* ⊘ *No dinner Sun.*

$ 🍴 **The Pantry.** *Diner.* Since 1948, this beloved, family-owned greasy spoon with a familiar blue neon sign has been pleasing budget-minded locals and visitors with consistently tasty diner fare, including buckwheat pancakes, *huevos consuelo* (a corn tortilla topped with two eggs, a spicy chile sauce, and cheese, with the Pantry's famous home fries), green-chile stew, tortilla burgers, and chicken-fried steak. **Known for:** huevos consuelo; great value; down-home atmosphere. [$] *Average main: $9* ✉ *1820 Cerrillos Rd., South Side* ☎ *505/986–0022* 🌐 *www.pantrysantafe.com.*

$ 🍴 **Ranch House.** *Barbecue.* Given New Mexico's deep ties to its easterly neighbor, the Lone Star State, it's hardly surprising that the region has some top-notch barbecue joints, including this bright, spacious contemporary adobe building with two large patios that looks a bit fancy but turns out superb fall-off-the-bone barbecue brisket, baby-back ribs, pulled pork, and smoked half-chicken. Fish tacos, steaks, burgers, and traditional New Mexican dishes round out the extensive menu. **Known for:** barbecue brisket; steaks; a well-priced afternoon happy hour. [$] *Average main: $17* ✉ *2571 Cristo's Rd., South Side* ☎ *505/424–8900* 🌐 *www.theranchhousesantafe.com.*

★ Fodor's Choice 🍴 **San Marcos Cafe.** *Café.* In Lone Butte, about
$ 20 miles south of Downtown Santa Fe along the northern
FAMILY end of the scenic Turquoise Trail, this funky spot is known for its creative fare and nontraditional setting—an actual feed store, with roosters, turkeys, and peacocks running about outside. In one of the two bric-a-brac–filled dining rooms, sample rich cinnamon rolls and such delectables as burritos stuffed with roast beef and potatoes and topped with green chile. **Known for:** the Feed Store burrito (with hash browns, bacon, cheese, chile, and egg); warm apple pie à la mode; offbeat farmyard setting. [$] *Average main: $9* ✉ *3877 NM 14, South Side* ☎ *505/471–9298* 🌐 *www.sanmarcosfeed.com* ⏲ *No dinner.*

$ 🍴 **Tecolote Café.** *Southwestern.* The mantra at this celebrated bakery and breakfast joint is "no toast," and you won't miss it. Since 1980, the bellies of locals and tourists alike have been satisfied with delicious meals founded primarily on northern New Mexican cuisine. **Known for:** green-chile stew; the Sheepherder's Breakfast; the bakery basket of fresh muffins and biscuits. [$] *Average main: $9* ✉ *1616 Saint Michaels Dr., South Side* ☎ *505/988–1362* 🌐 *www.tecolotecafe.com* ⏲ *Closed Mon. No dinner.*

WHERE TO STAY

Updated by Andrew Collins

IN SANTA FE YOU CAN ensconce yourself in quintessential Southwestern style or anonymous hotel-chain decor, depending on how much you want to spend—the city has costlier accommodations than anywhere else in the Southwest. Cheaper options are available on Cerrillos (pronounced sir- *ee*-yos) Road, the rather unattractive business thoroughfare southwest of Downtown. Quality varies greatly on Cerrillos, but some of the best-managed, most attractive properties are (from roughly most to least expensive) the DoubleTree, Hyatt Place, Courtyard Marriott, Hampton Inn, Best Western Plus, Comfort Suites, and the Econolodge. You generally pay more as you get closer to the Plaza, but for many visitors it's worth it to be within walking distance of many attractions. Some of the best deals are offered by bed-and-breakfasts—many of those near the Plaza offer much better values than the big, touristy hotels. Rates drop, often from 30% to 50%, from November to April (excluding Thanksgiving and Christmas).

RENTALS AND RENTAL AGENCIES

In addition to the usual array of inns and hotels here, Santa Fe has a wide range of long- and short-term vacation rentals. Rates generally range from $150 to $300 per night for double-occupancy units, with better values at some of the two- to four-bedroom properties. Many have fully stocked kitchens. Another route is to rent a furnished condo or casita at one of several compounds geared to travelers seeking longer stays. Here are some top vacation-rental options in town.

★ $$$ FAMILY Fodor'sChoice 🏨 **Campanilla Compound.** *Rental.* A luxurious, secluded, yet centrally located tract of about 15 spacious one- and-two-bedroom vacation rentals on a hill just north of Downtown. $ *Rooms from: $250* ✉ *334 Otero St., North Side* ☎ *505/988–7585* 🌐 *www.campanillacompound.com* ⇨ *15 units* 🍴 *No meals.*

$$ FAMILY 🏨 **Fort Marcy Suites.** *Rental.* On a bluff just a 10-minute walk northeast of the Plaza with great views, this large, older compound comprises individually furnished units that accommodate two to six guests and come with full kitchens, wood fireplaces, DVDs, and CD stereos. ✉ *321 Kearney Ave., North Side* ☎ *888/570–2775* 🌐 *www.allseasonsresortlodging.com* ⇨ *100 units* 🍴 *No meals.*

$ 🏨 **Kokopelli Property Management.** *Rental.* A large, well-established agency, Kokopelli represents more than 70 vacation rentals in town, including everything from cozy two-bedroom casitas that rent for as low as $140 per day to ultra-posh mountain compounds that will set you back $850 per day during the busy months. ✉ *Santa Fe* ☎ *888/988–7244, 505/988–7244* 🌐 *www.kokoproperty.com* 🍴 *No meals.*

WHAT IT COSTS				
	$	$$	$$$	$$$$
Hotels	under $110	$110–$180	$181–$260	over $260

Prices are for two people in a standard double room in high season, excluding 12%–13% tax.

Hotel reviews have been shortened. For full information, visit Fodors.com.

4

THE PLAZA

$$$ 🏨 **Drury Plaza Hotel.** *Hotel.* One of Downtown Santa Fe's largest and most impressive hotels, this upscale property with a dramatic rooftop bar and pool opened in 2014 next to St. Francis Cathedral inside the masterfully transformed Territorial Revival–style former St. Vincent's Hospital. **Pros:** beautiful, light-filled public spaces; steps from Canyon Road and the Plaza; spacious rooms. **Cons:** parking is valet only and costs $16; some room amenities are a bit ordinary for an upscale hotel. [$] *Rooms from: $259* ✉ *828 Paseo de Peralta, The Plaza* ☎ *505/424–2175, 855/823–3954* 🌐 *www.druryhotels.com* 🛏 *182 rooms* 🍴 *Breakfast.*

$$$ 🏨 **Eldorado Hotel & Spa.** *Hotel.* Because it's the closest thing Santa Fe has to a convention hotel, the Eldorado sometimes gets a bad rap, but it's actually quite inviting, with individually decorated rooms and stunning mountain views. **Pros:** attractive accommodations three blocks from Plaza; great view from rooftop pool (especially at sunset); fun bar with great late-night food menu. **Cons:** staff's attention to service varies considerably; can be very expensive during busy periods. [$] *Rooms from: $235* ✉ *309 W. San Francisco St., The Plaza* ☎ *505/988–4455, 800/955–4455* 🌐 *www.eldoradohotel.com* 🛏 *213 rooms* 🍴 *No meals.*

$$ 🏨 **Hotel Chimayo de Santa Fe.** *Hotel.* Among the handful of
FAMILY mid-price, full-service hotels within a couple of blocks of the Plaza, this attractive, Territorial-style adobe hotel with a mix of spacious standard rooms and even bigger suites is a terrific option, especially given the extensive amenities available in many units—wet bars, kitchenettes, spacious sitting areas. **Pros:** unbeatable location; spacious rooms and

extensive in-room perks are nice for families or groups; the hotel offers free Downtown walking tours May–October. **Cons:** in a crowded part of Downtown; no pool or gym. [$] *Rooms from: $160* ✉ *125 Washington Ave., The Plaza* ☎ *505/988–4900, 877/901–7666* 🌐 *www.hotelchimayo.com* 🛏 *54 rooms* 🍴 *No meals.*

$$ 🏨 **Hotel St. Francis.** *Hotel.* Just one block south of the Plaza, this stately three-story hotel retains a historic vibe but has been given a modern flair—with expansive stone floors, plaster walls, and spare furnishings lit by massive pillar candles at night, the lobby feels a bit like a Tuscan monastery. **Pros:** a stylish, contemporary vibe in a historic building; two blocks from the Plaza and near many shops; excellent dining and nightlife on-site. **Cons:** service can be spotty; some rooms (and especially bathrooms) are quite small. [$] *Rooms from: $179* ✉ *210 Don Gaspar Ave., The Plaza* ☎ *505/983–5700, 877/901–7666* 🌐 *www.hotelstfrancis.com* 🛏 *80 rooms* 🍴 *No meals.*

$$$ **FAMILY** 🏨 **Inn and Spa at Loretto.** *Hotel.* This plush, oft-photographed, pueblo-inspired property attracts a loyal clientele, many of whom swear by the friendly staff and high decorating standards. **Pros:** ideal location; gorgeous grounds and pool; distinctive architecture. **Cons:** expensive parking and resort fees; bathrooms feel a bit ordinary, small, and dated, and they also lack counter space. [$] *Rooms from: $252* ✉ *211 Old Santa Fe Trail, The Plaza* ☎ *505/988–5531, 866/582–1646* 🌐 *www.hotelloretto.com* 🛏 *134 rooms* 🍴 *No meals.*

★ **$$** Fodor's Choice 🏨 **Inn of the Governors.** *Hotel.* This rambling, reasonably priced hotel by the Santa Fe River is staffed by a polite, enthusiastic bunch. **Pros:** close to Plaza; year-round, heated pool; free parking (unusual for Downtown). **Cons:** standard rooms are a bit small; some rooms view parking lot. [$] *Rooms from: $179* ✉ *101 W. Alameda St., The Plaza* ☎ *505/982–4333, 800/234–4534* 🌐 *www.innofthegovernors.com* 🛏 *100 rooms* 🍴 *Breakfast.*

$$ 🏨 **Inn on the Paseo.** *B&B/Inn.* This handily situated inn has fairly simple, if in some cases compact, rooms, but they're clean and light, some have hardwood floors, and all have pleasing Southwestern furnishings and color schemes—the best units even have fireplaces and private patios. **Pros:** just a few blocks from the Plaza; friendly, helpful staff. **Cons:** rooms facing the road receive some traffic noise. [$] *Rooms from: $140* ✉ *630 Paseo de Peralta, The Plaza* ☎ *505/984–8200, 855/984–8200* 🌐 *www.innonthepaseo.com* 🛏 *18 rooms* 🍴 *Breakfast.*

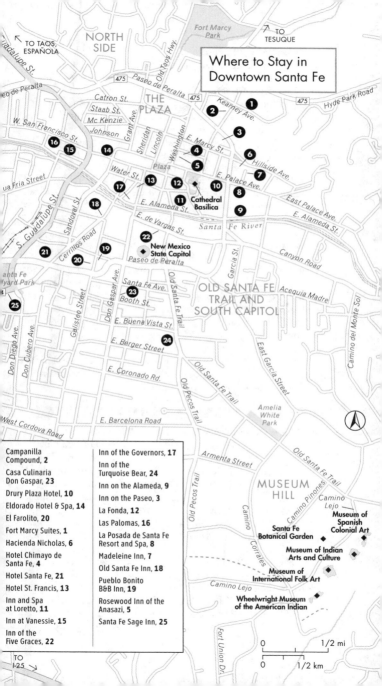

← TO TAOS, ESPAÑOLA

NORTH SIDE

Fort Marcy Park

↗ TO TESUQUE

Where to Stay in Downtown Santa Fe

Guadalupe St.

eo de Peralta

Paseo Old Taos Hwy.

Paseo de Peralta

Hyde Park Road

475

THE PLAZA

Catron St.

Staab St.

Mc Kenzie

Johnson

W. San Francisco St.

1

Kearney Ave.

2

3

E. Marcy St.

4

6

Hillside Ave.

5

7

E. Palace Ave.

16 **15**

14

Grant Ave.

Sheridan

Lincoln

Washington

Plaza

Water St.

13 **12**

10

8

East Palace Ave.

ua Fria Street

S. Guadalupe St.

17

18

E. Alameda St.

11 Cathedral Basilica

9

E. Alameda St.

Sandoval St.

Cerrillos Road

E. de Vargas St.

Santa Fe River

22

New Mexico State Capitol

Garcia St.

Canyon Road

21

19

20

Galisteo Street

Paseo de Peralta

anta Fe yard Park

OLD SANTA FE TRAIL AND SOUTH CAPITOL

Acequia Madre

25

Don Gaspar Ave.

Santa Fe Ave.

23

Booth St.

Don Diego Ave.

Don Cubero Ave.

E. Buena Vista St.

Old Santa Fe Trail

Garcia Street

Camino del Monte Sol

24

E. Berger Street

E. Coronado Rd.

East

West Cordova Road

E. Barcelona Road

Old Pecos Trail

Amelia White Park

Old Santa Fe Trail

Armenta Street

Camino Pinones

Old Santa Fe Trail

Camino Lejo

MUSEUM HILL

TO I-25 →

Campanilla Compound, **2**	Inn of the Governors, **17**
Casa Culinaria Don Gaspar, **23**	Inn of the Turquoise Bear, **24**
Drury Plaza Hotel, **10**	Inn on the Alameda, **9**
Eldorado Hotel & Spa, **14**	Inn on the Paseo, **3**
El Farolito, **20**	La Fonda, **12**
Fort Marcy Suites, **1**	Las Palomas, **16**
Hacienda Nicholas, **6**	La Posada de Santa Fe Resort and Spa, **8**
Hotel Chimayo de Santa Fe, **4**	Madeleine Inn, **7**
Hotel Santa Fe, **21**	Old Santa Fe Inn, **18**
Hotel St. Francis, **13**	Pueblo Bonito B&B Inn, **19**
Inn and Spa at Loretto, **11**	Rosewood Inn of the Anasazi, **5**
Inn at Vanessie, **15**	Santa Fe Sage Inn, **25**
Inn of the Five Graces, **22**	

Museum of Spanish Colonial Art

Santa Fe Botanical Garden

Museum of Indian Arts and Culture

Museum of International Folk Art

Camino Lejo

Wheelwright Museum of the American Indian

Fort Union Dr.

Camino Corrales

0   1/2 mi

0   1/2 km

★ Fodor'sChoice 🏨 **La Fonda.** *Hotel.* This venerable Downtown landmark completed its biggest renovation in nearly a century in 2013, its rooms upgraded with more modern amenities and better climate controls, but with a warm, artful design—including whimsical painted headboards and handcrafted furniture—that's faithful to the vision of Mary Elizabeth Jane Colter, the vaunted architect responsible for the hotel's elegant Southwestern aesthetic. **Pros:** iconic building steeped in history; free hotel history and art tours are offered several days a week; Plaza is right outside the door. **Cons:** lobby often packed with tourists and nonguests; fitness facilities are modest for an upscale hotel. [$] *Rooms from: $239* ✉ *100 E. San Francisco St., The Plaza* ☎ *505/982–5511, 800/523–5002* 🌐 *www.lafondasantafe.com* 🛏 *163 rooms* 🍴 *No meals.*
$$$

★ Fodor'sChoice 🏨 **Rosewood Inn of the Anasazi.** *Hotel.* This posh and artfully designed boutique hotel steps from the Plaza is one of Santa Fe's finest, with superb architectural detail, top-notch service, and a much-celebrated restaurant and bar. **Pros:** staff is thorough, gracious, and highly professional; superb restaurant and charming bar; beautiful, lodge-like public spaces that are ideal for conversation or curling up with a book. **Cons:** standard rooms are a bit small for the price; few rooms have balconies; no hot tub or pool. [$] *Rooms from: $390* ✉ *113 Washington Ave., The Plaza* ☎ *505/988–3030, 888/767–3966* 🌐 *www.rosewoodhotels.com* 🛏 *58 rooms* 🍴 *No meals.*
$$$$

OLD SANTA FE AND SOUTH CAPITOL

$$$ 🏨 **Casa Culinaria Don Gaspar.** *B&B/Inn.* One of the city's most charming little finds, this exquisitely landscaped and attractively decorated compound is on a pretty residential street a half mile south of the Plaza. **Pros:** some units have fully equipped kitchens; the owners offer superb breakfasts and cooking classes; lush gardens. **Cons:** occasional noise from nearby elementary school. [$] *Rooms from: $217* ✉ *623 Don Gaspar Ave., Old Santa Fe Trail and South Capitol* ☎ *505/986–8664, 888/986–8664* 🌐 *www.ccsantafe.com* 🛏 *10 rooms* 🍴 *Breakfast.*

$$$ 🏨 **El Farolito.** *B&B/Inn.* All the beautiful Southwestern and Mexican furniture in this small, upscale compound is custom-made, and all the art and photography original. **Pros:** attentive service; half of the casitas have private patios, and half have shared patio areas; ample free off-street parking. **Cons:** no on-site pool or hot tub. [$] *Rooms from: $195*

✉ *514 Galisteo St., Old Santa Fe Trail and South Capitol* ☎ *505/988–1631, 888/634–8782* ⊕ *www.farolito.com* ⤷ *7 rooms, 1 suite* ⦿ *Breakfast.*

★ **Fodor's**Choice ⊡ **Inn of the Five Graces.** *B&B/Inn.* There isn't
$$$$ another property in Santa Fe to compare to this sumptuous yet relaxed inn with an unmistakable East-meets-West feel. **Pros:** tucked into a quiet, ancient neighborhood; loads of cushy perks and in-room amenities; fantastic staff—attentive but not overbearing. **Cons:** very steep rates. $ *Rooms from: $575* ✉ *150 E. DeVargas St., Old Santa Fe Trail and South Capitol* ☎ *505/992–0957, 866/992–0957* ⊕ *www. fivegraces.com* ⤷ *23 suites* ⦿ *Breakfast.*

★ **Fodor's**Choice ⊡ **Inn of the Turquoise Bear.** *B&B/Inn.* In the
$$ 1920s, poet Witter Bynner played host to an eccentric circle of artists and intellectuals, as well as some wild parties in his mid-19th-century Spanish–Pueblo Revival home, which is now a superb bed-and-breakfast with a great location a few blocks from the capitol; in sum, it's the quintessential Santa Fe inn. **Pros:** gorgeous grounds and a house steeped in local history; gracious, knowledgeable staff; generous gourmet breakfasts. **Cons:** no pool or hot tub on-site; quirky layout of some rooms isn't for everyone; the least expensive rooms share a bath. $ *Rooms from: $155* ✉ *342 E. Buena Vista, Old Santa Fe Trail and South Capitol* ☎ *505/983–0798, 800/396–4104* ⊕ *www.turquoisebear. com* ⤷ *13 rooms* ⦿ *Breakfast.*

$$ ⊡ **Pueblo Bonito B&B Inn.** *B&B/Inn.* Rooms in this reasonably priced 1873 adobe compound have handmade and hand-painted furnishings, Navajo weavings, brick and hardwood floors, sand paintings and pottery, locally carved santos (Catholic saints), and Western art. **Pros:** intimate, cozy inn on peaceful grounds; excellent value. **Cons:** bathrooms tend to be small; on a slightly noisy street. $ *Rooms from: $135* ✉ *138 W. Manhattan Ave., Old Santa Fe Trail and South Capitol* ☎ *505/984–8001, 800/461–4599* ⊕ *www. pueblobonitoinn.com* ⤷ *19 rooms* ⦿ *Breakfast.*

EAST SIDE AND CANYON ROAD

★ **Fodor's**Choice ⊡ **Hacienda Nicholas.** *B&B/Inn.* This classic
$$ Santa Fe hacienda is just blocks from the Plaza yet set in a quiet residential area and sheltered from outside noises by thick adobe walls. **Pros:** reasonable rates for such a lovely, upscale inn; the inn uses eco-friendly products and practices. **Cons:** no hot tub or pool, but guests have privileges at El Gancho Health Club (a 15-minute drive). $ *Rooms*

from: $155 ✉ 320 E. Marcy St., East Side and Canyon Road ☎ 505/986–1431, 888/284–3170 🌐 www.haciendanicholas.com ⇆ 7 rooms 🍴 Breakfast.

★ Fodor's Choice 🏨 **Inn on the Alameda.** *Hotel.* Within an easy walk
$$$ of both the Plaza and Canyon Road, this mid-priced charmer with spacious Southwest-style rooms is one of the city's best small hotels. **Pros:** the solicitous staff is first-rate; excellent, expansive breakfast buffet and afternoon snacks; free parking. **Cons:** rooms closest to Alameda can be a bit noisy; no pool. [$] *Rooms from: $189 ✉ 303 E. Alameda St., East Side and Canyon Road ☎ 505/984–2121, 888/984–2121 🌐 www.innonthealameda.com ⇆ 69 rooms 🍴 Breakfast.*

$$$$ 🏨 **La Posada de Santa Fe Resort and Spa.** *Resort.* Rooms on
FAMILY the beautiful, quiet grounds of this hotel vary greatly in size and configuration, but the level of luxury befits the somewhat steep rates, especially given the considerable amenities and appealing East Side location. **Pros:** numerous amenities, including a top-notch spa and restaurant; a few blocks from Plaza and similarly close to Canyon Road; a large pool. **Cons:** resort can sometimes feel crowded; daily resort fee. [$] *Rooms from: $285 ✉ 330 E. Palace Ave., East Side and Canyon Road ☎ 505/986–0000, 855/210–7210 🌐 www.laposadadesantafe.com ⇆ 157 rooms 🍴 No meals.*

★ Fodor's Choice 🏨 **Madeleine Inn.** *B&B/Inn.* Santa Fe hasn't
$$ always been a town of pseudo-pueblo buildings, and this lovely Queen Anne Victorian is a dramatic reminder of the city's more eclectic architectural heritage. **Pros:** excellent value; good mix of historic charm and modern perks (iPods, flat-screen TVs); eco-friendly. **Cons:** the floral Victorian vibe isn't for everyone; no elevators in this three-story house. [$] *Rooms from: $155 ✉ 106 Faithway St., East Side and Canyon Road ☎ 505/982–3465, 888/877–7622 🌐 www.madeleineinn.com ⇆ 7 rooms 🍴 Breakfast.*

RAILYARD DISTRICT

★ Fodor's Choice 🏨 **Hotel Santa Fe.** *Hotel.* Picurís Pueblo has con-
$$ trolling interest in this handsome Pueblo-style three-story hotel on the Railyard District's edge and a 15-minute walk from the Plaza. **Pros:** professional, helpful staff; lots of amenities; easy access to Railyard District's trendy shopping and dining. **Cons:** standard rooms are a bit small; resort fee. [$] *Rooms from: $165 ✉ 1501 Paseo de Peralta, Railyard District ☎ 505/982–1200, 855/825–9876 🌐 www.hotelsantafe.com ⇆ 131 rooms 🍴 No meals.*

★ Fodor'sChoice **Old Santa Fe Inn.** *Hotel.* This contemporary motor court–style inn looks from the outside like an attractive, if fairly ordinary, adobe motel, but it has stunning and spotless rooms with elegant Southwestern decor. **Pros:** rooms are more inviting than several more-expensive Downtown hotels; short walk to the Plaza; free parking. **Cons:** rooms set around parking lot. *$ Rooms from: $175 ✉ 201 Montezuma Ave., Railyard District ☎ 505/995–0800, 855/244–6626 🌐 www.oldsantafeinn.com ⇨ 58 rooms 🍴 Breakfast.*
$$

$$ **Santa Fe Sage Inn.** *Hotel.* On the southern edge of the Railyard District, this smartly renovated motel offers affordable comfort, surprisingly attractive (given the reasonable rates) Southwestern decor, and a location that's just about a 15-minute walk from the Plaza. **Pros:** comfortable and affordable; small but nice pool; close to Railyard District attractions and galleries. **Cons:** rooms nearest the street can be noisy; $5 nightly parking charge. *$ Rooms from: $128 ✉ 725 Cerrillos Rd., Railyard District ☎ 505/982–5952, 866/433–0335 🌐 www.santafesage-inn.com ⇨ 155 rooms 🍴 Breakfast.*
FAMILY

4

WEST OF THE PLAZA

$$$$ **Inn at Vanessie.** *B&B/Inn.* The large rooms in this handsome adobe compound 2½ blocks from the Plaza are decorated with reed shutters, antique pine beds, viga-beam ceilings, hand-stenciled artwork, wood or brick floors, and a blend of cowboy, Hispanic, and Native American art and artifacts. **Pros:** elegant decor; free parking; popular restaurant and live-music venue next door. **Cons:** grounds are restricted—the inn overlooks a parking lot; steep rates. *$ Rooms from: $285 ✉ 427 W. Water St., West of the Plaza ☎ 505/984–1193, 🌐 www.vanessiesantafe.com ⇨ 18 rooms 🍴 Breakfast.*

$$ **Las Palomas.** *B&B/Inn.* It's a pleasant 10-minute walk west of the Plaza to reach this group of properties consisting of a few historic, luxurious compounds, one of them Spanish Pueblo–style adobe, another done in the Territorial style, and others ranging from rooms in renovated Victorian houses to contemporary condos with up to three bedrooms. **Pros:** kid-friendly, with swings and a play yard; on-site fitness center; most units feel very private and self-contained. **Cons:** big variations among the accommodations; no hot tub or pool on-site (guests may use pool at the Hotel Santa Fe). *$ Rooms from: $139 ✉ 460 W. San Francisco St., West of the Plaza ☎ 505/982–5560, 855/982–5560 🌐 www.laspalomas.com ⇨ 63 units 🍴 Breakfast.*

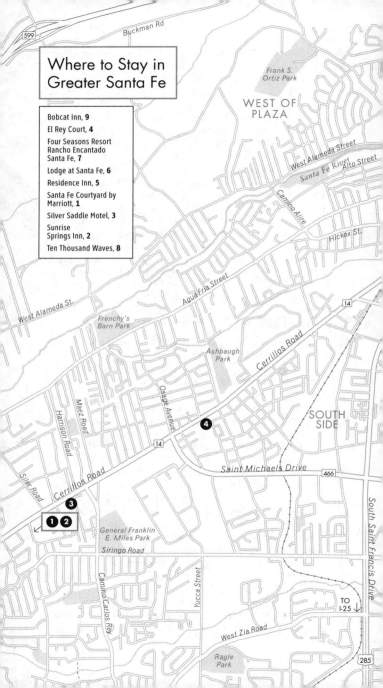

Where to Stay in Greater Santa Fe

Bobcat Inn, **9**

El Rey Court, **4**

Four Seasons Resort Rancho Encantado Santa Fe, **7**

Lodge at Santa Fe, **6**

Residence Inn, **5**

Santa Fe Courtyard by Marriott, **1**

Silver Saddle Motel, **3**

Sunrise Springs Inn, **2**

Ten Thousand Waves, **8**

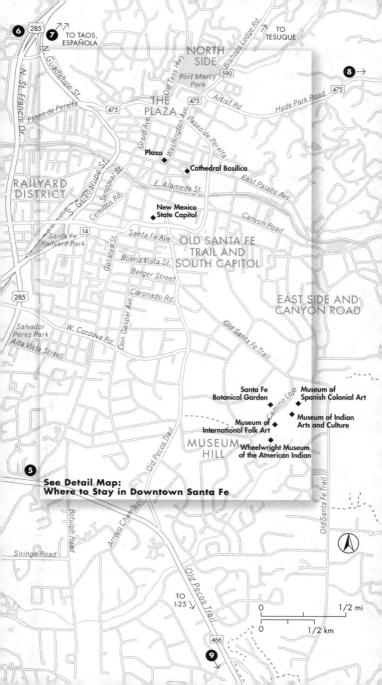

6 285

7 ↗↗ TO TAOS,
ESPAÑOLA

TO
TESUQUE

N. St. Francis Dr.
N. Guadalupe St.
Paseo de Peralta

NORTH
SIDE

Fort Marcy
Park

590

Old Taos Hwy.

Bishops Lodge Rd.

8 →

Artist Rd.

Hyde Park Road

475

THE
PLAZA

475

Grant Ave.
Washington Ave.
Paseo de Peralta

475

Plaza ◆
◆ Cathedral Basilica

RAILWAY
DISTRICT

Sandoval St.
S. Guadalupe St.

E. Alameda St.

East Palace Ave.

Cerrillos Rd.

New Mexico
State Capitol ◆

Canyon Road

14
Santa Fe
Railyard Park

Galisteo St.

Santa Fe Ave.

OLD SANTA FE
TRAIL AND
SOUTH CAPITOL

Buena Vista St.

285

Berger Street

Coronado Rd.

EAST SIDE AND
CANYON ROAD

Don Gaspar Ave.

Salvador
Perez Park
Alta Vista Street

W. Cordova Rd.

Old Santa Fe Trail

Santa Fe
Botanical Garden

Camino Lejo

Museum of
Spanish Colonial Art
◆

◆ Museum of Indian
Arts and Culture

Old Pecos Trail

◆ Museum of
International Folk Art

Old Santa Fe Trail

5 See Detail Map:
Where to Stay in Downtown Santa Fe

MUSEUM
HILL

◆ Wheelwright Museum
of the American Indian

Botulph Road

Arroyo Chamiso

Siringo Road

TO
I-25

Old Pecos Trail

0   1/2 mi

0   1/2 km

466

9 ↓

NORTH SIDE

★ Fodor's Choice **Four Seasons Resort Rancho Encantado Santa Fe.** *Resort.* This secluded and stunning luxury compound on a dramatic, sunset-facing bluff in the Sangre de Cristo foothills exemplifies the Four Seasons brand's famously flawless sense of gracious hospitality and efficiency. **Pros:** freestanding couples spa suites; complimentary minibar (nonalcoholic beverages only); stunning rooms and views. **Cons:** several of the private terraces overlook parking lots; remote location. [$] *Rooms from: $490* ✉ *198 NM 592, North Side* ☎ *505/946–5700, 855/674–5401* 🌐 *www.fourseasons.com/santafe* ⇨ *65 rooms* 🍴 *No meals.*
$$$$

$$ **Lodge at Santa Fe.** *Hotel.* Rooms at this mid-price property have pleasant Southwestern furnishings and earth-tone fabrics. **Pros:** away from the crowds and noise of the Plaza; nice mountain views from some rooms. **Cons:** room decor and bathrooms are a bit dated; not much within walking distance. [$] *Rooms from: $152* ✉ *750 N. St. Francis Dr., North Side* ☎ *505/992–5800, 888/563–4373* 🌐 *www.lodgeatsantafe.com* ⇨ *125 rooms* 🍴 *No meals.*
FAMILY

★ Fodor's Choice **Ten Thousand Waves.** *B&B/Inn.* Devotees appreciate the authentic *onsen* (Japanese-style baths) atmosphere of this 20-acre Japanese-inspired spa and boutique resort in the picturesque foothills a few miles northeast of town. **Pros:** artful, unfussy furnishings; outstanding restaurant; a soothing, spiritual vibe pervades. **Cons:** a bit remote; the spa and baths can get crowded with day visitors. [$] *Rooms from: $215* ✉ *3451 Hyde Park Rd., 4 miles northeast of the Plaza, North Side* ☎ *505/982–9304* 🌐 *www.tenthousandwaves.com* ⇨ *13 cottages* 🍴 *Breakfast.*
$$$

SOUTH SIDE

$$ **Bobcat Inn.** *B&B/Inn.* A delightful, affordable, country hacienda that's a 15-minute drive southeast of the Plaza, this adobe bed-and-breakfast sits amid 10 secluded acres of piñon and ponderosa pine, with grand views of the Ortiz Mountains and the area's high-desert mesas. **Pros:** gracious inn and secluded location; wonderful hosts. **Cons:** located well outside town. [$] *Rooms from: $135* ✉ *442 Old Las Vegas Hwy., South Side* ☎ *505/988–9239* 🌐 *www.bobcatinn.com* ⇨ *5 rooms* 🍴 *Breakfast.*

★ Fodor'sChoice 🏨 **El Rey Court.** *Hotel.* The kind of place where
$$ Lucy and Ricky might have stayed during one of their
FAMILY cross-country adventures, the El Rey was built in 1936
but has been brought gracefully into the 21st century,
its rooms and bathrooms handsomely updated without
losing any period charm. **Pros:** excellent price for a dis-
tinctive, charming property; nicely landscaped grounds;
in most cases you can pull your car right up to your room.
Cons: rooms closest to Cerrillos Road can be noisy; some
rooms are quite dark. Ⓢ *Rooms from: $135* ✉ *1862 Cer-
rillos Rd., South Side* ☎ *505/982–1931* ⊕ *www.elreycourt.
com* ⤳ *86 rooms* ⊘*Breakfast.*

$$ 🏨 **Residence Inn.** *Hotel.* This compound consists of clusters
of three-story adobe town houses with pitched roofs and
tall chimneys. **Pros:** complimentary full breakfast; evening socials; grocery-shopping service. **Cons:** not within
easy walking distance of many restaurants or attractions.
Ⓢ *Rooms from: $169* ✉ *1698 Galisteo St., South Side*
☎ *505/988–7300, 800/331–3131* ⊕ *www.marriott.com/
safnm* ⤳ *120 suites* ⊘*Breakfast.*

$$ 🏨 **Santa Fe Courtyard by Marriott.** *Hotel.* This reliable mid-
range chain property along prosaic Cerrillos Road stands
out for its high standards of comfort and service, even
though it looks like a lot of the others: clad in faux adobe
and surrounded by parking lots and strip malls. **Pros:** rooms
have the usual chain doodads: mini-refrigerators, coffee-
makers, and hair dryers. **Cons:** hotel lacks character; on
an unattractive stretch of Cerrillos Road; a 10-minute
drive from Plaza. Ⓢ *Rooms from: $116* ✉ *3347 Cerrillos
Rd., South Side* ☎ *505/473–2800, 800/777–3347* ⊕ *www.
marriott.com* ⤳ *213 rooms* ⊘*No meals.*

★ Fodor'sChoice 🏨 **Silver Saddle Motel.** *Hotel.* This low-slung
$ adobe property significantly transcends the generally sketchy
quality of the several other budget motels along Cerril-
los Road, thanks to the tireless efforts of its owner. **Pros:**
super-affordable; good-sized rooms, some with refrigera-
tors; friendly, helpful staff. **Cons:** rooms toward the front
get noise from Cerrillos Road; very few frills; a 15-minute
drive from the Plaza. Ⓢ *Rooms from: $65* ✉ *2810 Cerrillos
Rd., South Side* ☎ *505/471–7663* ⊕ *www.santafesilversad-
dlemotel.com* ⤳ *27 rooms* ⊘*Breakfast.*

★ Fodor'sChoice 🏨 **Sunrise Springs Inn.** *Resort.* This tranquil
$$$$ 70-acre resort offers 32 rooms overlooking verdant gar-
dens and 20 casitas with gas fireplaces and secluded patios,
plus a first-rate spa focused on energy healing and inte-
grative medicine, open-air private and communal soaking

tubs, yoga and fitness studios, a sweat lodge and sacred medicine wheel, and an outstanding restaurant—Blue Heron—serving healthful, locally sourced contemporary fare. **Pros:** restaurant uses organic vegetables and herbs grown on-site; the cottonwood-shaded soaking tubs are unbelievably soothing; superb spa with an extensive list of treatments—including playing with puppies in training to become service dogs. **Cons:** a 20-minute drive away from Downtown. [$] *Rooms from: $265* ✉ *242 Los Pinos Rd., South Side* ☎ *505/471–3600, 800/704–0531* 🌐 *www.sunrisesprings.ojospa.com* 🛏 *52 rooms* 🍴 *Breakfast.*

NIGHTLIFE AND PERFORMING ARTS

Updated by Andrew Collins

FEW SMALL CITIES IN AMERICA can claim an arts scene as thriving as Santa Fe's—with opera, symphony, and theater in splendid abundance. The music acts here tend to be high caliber, but rather sporadic. Santa Fe has a decent, and steadily improving, crop of bars, many specializing in craft beers and artisan cocktails, but evening carousing tends to wind down early, and this is not a destination for clubbing and dancing. When popular acts do occasionally come to town, the whole community shows up and dances like there's no tomorrow. A super, eight-week series of music on the Plaza bandstand runs through the summer with performances four nights a week. Gallery openings, poetry readings, plays, and dance concerts take place year-round, not to mention the famed opera and chamber-music festivals. Check the arts and entertainment listings in Santa Fe's daily newspaper, the *New Mexican* (⊕*www.santafenewmexican.com*), particularly on Friday, when the arts and entertainment section, "Pasatiempo," is included, or check the weekly *Santa Fe Reporter* (⊕*www.sfreporter.com*) for shows and events. As you might suspect, activities peak in the summer.

NIGHTLIFE

Culturally endowed though it is, Santa Fe has a pretty mellow nightlife scene; its key strength is live music, which is presented at numerous bars, hotel lounges, and restaurants. Regionally renowned blues, jazz, folk, country and other acts wander into town, and members of blockbuster bands have been known to perform unannounced at small clubs while vacationing in the area. But on most nights your best bet might be quiet cocktails beside the flickering embers of a piñon fire or under the stars out on the patio.

BARS AND LOUNGES

Agave Lounge. The side bar at the Hotel Eldorado is stylish and contemporary, making it just as much of a hit with locals and nonguests as with those staying on property. The well-made cocktails, natty decor, happy hour deals, and stellar late-night bar-food menu (seared tuna with avocado, street tacos) are among Agave's key assets. ✉ *Eldorado Hotel, 309 W. San Francisco St., The Plaza* ☎ *505/995–4530* ⊕ *www.eldoradohotel.com/agave-lounge.*

★ **Fodor's Choice Bell Tower Bar.** The lofty rooftop perch at historic Hotel La Fonda is open only from mid-spring through mid-fall, but during the warmer months it's one of the loveliest places in town to sip cocktails while watching the sunset and surrounding mountains. Year-round, you can also enjoy outstanding margaritas and tasty bar food in lively La Fiesta Lounge, just off the hotel lobby, which also features live music. ✉ *Hotel La Fonda, 100 E. San Francisco St., The Plaza* ☎ *505/982–5511* ⊕ *www.lafondasantafe.com.*

Cowgirl BBQ. This rollicking barbecue and burgers joint is one of the most popular places in town for live blues, country, rock, folk, and even karaoke. The bar is friendly and the cheap happy hour margaritas provide a lot of bang for the buck. The fun pool hall can get wild as the night gets late. ✉ *319 S. Guadalupe St., Railyard District* ☎ *505/982–2565* ⊕ *www.cowgirlsantafe.com.*

Del Charro. The laid-back saloon at Downtown's Inn of the Governors serves a fine green-chile cheeseburger, plus quality margaritas and the like. It's less fancy than some of the other hotel bars in town, with old-fashioned Western decor, dark-wood paneling (warmed by the glow of a wood-burning fireplace), and an airy patio. ✉ *Inn of the Governors, 101 W. Alameda St., The Plaza* ☎ *505/954–0320* ⊕ *www. delcharro.com.*

Draft Station. Beer aficionados can sample a remarkable variety of New Mexican craft brews—including selections from Marble Brewery, La Cumbre, Bosque Brewing, and Chama River Brewing—at this cheery spot with a large balcony overlooking the Plaza. You can order pizza to enjoy with your beer from Rooftop Pizzeria, which is just down the hall. There's an Albuquerque branch, too. ✉ *60 E. San Francisco St., Santa Fe Arcade, 2nd fl., The Plaza* ☎ *505/983–6443* ⊕ *www.draft-station.com.*

★ Fodor'sChoice **Duel Brewing.** Sip superb Belgian-style ales, including a number of aromatic seasonal saisons, at the craft brewery bar and tasting room down the street from the famed Meow Wolf art installation, whose bar also features Duel Brewing beers. Exceptionally tasty sandwiches as well as charcuterie and cheese boards complement the brews. ✉ *1228 Parkway Dr., South Side* ☎ *505/474–5301* ⊕ *www.duelbrewing.com.*

★ Fodor'sChoice **El Farol.** With its long front portal and expansive back patio, this ancient adobe restaurant is a lovely spot to enjoy the afternoons and evenings of summer. The roomy, rustic lounge has a true Old West atmosphere—there's been a bar on the premises since 1835—and you can order some fine Spanish brandies and sherries in addition to cold beers, sangria, and margaritas, and the kitchen turns out authentic Spanish fare, from hearty paellas to lighter tapas. It's a great place to see a variety of music, including first-rate flamenco dinner shows; the dance floor fills up with a friendly crowd. ⊠ *808 Canyon Rd., East Side and Canyon Road* ☎ *505/983–9912* ⊕ *www.elfarolsf.com.*

★ **Fodor'sChoice Santa Fe Spirits Downtown Tasting Room.** One of the Southwest's most acclaimed artisan distilleries, known for Expedition Vodka, Apple Brandy, Slow Burn Smoked Gin Liqueur, and several other robust elixirs, operates this convivial tasting room and cocktail bar with comfy leather bar stools and sofas. On warm evenings, sip drinks on the lovely patio. Distillery tours, by reservation, are available at the main production facility out near the airport. ⊠ *308 Read St., Railyard District* ☎ *505/780–5906* ⊕ *www.santafespirits.com.*

Second Street Brewery. This long-popular brewpub has three locations in town, including a spiffy new branch on the South Side by Meow Wolf. The outpost at the Railyard is especially popular and within easy walking distance of Downtown hotels. At all venues, there's great live music (usually rock or folk) or DJs many nights, patios, and a rotating selection of terrific beers. A substantial food menu includes good burgers and pub favorites. ⊠ *1607 Paseo de Peralta, in back of farmers' market bldg., Railyard District* ☎ *505/989–3278* ⊕ *www.secondstreetbrewery.com.*

★ **Fodor'sChoice Secreto Lounge.** This beautifully designed bar inside the historic Hotel St. Francis makes some of the best and most interesting craft cocktails in the state, including a classic Manhattan with clove tincture spritzed over the top, and a smoked-sage margarita. There's a nice selection of appetizers and light entrées, as well, prepared by the kitchen at the hotel's Tabla de Los Santos restaurant. Just across the hotel lobby, you can also sample superb New Mexico wines at Gruet Winery Tasting Room. ⊠ *210 Don Gaspar Ave., The Plaza* ☎ *505/983–5700* ⊕ *www.hotelstfrancis.com.*

Tonic. At this intimate, high-ceilinged bar with a dapper art deco interior, sip deftly crafted cocktails and listen to some of the best jazz acts in town. It's one of the few late-night spots serving bar food until 1 most evenings. ⊠ *103 E. Water St., The Plaza* ☎ *505/982–1189* ⊕ *www.facebook. com/tonicsantafe.*

PERFORMING ARTS

The performing arts scene in Santa Fe blossoms in summer when the calendar fills with classical and jazz performances, Shakespeare productions at various venues, experimental theater at Santa Fe Playhouse, and nearly 80 free concerts on the Plaza.... "Too many choices!" is the biggest complaint. The rest of the year things quiet down a bit, but several notable performing-arts groups are prolific from fall through spring, including Performance Santa Fe, Santa Fe Pro Musica, Santa Fe Symphony, and fantastic flamenco performances. The "Pasatiempo" section of the *Santa Fe New Mexican*'s Friday edition, which is also distributed as a free stand-alone in newspaper stands around town, or the *Santa Fe Reporter*, released on Wednesday, are great sources for current happenings.

ARTS CENTERS

Center for Contemporary Arts (CCA). The city's most interesting multiuse arts venue, the Center for Contemporary Arts (CCA) presents indie and foreign films, art exhibitions, provocative theater, and countless workshops and lectures. ✉ *1050 Old Pecos Trail, Old Santa Fe Trail and South Capitol* ☎ *505/982–1338* ⊕ *www.ccasantafe.org.*

CONCERT VENUES

★ Fodor'sChoice **Lensic Performing Arts Center.** Santa Fe's vintage Downtown movie house has been fully restored and converted into the 850-seat Lensic Performing Arts Center. The grand 1931 building, with Moorish and Spanish Renaissance influences, hosts the Santa Fe Symphony, theater, classic films, lectures and readings, noted world, pop, and jazz musicians, and many other prominent events. ✉ *211 W. San Francisco St., The Plaza* ☎ *505/988–7050* ⊕ *www.lensic.com.*

St. Francis Auditorium. This historic space with colorful murals inside the Museum of Fine Arts is a top venue for many cultural events, such as theatrical productions and concerts. ✉ *107 W. Palace Ave., The Plaza* ☎ *505/476–5072* ⊕ *www.nmartmuseum.org.*

DANCE

Aspen Santa Fe Ballet. The esteemed company presents several ballet performances throughout the year at the Lensic Performing Arts Center. ✉ *Santa Fe* ☎ *505/988–1234* ⊕ *www.aspensantafeballet.com.*

El Flamenco. Several organizations produce flamenco concerts around town, including the prestigious Entreflamenco Company, which performs at El Flamenco restaurant a few blocks from the Plaza. ✉ *135 W. Palace Ave., The Plaza* ☎ *505/209–1302* ⊕ *www.entreflamenco.com.*

FILM

★ Fodor'sChoice **Jean Cocteau Cinema.** Author and longtime Santa Fe resident George R. R. Martin, of *Game of Thrones* fame, has restored this intimate, funky Railyard District art-movie house. This single-screen theater is a great place to catch first-run films, indie flicks, and cult classics. ✉ *418 Montezuma Ave., Railyard District* ☎ *505/466–5528* ⊕ *www.jeancocteaucinema.com.*

Santa Fe Film Festival. With the film industry booming in New Mexico, this five-day event held in mid-February has become increasingly well attended, and film screenings, workshops, and discussion panels take place at venues around the city. Movie buffs should also mark their calendars for the Santa Fe Independent Film Festival (⊕ *www.santafeindependentfilmfestival.com*), which takes place over four days in mid-October, with an emphasis, of course, on indie flicks. ✉ *Santa Fe* ☎ *505/216–6063* ⊕ *www.santafe-filmfestival.com.*

Violet Crown Cinema. This state-of-the-art multiscreen cinema in the Railyard District shows everything from blockbusters to indie and vintage movies and offers a restaurant and bar featuring craft brews and ciders, fine wine, and sophisticated food options, which you can eat in the theaters. Reserved seating means never having to settle for a bad row. ✉ *1606 Alcaldesa St., Railyard District* ☎ *505/216–5678* ⊕ *santafe.violetcrown.com.*

MUSIC

New Mexico Jazz Festival. Begun in 2006 and now widely acclaimed, this nearly monthlong festival presents numerous concerts in both Santa Fe and Albuquerque from mid-July through early August. Recent performers have included Stanley Clarke, the Yellowjackets, Dianne Reeves, and Allen Toussaint. ⊠ *Santa Fe* ☎ *505/268–0044* ⊕ *www.outpostspace.org.*

Performance Santa Fe. From September through May, the venerable organization (aka Santa Fe Concert Association) founded in 1937 presents symphony and solo classical concerts, lectures, dance recitals, opera, and family-minded shows at several venues around town, including the Lensic, St. Francis Auditorium, and United Church of Santa Fe. The organization has brought a number of prestigious talents to Santa Fe over the years, including Wynton Marsalis, Kronos Quartet, and the Academy of St. Martin in the Fields Chamber Ensemble. ⊠ *324 Paseo de Peralta* ☎ *505/984–8759* ⊕ *www.performancesantafe.org.*

Santa Fe Bandstand Concerts. Tuesday through Saturday nights throughout July and August, free concerts are staged at the bandstand in Downtown's festive and historic Plaza or occasionally at Swan Park on the South Side (off NM 599). A number of nationally noteworthy artists have appeared for this event, where the music ranges from Spanish guitar to blues to rockabilly. ⊠ *Old Santa Fe Trail at Palace Ave., The Plaza* ☎ *505/986–6054* ⊕ *www.santafebandstand.org.*

★ **Fodor's**Choice **Santa Fe Chamber Music Festival.** This outstanding festival runs mid-July through late August, with performances nearly every night at the art-filled St. Francis Auditorium, or, occasionally, the Lensic Performing Arts Center. There are also free youth-oriented concerts given on several summer mornings. ⊠ *Santa Fe* ☎ *505/983–2075, 888/221–9836* ⊕ *www.santafechambermusic.com.*

Santa Fe Desert Chorale. Performances take place over about three weeks in late July and early August at a variety of intriguing venues, from the Cathedral Basilica St. Francis to Loretto Chapel. This highly regarded singing group, which was started in 1982, also performs during the December holiday season. ⊠ *Santa Fe* ☎ *505/988–2282, 800/244–4011* ⊕ *www.desertchorale.org.*

★ **Fodor's**Choice **Santa Fe Opera.** To watch opera in this strikingly modern structure—a 2,128-seat, indoor-outdoor amphitheater with excellent acoustics and sight lines—is a memorable visual and auditory experience. Carved into the natural curves of a hillside 7 miles north of the Plaza, the opera overlooks mountains, mesas, and sky. Add some of the most acclaimed operatic talents from Europe and the

United States, and you begin to understand the excitement that builds every June. This world-renowned company presents five works in repertory each summer—a blend of seasoned classics, neglected masterpieces, and world premieres. Many evenings sell out far in advance, but less expensive standing-room tickets are often available on the day of the performance. A favorite pre-opera pastime is tailgating in the parking lot before the evening performance—many guests set up elaborate picnics of their own, but you can also preorder picnic meals at the opera website or by calling 24 hours in advance. Alternatively, you can dine at the Preview Dinner, set up 2½ hours before each performance by the Guilds of the Santa Fe Opera. These meals include a large spread of very good food along with wine, held on the opera grounds. During dessert, a prominent local expert on opera gives a talk about the evening's performance. The Preview Dinner is by reservation only and the cost is $70 per person. ⊠ *301 Opera Dr., off U.S. 285/84, North Side* ☎ *505/986–5900, 800/280–4654* ⊕ *www.santafeopera.org.*

Santa Fe Pro Musica. First-rate orchestra and chamber concerts are given at St. Francis Auditorium and the Lensic Performing Arts Center by the Grammy-nominated Santa Fe Pro Musica from September through April. Baroque and other classical compositions are the normal fare; the annual Christmas performance, held at Loretto Chapel, is a highlight. ⊠ *Santa Fe* ☎ *505/988–4640, 505/988–1234 ticket office* ⊕ *www.sfpromusica.org.*

Santa Fe Symphony. This highly respected symphony performs about 10 concerts each season (September to May) in the Lensic Performing Arts Center. ⊠ *Santa Fe* ☎ *505/983–3530, 800/480–1319* ⊕ *www.santafesymphony.org.*

THEATER

Santa Fe Playhouse. The oldest extant theater company west of the Mississippi, the Santa Fe Playhouse occupies a converted 19th-century adobe stable and has been presenting an adventurous mix of avant-garde pieces, classical drama, and musical comedy since 1922—the season runs year-round. The Fiesta Melodrama—a spoof of the Santa Fe scene—pokes sly fun from late August to mid-September. ⊠ *142 E. De Vargas St., Old Santa Fe Trail and South Capitol* ☎ *505/988–4262* ⊕ *www.santafeplayhouse.org.*

SHOPS AND SPAS

Updated by Andrew Collins

SANTA FE HAS BEEN A trading post for eons. Nearly a thousand years ago the great pueblos of the Chacoan civilizations were strategically located between the buffalo-hunting tribes of the Great Plains and the Indians of Mexico. Native Americans in New Mexico traded turquoise and other valuables with Indians from Mexico for metals, shells, parrots, and other exotic items. After the arrival of the Spanish and the West's subsequent development, Santa Fe became the place to exchange silver from Mexico and natural resources from New Mexico for manufactured goods, whiskey, and greenbacks from the United States. The construction of the railroad in 1880 brought Santa Fe access to all kinds of manufactured goods.

The trading legacy remains, but now Downtown Santa Fe caters increasingly to those looking for handmade furniture and crafts, and bespoke apparel and accessories. Sure, a few chains have moved in and a handful of fairly tatty souvenir shops still proliferate, but shopping in Santa Fe consists mostly of high-quality, one-of-a-kind independent stores. Canyon Road, packed with internationally acclaimed galleries, is the perfect place to browse for art and collectibles. The Downtown blocks around the Plaza have unusual gift and curio shops, as well as clothiers and shoe stores that range from theatrical to conventional. You'll find quite a few art galleries here, too. The hip, revitalized Railyard District (sometimes referred to as the Guadalupe District), less touristy than the Plaza, is on Downtown's southwest perimeter and includes a wide-ranging mix of trendy boutiques, gift shops, and avant-garde contemporary art galleries—it's arguably the most eclectic of Santa Fe's shopping areas.

SHOPS

ANTIQUES, GIFTS, AND HOME FURNISHINGS

Array. In this cozy Railyard District shop you'll find a well-curated selection of home goods—tableware, candles and folk art from Mexico, tote bags, toys, and even a few antiques. Note the very nice selection of lotions and body-care products made in New Mexico. ⊠ *322 S. Guadalupe St., Railyard District* ☎ *505/699–2760* ⊕ *www.arrayhome. com* ☉ *Oct.–Mar., closed Sun.*

Arrediamo. One of the top spots in the Southwest for handmade Turkish, Persian, and Afghan rugs, Arrediamo also carries a fine selection of authentic Navajo rugs and textiles. ⊠ *214 Galisteo St., The Plaza* ☎ *505/820–2331* ⊕ *www. arrediamo.com.*

Casa Nova. A spacious shop that sells functional and decorative art from around the world, Casa Nova deftly mixes colors, textures, and cultural icons—old and new—from stylish pewter tableware from South Africa to vintage hand-carved ex-votos (votive offerings) from Brazil. There is a major emphasis here on goods produced by artists and cooperatives focused on sustainable economic development. ⊠ *530 S. Guadalupe St., Railyard District* ☎ *505/983–8558* ⊕ *www.casanovagallery.com* ☉ *Closed Sun.*

Design Warehouse. A welcome antidote to Santa Fe's preponderance of shops selling Native American and Spanish-colonial antiques, Design Warehouse carries hip, contemporary furniture, kitchenware, home accessories, and other sleek knickknacks, including vaunted brands like Alessi, Knoll, and Normann Copenhagen. Note the select collection of amusing books for kids and adults. ⊠ *101 W. Marcy St., The Plaza* ☎ *505/988–1555* ⊕ *www. designwarehousesantafe.com.*

★ Fodor'sChoice **Doodlet's.** Check out the whimsical collection of stuff: pop-up books, silly postcards, tin art, hooked rugs, and stringed lights. Wonderment is in every display case, drawing the eye to the unusual. There's something for just about everyone at this delightfully quirky shop, and often it's affordable. ⊠ *120 Don Gaspar Ave., The Plaza* ☎ *505/983–3771* ⊕ *www.doodlets.com.*

★ Fodor'sChoice **Jackalope.** You could easily spend a couple of
FAMILY hours wandering through this legendary indoor-outdoor bazaar, which sprawls over 7 acres, incorporating several pottery barns, a furniture store, endless aisles of knickknacks from Latin America and Asia, a huge greenhouse, and a prairie dog village (a fun diversion if you have kids along). There's also an area where craftspeople, artisans, and others sell their wares—sort of a mini flea market. ⊠ *2820 Cerrillos Rd., South Side* ☎ *505/471–8539* ⊕ *www. jackalope.com.*

La Mesa. La Mesa has become well known for showcasing contemporary handcrafted, mostly functional, works by more than two dozen, mostly local, artists including Kathy O'Neill, Gregory Lomayesva, and Ritchie Mole. Collections include dinnerware, glassware, pottery, lighting, fine art, and accessories. ✉ *225 Canyon Rd., East Side and Canyon Road* ☎ *505/984–1688* ⊕ *www.lamesaofsantafe.com.*

Pandora's. Beautiful, carefully curated items for the home—some produced regionally and others from Peru, Uzbekistan, the Congo, and other far-flung lands—are the specialty of this colorful boutique in DeVargas Center. Keep an eye out for quilts made by a weaving co-op in Vietnam and brightly colored Missoni bath linens. ✉ *173 Paseo de Peralta, West of the Plaza* ☎ *505/982–3298* ⊕ *www. pandorasantafe.com.*

ART GALLERIES

Over the past three decades, Santa Fe has outgrown its reputation as a provincial, albeit respected, market for traditional Southwest art. Galleries carrying works by both vintage and contemporary artists who specialize in Western landscapes and scenes still thrive, but Santa Fe now rivals cities many times its size when it comes to edgy, provocative, and often high-priced abstract and contemporary works in every imaginable media. The following are only a limited but notable sampling of the roughly 200 galleries in greater Santa Fe—with the best of representational, nonobjective, Native American, Latin American, cutting-edge, photographic, and soulful works that defy categorization. *The Collectors Guide to Santa Fe, Taos, and Albuquerque* is a good resource for learning about more galleries; you can pick up this free publication at hotels and shops around town, or browse listings online at ⊕ *www.collectorsguide.com.* Check the "Pasatiempo" pullout in the *Santa Fe New Mexican* on Friday for a preview of weekly gallery openings.

★ Fodor'sChoice **Andrew Smith Gallery.** This highly esteemed photo gallery deals in works by Edward S. Curtis and other 19th-century chroniclers of the American West. Other major figures are Ansel Adams, Edward Weston, O. Winston Link, Henri Cartier-Bresson, Eliot Porter, Laura Gilpin, Dorothea Lange, Alfred Stieglitz, Annie Liebovitz, and regional artists like Barbara Van Cleve. ✉ *122 Grant Ave., The Plaza* ☎ *505/984–1234* ⊕ *www.andrewsmithgallery. com* ☉ *Closed Sun.*

Art of Russia Gallery. The art communities of Santa Fe and Taos have a surprisingly strong connection with those of Russia, and this Canyon Road space carries a particularly strong collection of works by contemporary and historic

Russian artists, including a number of Impressionist paintings. A highlight here is the selection of USSR propaganda posters. ⊠ *225 Canyon Rd., East Side and Canyon Road* ☎ *505/466–1718* ⊕ *www.artofrussiagallery.com.*

Bellas Artes. A sophisticated gallery with a serene sculpture garden, Bellas Artes has a captivating collection of ceramics, paintings, photography, and sculptural work, and represents internationally renowned artists like Judy Pfaff, David Kimball Anderson, and Olga de Amaral. The vanguard modernist work of sculptor Ruth Duckworth is also well represented. ⊠ *653 Canyon Rd., East Side and Canyon Road* ☎ *505/983–2745* ⊕ *www.bellasartesgallery. com* ⊙ *Closed Sun. and Mon.*

Charlotte Jackson Fine Art. This Railyard District notable focuses primarily on monochromatic "radical" painting and sculpture and is set in a fantastic, open space in a renovated warehouse. Many of the pieces here are large-scale, with "drama" the guiding force. Joe Barnes, William Metcalf, Constance DeJong, and Winston Roeth are among the artists producing minimalist works dealing with light and space. ⊠ *554 S. Guadalupe St., Railyard District* ☎ *505/989–8688* ⊕ *www.charlottejackson.com* ⊙ *Sun. and Mon. by appointment only.*

EVOKE Contemporary. In a striking, high-ceilinged space in the Railyard District, EVOKE ranks among the more diverse contemporary galleries in town, with works by renowned landscape painters (Lynn Boggess, Michael Workman, and the late Louisa McElwain), outsider folk art by Nicholas Herrera, surrealist portraits by self-taught painter Jorge Santos, and intricate sgraffiti by Alice Leora Briggs. ⊠ *550 S. Guadalupe St., Railyard District* ☎ *505/995–9902* ⊕ *www. evokecontemporary.com.*

★ Fodor'sChoice **Gerald Peters Gallery.** Santa Fe's most impressive gallery of American and European art from the 19th century to the present. Contained within are works by Max Weber, Albert Bierstadt, Frederic Remington, the Taos Society, the New Mexico modernists, and Georgia O'Keeffe, as well as contemporary artists. ⊠ *1011 Paseo de Peralta, East Side and Canyon Road* ☎ *505/954–5700* ⊕ *www.gpgallery.com* ⊙ *Closed Sun.*

Giacobbe-Fritz. Stop inside this late-1890s adobe building to admire a truly diverse collection of paintings, drawings, and sculpture, much of it with a regional and traditional approach, including impressionist New Mexico landscapes by Connie Dillman and whimsical bronze sculptures of burros, bats, and other animals by Copper Tritscheller. The owners also operate the excellent GF Contemporary, across the street, which focuses more on modern and abstract works. ⊠ *702 Canyon Rd., East Side and Canyon Road* ☎ *505/986–1156* ⊕ *www.giacobbefritz.com.*

★ **Fodor'sChoice** **LewAllen Galleries.** Set in a dramatic 14,000-square-foot neo-industrial building beside the farmers' market in the Railyard District, this leader in both contemporary and modern art carries works by such icons as Alexander Calder, Claes Oldenburg, and Andy Warhol. You'll also find a dazzling collection of abstract sculpture, photography, and paintings by up-and-coming regional and international talents. ⊠ *1613 Paseo de Peralta, Railyard District* ☎ *505/988–3250* ⊕ *www.lewallengalleries. com* ⊘ *Closed Sun.*

★ **Fodor'sChoice** **Manitou Galleries.** This respected gallery near the Plaza carries mostly contemporary representational paintings and sculptures by such world-class artists as Jie-Wei Zhou and Martha Pettigrew; they also have photographs by Edward Curtis. Manitou has a second location, every bit as impressive, at 225 Canyon Road. ⊠ *123 W. Palace Ave., The Plaza* ☎ *505/986–0440* ⊕ *www.manitougalleries.com.*

Meyer Gallery. One of the oldest and most prestigious galleries in the Southwest, Meyer is a good place to begin a stroll up Canyon Road—it's at the bottom of the hill, and the work shown in this expansive gallery gives a good sense of the traditional Santa Fe art scene. ⊠ *225 Canyon Rd., East Side and Canyon Road* ☎ *505/983–1434* ⊕ *www. meyergalleries.com.*

Monroe Gallery. In this attractive storefront space a couple of blocks from the Plaza, you can admire works by the most celebrated black-and-white photographers of the 20th century, including Margaret Bourke-White, Berenice Abbott, and Alfred Eisenstaedt. The focus is on humanist and photojournalist-style photography, and many iconic images are available for purchase. ⊠ *112 Don Gaspar Ave., The Plaza* ☎ *505/992–0800* ⊕ *www.monroegallery.com.*

Nedra Matteucci Galleries. One of the Southwest's premier galleries, Matteucci Galleries exhibits works by California regionalists, members of the early Taos and Santa Fe schools, and masters of American impressionism and modernism. Spanish-colonial furniture, Indian antiquities, and a fantastic sculpture garden are other draws of this well-respected establishment. The old adobe building that the gallery is in is a beautifully preserved example of Santa Fe–style architecture. Matteucci also owns Morning Star Gallery around the corner at 513 Canyon Road. ✉ *1075 Paseo de Peralta, East Side and Canyon Road* ☎ *505/982–4631* ⊕ *www.matteucci.com* ⊙ *Closed Sun.*

Peyton Wright. Tucked inside the historic Spiegelberg house, this gallery represents some of the most talented emerging and established contemporary artists in the country; historic notables featured here include Dorothy Brett, Robert Motherwell, Joseph Stella, and William Shuster as well as antique and even ancient New Mexican, Russian, and Latin works. ✉ *237 E. Palace Ave., The Plaza* ☎ *505/989–9888* ⊕ *www.peytonwright.com* ⊙ *Closed Sun.*

FAMILY **Shidoni Gallery and Sculpture Garden.** This picturesque compound on the grounds of an old chicken ranch in rural Tesuque is home to a rambling sculpture garden and a gallery (Shidoni's famous foundry closed in 2016 due to financial challenges). On sunny afternoons, there are few more picturesque places to admire art than the tranquil garden, in which you'll find dazzling large-scale works in bronze and other metals. The gallery shows a variety of crafts and other works, from wood carvings to fiber. ✉ *1508 Bishop's Lodge Rd., 5 miles north of the Plaza, North Side* ☎ *505/988–8001* ⊕ *www.shidoni.com* ⊙ *Closed Sun.*

Ventana Fine Art. Set in a dramatic and expansive Victorian redbrick schoolhouse on Canyon Road, Ventana has been at the forefront of Santa Fe's constantly shifting contemporary art scene since the mid-1980s. The gallery represents notable talents like Doug Dawson, John Axton, and John Nieto, and there's a lovely sculpture garden adjacent. ✉ *400 Canyon Rd., East Side and Canyon Road* ☎ *505/983–8815, 800/746–8815* ⊕ *www.ventanafineart.com.*

VIVO Contemporary. Distinct in that it focuses solely on Santa Fe artists who produce contemporary works, VIVO also offers some very interesting programming from its handsome two-level space on Canyon Road, including an annual show featuring paintings and poems together. Rachel Darnell's Japanese-inspired abstracts and Joy Campbell's imaginative "book art" constructions (which use ornately folded paper) are among the gallery's highlights. ✉ *725 Canyon Rd., East Side and Canyon Road* ☎ *505/982–1320* ⊕ *www.vivocontemporary.com.*

Zane Bennett Contemporary Art. The sleek design of this airy, two-story gallery with a skylighted atrium is a fitting venue for the cutting-edge photography, paintings, sculptures, and mixed-media works within. Zane Bennett has carried works by icons (Helen Frankenthaler, Sol LeWitt) but also presents rotating shows focused on everything from up-and-coming Native artists to the works of noted American pop artist Jim Dine. ⊠ *435 S. Guadalupe St., Railyard District* ☎ *505/982–8111* ⊕ *www.zanebennettgallery.com* ⊗ *Closed Sun. and Mon.*

BOOKS

Several shops in Santa Fe sell used books, and a handful of high-quality shops carry the latest releases from mainstream and small presses.

★ Fodor'sChoice **Collected Works Book Store.** You'll find a great selection of art and travel books here, including a generous selection of titles on Southwestern art, architecture, and general history, as well as the latest in contemporary literature. In an large, inviting space close to the Plaza, you can enjoy organic lattes, snacks, and sandwiches in a small branch of superb Iconik Coffee Roasters, which also presents readings and music. The patio invites long, leisurely reads. The proprietress, Dorothy Massey, and her staff are well loved for their knowledge and helpfulness. ⊠ *202 Galisteo St., The Plaza* ☎ *505/988–4226* ⊕ *www. collectedworksbookstore.com.*

Garcia Street Books. This outstanding independent shop is strong on art, architecture, cookbooks, literature, and regional Southwestern works—it's a block from the Canyon Road galleries and hosts frequent talks by authors under its portal during the summer. ⊠ *376 Garcia St., East Side and Canyon Road* ☎ *505/986–0151* ⊕ *www. garciastreetbooks.com.*

★ Fodor'sChoice **Photo-eye Bookstore and Gallery.** The place to go for an almost unbelievable collection of new, rare, and out-of-print photography books; the staff is made up of photographers who are excellent sources of information and advice on great spots to shoot in and around Santa Fe. The impressive gallery in the Railyard District (*541 S. Guadalupe St.*) presents fine photography. ⊠ *376 Garcia St., East Side and Canyon Road* ☎ *505/988–5152* ⊕ *www. photoeye.com.*

Travel Bug. Here you'll find a huge array of guides and books about travel, and USGS and other maps. You'll also find all sorts of gadgets for hikers and backpackers. There's also a cozy coffeehouse (excellent java) with Wi-Fi. ⊠ *839 Paseo de Peralta, The Plaza* ☎ *505/992–0418* ⊕ *www.map-sofnewmexico.com.*

CLOTHING AND ACCESSORIES

Many tourists arrive in clothing from mainstream department stores and leave bedecked in Western garb. Although it's not difficult to find getups Annie Oakley herself might have envied, you'll see that at most boutiques in town Western gear is mixed with pieces from all over the globe to create a more eclectic and cosmopolitan Santa Fe style. There are artists of every bent in this town and the surrounding areas, not only putting paint to canvas, but also creating jewelry, clothing, hats, shoes, and other accessories. Informed by cultural traditions but as cutting edge and innovative as anything you'll find in New York or San Francisco, the contemporary jewelry coming from Native American artists like Cody Sanderson and Pat Pruitt is incredible.

★ Fodor's Choice **Back at the Ranch.** This cozy space in an old, creaky-floored adobe is stocked with perhaps the finest handmade cowboy boots you will ever see—in every color, style, and embellishment imaginable. Other finds, like funky ranch-style furniture, 1950s blanket coats, jewelry, and belt buckles are also sold. The staff is top-notch and the boots are breathtaking. ⊠ *209 E. Marcy St., The Plaza* ☎ *505/989–8110* ⊕ *www.backattheranch.com.*

★ Fodor's Choice **Double Take.** This rambling 25,000-square-foot shop ranks among the best consignment stores in the West, carrying elaborately embroidered vintage cowboy shirts, hundreds of pairs of boots, funky old prints, and amazing vintage Indian pawn and Mexican jewelry. The store comprises several sections that also include contemporary clothing and accessories for men and women and a pottery showroom. ⊠ *320 Aztec St., Railyard District* ☎ *505/989–8886* ⊕ *www.santafedoubletake.com* ☉ *Closed Sun.*

Mirá. The women's clothing here is edgy and eclectic, combining the adventurous spirit of New Mexico with global contemporary fashion. The shop has jewelry, accessories, and collectibles from Latin America, the Flax line of natural-fiber clothing, and knockout dresses and separates not sold anywhere else in town. ⊠ *101 W. Marcy St., The Plaza* ☎ *505/988–3585* ⊕ *mirasantafe.com.*

★ **Fodor'sChoice O'Farrell Hats.** Scott O'Farrell (son of the shop's late founder, Kevin) and his highly trained staff carry on the tradition of producing carefully designed and constructed classic Western hats. The one-of-a-kind beaver-felt cowboy hats make the ultimate Santa Fe keepsake. This level of quality comes at a cost, but devoted customers—who have included everyone from cattle ranchers to U.S. presidents—swear by O'Farrell's artful creations. ⊠ *111 E. San Francisco St., The Plaza* ☎ *505/989–9666* ⊕ *www.ofarrell-hatco.com* ⊗ *Closed Sun.*

Red River Mercantile. This small but well-stocked space is one of the best spots in town for rugged and stylish—but casual—men's wear, along with backpacks, computer bags, watches, wallets, and other accessories. Well-established brands like Filson, Pendleton, Howler Brothers, and Grayer's fill the aisles, and the staff is extremely helpful. ⊠ *235 Don Gaspar Ave., The Plaza* ☎ *505/992–1233.*

FOOD, DRINK, AND COOKWARE

In addition to traditional gift shops selling gourmet goodies and candies, you'll find an increasing number of shops in Santa Fe specializing in high-quality edibles and craft beverages (wine, beer, liquor, coffee). *See the Day Trips from Santa Fe chapter for information on the top wineries in the region, most of which are north of Santa Fe, en route to Taos, and see the Santa Fe Nightlife and Performing Arts chapter for listings of brewpubs that not only serve fine local beers on premises but also sell them to go.*

★ **Fodor'sChoice Kakawa.** You're unlikely to ever have tasted any-
FAMILY   thing like the divine, agave-sweetened, artisanal creations that emerge from this shop. Historically accurate chocolate drinks, like the Aztec Warrior Elixir, divine caramels, and agave-sweetened, gluten-free chocolate baked goods are served in this cozy, welcoming establishment that's as much an educational experience as a chance to indulge in exceptional sweets. ⊠ *1050 Paseo de Peralta* ☎ *505/982–0388* ⊕ *www.kakawachocolates.com.*

Las Cosas Kitchen Shoppe & Cooking School. In DeVargas shopping center, Las Cosas Kitchen Shoppe stocks a fantastic selection of cookery, tableware, and kitchen gadgetry and gifts. The shop is also renowned for its cooking classes, which touch on everything from high-altitude baking to Asian-style grilling. ⊠ *De Vargas Mall, 181 Paseo de Peralta, at N. Guadalupe St., West of the Plaza* ☎ *505/988–3394, 877/229–7184* ⊕ *www.lascosascooking.com.*

★ **Fodor's**Choice **Todos Santos.** This tiny candy shop in the 18th-century courtyard of Sena Plaza sells must-be-seen-to-be-believed works of edible art, including chocolate milagros and altar pieces gilded with 23-karat gold or silver leaf. Truffles come in exotic flavors, like tangerine chile, rose caramel, and lemon verbena. The buttery, spicy, handmade chipotle caramels melt in your mouth. Amidst the taste sensations and quirky folk art are amazing and delightful customized Pez dispensers from Albuquerque folk artist Steve White and astonishing, intricate recycled paper creations from local phenom Rick Phelps. ⊠ *125 E. Palace Ave., The Plaza* ☎ *505/982–3855.*

JEWELRY

Eidos. Check out "concept-led" minimalist contemporary jewelry from European designers and Deborah Alexander and Gordon Lawrie, who own the store. It's a lovely, contemporary space with a fascinating array of materials, good range of prices, and helpful staff. ⊠ *508A Camino de la Familia, Railyard District* ☎ *505/992–0020* ⊕ *www.eidosjewelry.com.*

LewAllen & LewAllen Jewelry. Father-and-daughter silversmiths Ross and Laura LewAllen run this impressive shop. Handmade jewelry ranges from whimsical to mystical inside their tiny space just off the Plaza. There's something for absolutely everyone in here, including delightful charms for your pet's collar. ⊠ *105 E. Palace Ave., The Plaza* ☎ *800/988–5112, 505/983–2657* ⊕ *www.lewallenjewelry.com.*

★ **Fodor's**Choice **Patina.** In this airy, museum-like space, you'll find outstanding contemporary jewelry, textiles, and sculptural objects of metal, clay, and wood. With a staff whose courtesy is matched by knowledge of the genre, artists-owners Ivan and Allison Barnett have used their fresh curatorial aesthetic to create a showplace for dozens of American and European artists they represent—many of whom are in permanent collections of museums such as MoMA. ⊠ *131 W. Palace Ave., The Plaza* ☎ *505/985–5925* ⊕ *www.patina-gallery.com.*

6

MARKETS

★ FodorsChoice **Santa Fe Farmers Market.** Browse through the
FAMILY vast selection of local produce, meat, flowers, honey, wine,
jams, and cheese—much of it organic—at the thriving Santa
Fe Farmers Market. Dozens of stalls are arranged inside a
snazzy, modern building in the Railyard and adjacent to it;
it's open year-round on Saturday mornings (7 am to 1 pm in
summer, 8 am to 1 pm in winter) and additionally on Tuesday mornings May through mid-December and Wednesday
evenings mid-June to late September. The lively space also
hosts an artisan market on Sundays from 10 to 4. It's a
great people-watching venue, with entertainment for kids
as well as food vendors selling terrific breakfast burritos,
green-chile bread, Taos Cow ice cream, and other goodies.
⊠ *1607 Paseo de Peralta, Railyard District* ☎ *505/983–4098*
⊕ *www.santafefarmersmarket.com.*

NATIVE AMERICAN ARTS AND CRAFTS

Andrea Fisher Fine Pottery. You can browse some of the
nation's finest examples of both historic and contemporary Native pottery at this gallery a couple of blocks east
of the Plaza and especially renowned for its collection of
pieces from San Ildefonso Pueblo legend Maria Martinez
and her illustrious family. ⊠ *100 W. San Francisco St., The
Plaza* ☎ *505/986–1234* ⊕ *www.andreafisherpottery.com.*

Keshi: The Zuni Connection. Since the early '80s, this gallery
specializing in beautiful animal fetishes carved out of turquoise, marble, onyx, and countless other materials has
served as a co-op art gallery for western New Mexico's
Zuni Pueblo. You'll find fetishes representing an astounding
variety of animals, from eagles to mountain lions to turtles,
plus fine jewelry and pottery. ⊠ *227 Don Gaspar Ave., The
Plaza* ☎ *505/989–8728* ⊕ *www.keshi.com.*

★ FodorsChoice **Morning Star Gallery.** Owned by the prestigious
Nedra Matteucci Galleries, this is a veritable museum of
Native American art and artifacts. An adobe shaded by a
huge cottonwood tree houses antique basketry, pre-1940
Navajo silver jewelry, Northwest Coast Native American
carvings, Navajo weavings, and art of the Plains Indians.
Prices and quality prohibit casual purchases, but the col-
lection is magnificent. ⊠ *513 Canyon Rd., East Side and
Canyon Road* ☎ *505/982–8187* ⊕ *www.morningstargallery.
com* ⊙ *Closed Sun.*

Rainbow Man. Established in 1945, this colorful, if a bit touristy, shop does business in an old, rambling adobe complex, part of which dates from before the 1680 Pueblo Revolt. The shop carries early Navajo, Mexican, and Chimayó textiles, along with photographs by Edward S. Curtis, a breathtaking collection of vintage pawn and Mexican jewelry, Day of the Dead figures, Oaxacan folk animals, New Mexican folk art, kachinas, and contemporary jewelry from local artists. The friendly staff possesses an encyclopedic knowledge of the art here. ⊠ *107 E. Palace Ave., The Plaza* ☎ *505/982–8706* ⊕ *www.therainbowman.com.*

★ **Fodor'sChoice Robert Nichols Gallery.** This long-running establishment on Canyon Road represents a remarkable group of Native American ceramics artists doing primarily non-traditional work. Diverse artists include Glen Nipshank, whose organic, sensuous shapes would be right at home in MoMA, and Diego Romero, whose Cochiti-style vessels are detailed with graphic-novel-style characters and sharp social commentary. It is a treat to see cutting-edge work that is clearly informed by indigenous traditions. ⊠ *419 Canyon Rd., East Side and Canyon Road* ☎ *505/982–2145* ⊕ *www.robertnicholsgallery.com.*

Shiprock Santa Fe. "Eclectic Modern Vintage" is Shiprock Santa Fe's tagline, and it accurately sums up their impressive collection of pottery, textiles, painting, furniture, and sculpture. The gallery is notable for its dedication to showcasing exquisite vintage pieces alongside vanguard contemporary works. ⊠ *53 Old Santa Fe Trail, 2nd fl., The Plaza* ☎ *505/982–8478* ⊕ *www.shiprocksantafe.com.*

SPAS

Santa Fe has established itself as a major spa destination. From intimate boutique spas to gleaming resort sanctuaries where you can spend days ensconced in beautiful surroundings with endless treatment options, there is a spa and a specialty for everyone in this town. Several of the larger, upscale hotels have spas, the best of which are included here. Note that one of the region's top spa destinations, Ojo Caliente, is about an hour's drive north of town and is a highlight, either as a day trip or overnight visit, for spa lovers (⇨ *see the Day Trips from Santa Fe chapter for more information*). Also, as of this writing, Bishop's Lodge Resort was undergoing a full-scale renovation, which will include its first-rate spa. It's expected to reopen in mid-2018. Visit ⊕ *www.bishopslodge.com* for the latest updates.

★ Fodor'sChoice **Spa at Four Seasons Resort Rancho Encantado.** Set on a hilltop with spectacular mountain views, this intimate oasis has 15 treatment rooms, some of the best-trained body workers and estheticians in the Southwest, and a full complement of salon services. You'll pay more at the Four Seasons Spa than at most other properties in town (it's $165 for a 50-minute massage), but there's a reason both hotel guests and locals rave about their experiences here. Specialties include regionally inspired treatments, like the Blue Corn and Honey Renewal body wrap. A few different private couples' retreat packages are offered, including the three-hour Mountain Spirit Initiation, which includes a sage smudge, clay body mask, foot and scalp massage, and a full-body hot-stone juniper-sage massage. Do stick around and enjoy time in the impressive fitness center or relaxing by the pool (closed winter). Many guests combine their spa day with lunch or dinner on the peaceful patio of the resort's outstanding restaurant, Terra. The resort's Adventure Center also offers all sorts of excursions designed to get your blood flowing, from mountain-biking to hiking at nearby waterfalls. ⊠ *198 NM 592, North Side* ☎ *505/946–5700* ⊕ *www.fourseasons.com/santafe/spa.*

Spa at Loretto. Dark, polished wood surfaces, amber lighting, and candlelit kiva-style fireplaces infuse Inn at Loretto's intimate spa with a relaxed, understated elegance—especially during Santa Fe's cool winter months, this is a particularly cozy, inviting space for a massage, and the central location near the Plaza makes it a convenient choice for guests of the many nearby hotels. The old-world decor of the five treatment suites (plus a couples suite), some with Vichy showers and antique claw-foot soaking tubs, are especially nice for enjoying one of the spa's half-day packages, including a deluxe 365-minute session that includes sage-scented bath, hot-stone massage, facial, milk-and-honey wrap, manicure and pedicure, and chakra balancing. These services can be booked individually, along with a high-altitude massage geared specifically to Santa Fe's 7,000-foot elevation, and the bracing Café Olé Indonesian coffee scrub. An 80-minute massage is $195, and half-day packages are $330–$775. The gym includes cardiovascular machines, free weights, and weight-training equipment. Yoga classes are offered as well. One drawback: common areas are very limited, as there are no steam rooms, saunas, or hot tubs. ⊠ *211 Old Santa Fe Trail, The Plaza* ☎ *505/984–7997* ⊕ *www.hotelloretto.com.*

★ **Fodor's**Choice **Spa Sage at La Posada de Santa Fe.** The first-rate 4,500-square-foot spa at this historic Downtown resort emphasizes regional ingredients in its extensive offerings of treatments and services, including a signature Spirit of Santa Fe body rub that uses ground blue corn as a skin exfoliant, and a body wrap using chocolate and red chiles from nearby Chimayó. The 15-minute Shea Butter facial wrap is a great way to combat the effects on the skin of New Mexico's sunny, high-desert climate. Hair and nail services are also available, and there's an expansive fitness center (24-hour access for hotel guests) with Cybex equipment and personal-training as well as private yoga sessions offered. After working out, or being worked on, go for a swim in the heated outdoor pool, or just soak up the Sangre de Cristo views on the rooftop terrace. There's also a poolside patio grill serving light fare. Rates start at $185 for an 80-minute massage. ⊠ *330 E. Palace Ave., East Side and Canyon Road* ☎ *505/986–0000* ⊕ *www.laposadadesantafe.com.*

★ **Fodor's**Choice **Sunrise Springs Spa Resort.** After an extended closure, Sunrise Springs and its wonderfully inviting spa—complete with an extensive system of both private and common soaking pools and an expressive arts studio (with painting, journaling, and other classes)—reopened in 2016 under the ownership of the famed Ojo Caliente spa resort, north of Santa Fe. Treatments with a holistic bent are offered, including Reiki, blue corn and prickly pear salt scrubs, and herbal towel compress therapy using Round Barn Apothecary products. A 50-minute custom massage costs $99.

Set amid a grove of cottonwood trees, the resort's *ojito* soaking tubs, one of which is mineral-infused, can be booked privately. A range of enriching activities, such as yoga, mindfulness meditation, and gardening, are also available. This upscale eco-resort unfolds over 70 green and serene acres, 15 miles southwest of Downtown Santa Fe. ⊠ *242 Los Piños Rd.* ☎ *505/780–8145* ⊕ *www.sunrisesprings.ojospa.com.*

★ **Fodor's**Choice **Ten Thousand Waves.** This renowned Japanese-style spa with outstanding facilities and treatments is just 10 minutes north of Santa Fe toward the ski basin, nestled peacefully among the piñon trees on a sheltered hillside. Primarily a day spa—the private and communal hot tubs, especially nice in the evening under a starry sky, are a popular option—Ten Thousand Waves also has 14 sleek

6

and inviting overnight casitas and a lovely *izakaya*-style restaurant, Izanami. The treatment rooms and spa facilities here are simple yet elegant, with a zenlike vibe—perfect for relaxing while undergoing a Yasuragi head and neck treatment, a salt-glow body exfoliation, or the Japanese organic facial, which includes a thorough neck and shoulder massage. If you've been skiing or hiking in the mountains up the road, stopping here on the way home is a great way to heal sore muscles. It's $119 for a 50-minute massage and $213–$473 for half-day packages. Nature walks are also offered. ⊠ *3451 Hyde Park Rd., East Side and Canyon Road* ☎ *505/982–9304* ⊕ *www.tenthousandwaves.com.*

Wo' P'in Spa at Buffalo Thunder Resort. At 16,000 square feet, the expansive Wo' P'in Spa at this Hilton-managed Pojoaque Tribe–owned gaming resort just north of Santa Fe is one of the largest in the state. With its huge outdoor pool and Roman baths–inspired indoor pool, swanky salon, and extensive manicure and pedicure options, Wo' P'in is more a place for pampering—in the style of a Vegas resort—than meditative serenity or spiritual enrichment. The spa can tailor any massage or treatment with a number of add-ons, ranging from reflexology sessions to deep-foot massage to sugar-scrub exfoliations. One recommended treatment is the mocha mud coffee scrub that ends with a coconut-chocolate body-butter application. This is one of the few spas in the region with Vichy shower treatments, but these are sometimes suspended when water restrictions are in effect (which is often in Santa Fe). It's $170 for an 80-minute massage. ⊠ *20 Buffalo Thunder Trail, off U.S. 285/84, Exit 177, North Side* ☎ *505/819–2140* ⊕ *www. buffalothunderresort.com.*

SPORTS AND THE OUTDOORS

Updated
by Andrew
Collins

WHEN IT COMES TO OUTDOOR adventure, Santa Fe is a four-season destination. Low humidity and, thanks to the high elevation, cool temperatures—even in summer, for the most part—make north-central New Mexico a mecca for hiking, biking, wildlife viewing, rafting, and golfing from late spring through autumn. During the winter months, snow sports dominate in the mountains above the city, and at renowned ski areas like Taos and Angel Fire, which are both within day-tripping distance (although better suited to overnight excursions).

Santa Fe National Forest lies right in the city's backyard and includes the Dome Wilderness (more than 5,000 acres in the volcanically formed Jémez Mountains) and the Pecos Wilderness (about 225,000 acres of high mountains, forests, and meadows at the southern end of the Rocky Mountains chain). The 12,500-foot Sangre de Cristo Mountains (the name translates as "Blood of Christ," for the red glow they radiate at sunset) fringe the city's east side. To the south and west, several less formidable mountain ranges punctuate the sweeping high desert. From the Plaza in the center of the city, you're within a 10-minute drive of truly rugged and breathtakingly beautiful wilderness.

New Mexico Public Lands Information Center. For a one-stop shop for information about recreation on public lands, which include national and state parks, contact the New Mexico Public Lands Information Center. It has maps, reference materials, licenses, permits, and myriad online resources—just about everything you need to plan an outdoor adventure in Santa Fe and the surrounding region. ✉ *301 Dinosaur Trail, South Side* ☎ *505/954–2002, 877/276–9404* ⊕ *www.publiclands.org.*

Santa Fe National Forest Office. For information on general conditions in the forest, including advisories about areas closed because of fires (unfortunately, these are a fairly regular occurrence each summer), call or visit the helpful website of the Santa Fe National Forest Office. ✉ *11 Forest La., South Side* ☎ *505/438–5300* ⊕ *www.fs.fed.us/r3/sfe.*

BICYCLING

You can pick up a map of bike trips—among them a 38-mile round-trip ride from Downtown Santa Fe to Ski Santa Fe at the end of NM 475—from the New Mexico Public Lands Information Center, *or at the bike shops listed below.* One excellent place to mountain bike is the Dale Ball Trail Network, which you can access from several points on the east side of town.

★ Fodor'sChoice **Mellow Velo.** This friendly bike shop near the Plaza offers group tours, privately guided rides, bicycle rentals ($30 per day for basic cruisers to $75 for top-of-the-line mountain and road bikes), and repairs. The helpful staff at this well-stocked shop can suggest a great way to spend a day—or seven! ✉ *132 E. Marcy St., The Plaza* ☎ *505/995–8356* ⊕ *www.mellowvelo.com.*

New Mexico Bike N' Sport. Here at this large shop by Trader Joe's you can rent or buy bikes of all kinds and shop the great selection of clothing and gear. Rates start at $25 daily, with good discounts for multiday rentals. Note that it's closed on Sundays. ✉ *524C W. Cordova Rd., South Side* ☎ *505/820–0809* ⊕ *www.nmbikensport.com.*

BIRD-WATCHING

★ Fodor'sChoice **Randall Davey Audubon Center.** At the end of
FAMILY Upper Canyon Road, at the mouth of the canyon as it wends into the foothills, the 135-acre Randall Davey Audubon Center harbors diverse birds (nearly 200 species have been identified) and other wildlife. Free guided nature walks are given most Saturday mornings at 8:30; there are also two major hiking trails that you can tackle on your own. The home and studio of Randall Davey, a prolific early Santa Fe artist, can be toured on Friday afternoons. There's also a nature bookstore. ✉ *1800 Upper Canyon Rd., East Side and Canyon Road* ☎ *505/983–4609* ⊕ *nm. audubon.org* ✐ *Docent-led tours of the historic Randall Davey House and Studio $5.*

WingsWest Birding Tours. For an informed insider's perspective, take a tour with WingsWest Birding Tours. Gregarious and knowledgeable guide Bill West leads regular early-morning or sunset tours throughout spring and summer in Santa Fe and elsewhere in New Mexico, including Santa Fe Ski Basin, Cochiti Lake, the Espanola Valley, the Sandia Mountains, the Jémez Mountains, Bosque del Apache National Wildlife Refuge, and several other spots known for bird-watching. West also leads popular tours in Mexico and Ecuador. ✉ *Santa Fe* ☎ *505/989–3804* ⊕ *www. wingswestbirding.com.*

7

FISHING

There's excellent fishing from spring through fall in the Rio Grande and the mountain streams that feed into it, as well as a short drive away along the Pecos River.

High Desert Angler. This is a superb fly-fishing outfitter and guide service, your one-stop shop for equipment rental, fly-fishing tackle, licenses, and advice. ⊠ *460 Cerrillos Rd., Railyard District* ☎ *505/988–7688, 888/988–7688* ⊕ *www. highdesertangler.com.*

GOLF

Marty Sanchez Links de Santa Fe. This outstanding, reasonably priced municipal facility has a beautifully groomed 18-hole layout and a shorter 9-hole executive course. These sweeping courses meander over high prairie west of Santa Fe and afford fine mountain views. ⊠ *205 Caja del Rio Rd., off NM 599, about 10 miles west of Plaza, South Side* ☎ *505/955–4400* ⊕ *www.linksdesantafe.com* ☜ *$30* ⚲ *18 holes, 6095 yds, par 72. 9 holes, 1615 yds, par 28* ☞ *Facilities: driving range, putting green, golf carts, pull carts, rental clubs, pro shop, golf lessons, restaurant, bar.*

HIKING

Hiking around Santa Fe can take you into high-altitude alpine country or into lunaresque high desert as you head south and west to lower elevations. For winter hiking, the gentler climates to the south are less likely to be snow packed, while the alpine areas tend to require snowshoes or cross-country skis. In summer, wildflowers bloom in the high country, and the temperature is generally at least 10 degrees cooler than in town. The mountain trails accessible at the base of the Ski Santa Fe area and at nearby Hyde Memorial State Park (near the end of NM 475) stay cool on even the hottest summer days. Weather can change with one gust of wind, so be prepared with extra clothing, rain gear, food, and lots of water. Keep in mind that the sun at 10,000 feet is very powerful, even with a hat and sunscreen. *See the Day Trips from Santa Fe chapter, for additional hiking areas near the city.*

For information about specific hiking areas, contact the New Mexico Public Lands Information Center.

★ Fodor's Choice **Aspen Vista.** Especially in autumn, when golden
FAMILY aspens shimmer on the mountainside, this trail up near
Santa Fe's ski area makes for a lovely hike. After walking
a few miles through thick aspen groves you come to panoramic views of Santa Fe. The path, which is well marked
and gradually inclines toward Tesuque Peak, becomes
steeper with elevation—also note that snow has been
reported on the upper portions of the trail as late as July.
In winter, after heavy snows, the trail is great for intermediate–advanced cross-country skiing. The full hike to the
peak makes for a long, rigorous day—it's 12 miles round-
trip and sees an elevation gain of 2,000 feet, but it's just
3½ miles to the spectacular overlook. Note that the Aspen
Vista Picnic Site is also the trailhead for the Alamo Vista
Trail, which leads to the summit of the ski area. ⊠ *Hyde
Park Rd. (NM 475), 2 miles before ski area, East Side and
Canyon Road* ✣ *Parking lot at Aspen Vista Picnic Site.*

★ Fodor's Choice **Atalaya Trail.** Spurring off the Dale Ball Trail
system, the steep but rewarding (and dog-friendly) Atalaya
Trail runs from the visitor parking lot of St. John's College,
up a winding, ponderosa pine–studded trail to the peak of
Mt. Atalaya, which affords incredible 270-degree views of
Santa Fe. The nearly 6-mile round-trip hike climbs almost
2,000 feet (to an elevation of 9,121 feet), so pace yourself.
The good news: the return to the parking area is nearly
all downhill. ⊠ *1160 Camino de Cruz Blanca, East Side
and Canyon Road.*

7

Dale Ball Foothills Trail Network. A favorite spot for a ramble,
with a vast system of trails, is the Dale Ball Foothills Trail
Network, a 24-mile network of paths that winds and wends
up through the foothills east of town and can be accessed
at a few points, including Hyde Park Road (en route to the
ski valley) and the upper end of Canyon Road, at Cerro
Gordo. There are trail maps and signs at these points, and
the trails are very well marked. ⊠ *East Side and Canyon
Road* ⊕ *www.sfct.org/trails/dale-ball-trails.*

HORSEBACK RIDING

New Mexico's rugged countryside has been the setting for
many Hollywood Westerns. Whether you want to ride the
range that Gregory Peck and Kevin Costner tamed or just
head out feeling tall in the saddle, you can do so year-round.

Bishop's Lodge. You can book magnificently scenic trail rides at this historic stable adjacent to 314-acre Bishop's Lodge Ranch resort on Santa Fe's North Side, in the Sangre de Cristo foothills. ✉ *1297 Bishop's Lodge Rd., North Side* ☎ *505/819–0095* ⊕ *www.bishopslodgestables.com.*

MULTIPURPOSE SPORTS CENTER

FAMILY **Genoveva Chavez Community Center.** The expansive, well-maintained community recreation center on the south side is a reasonably priced (adults $7 per day) facility with a regulation-size ice rink (rentals available), an enormous gym, indoor running track, 50-meter pool, leisure pool with waterslide and play structures, aerobics, and more. ✉ *3221 Rodeo Rd., South Side* ☎ *505/955–4001* ⊕ *www. chavezcenter.com.*

RIVER RAFTING

If you want to watch birds and wildlife along the banks, try the laid-back floats along the Rio Chama or the Rio Grande's White Rock Canyon. The season generally runs from April to October. More rugged white-water rafting adventures take place from spring through early summer, farther north along the Rio Grande. Most outfitters have overnight package plans, and all offer half- and full-day trips. Be prepared to get wet, and wear secure water shoes.

Bureau of Land Management (BLM), Taos Field Office. For a list of outfitters who guide trips on the Rio Grande and the Rio Chama, contact the Bureau of Land Management (BLM), Taos Resource Area Office, or stop by the Rio Grande Gorge Visitor Center along NM 68 (on the "Low Road" to Taos), 16 miles south of Taos in the small village of Pilar, the launching point for many rafting trips on the Rio Grande. The visitor center is also an official part of the 242,500-acre Rio Grande del Norte National Monument, created in 2013 and administered by the BLM. ✉ *226 Cruz Alta Rd., Taos* ☎ *575/758–8851 Taos field office, 575/751–4899 Rio Grande Gorge visitor center* ⊕ *www.blm.gov.*

FAMILY **Kokopelli Rafting Adventures.** This respected outfitter offers half-day, full-day, and multiday river trips down the Rio Grande and Rio Chama. ✉ *1401 Maclovia St., Unit A, South Side* ☎ *505/983–3734* ⊕ *www.kokopelliraft.com.*

★ **Fodor's**Choice **New Wave Rafting.** Look to this company
FAMILY founded in 1980 for full-day, half-day, and overnight river
trips on the Rio Chama and Rio Grande, as well as fly-fishing trips, from its riverside location in Embudo, 45 miles
north of Santa Fe, on the Low Road to Taos. You can also
rent funyaks and paddle easier stretches of rapids yourself.
⊠ *2110 NM 68, mile marker 21, Embudo* ☎ *800/984–1444*
⊕ *www.newwaverafting.com.*

FAMILY **Santa Fe Rafting Company and Outfitters.** This well-known
tour company leads day trips down the Rio Grande and
the Chama River and customizes rafting tours. Tell them
what you want—they'll figure out a way to do it. ⊠ *1000
Cerrillos Rd., South Side* ☎ *505/988–4914, 888/988–4914*
⊕ *www.santaferafting.com.*

SKIING

You may want to rent skis or snowboards in town the
afternoon before the day you hit the slopes so you don't
waste any time waiting during the morning rush.

Alpine Sports. This centrally located shop rents downhill and
cross-country skis and snowboards. ⊠ *121 Sandoval St.,
The Plaza* ☎ *505/983–5155* ⊕ *www.alpinesportsonline.com.*

Cottam's Ski Shop. Stop by this long-established outfitter with
additional locations in Taos and Angel Fire on your way up
to the ski valley; they rent all manner of winter gear, including skis, snowboards, sleds, and snowshoes. ⊠ *740 Hyde
Park Rd., East Side and Canyon Road* ☎ *505/982–0495*
⊕ *www.cottamsskishops.com.*

Ski Santa Fe. Open roughly from late November through
early April, this is a fine, somewhat underrated, midsize
operation that receives an average of 225 inches of snow
a year and plenty of sunshine. It's one of America's highest
ski areas—the 12,000-foot summit has a variety of terrain
and seems bigger than its 1,725 feet of vertical rise and
660 acres. There are some great powder stashes, tough
bump runs, and many wide, gentle cruising runs. The 83
trails are ranked 20% beginner, 40% intermediate, and
40% advanced; there are seven lifts. Snowboarders are
welcome, and there's the Norquist Trail for cross-country
skiers. Chipmunk Corner provides day care and super-
vised kids' skiing. The ski school is excellent. Rentals, a
ski shop, and a good restaurant round out the amenities at
bright and modern La Casa Lodge base-camp, and Tote-

moff's Bar and Grill is a welcome mid-mountain option. The area is fun for hiking during the summer months, and the Super Chief Quad Chair operates from late August through mid-October, catering to hikers and shutterbugs eager to view the high-mountain fall foliage, including acres of shimmering golden aspens. ✉ *End of NM 475, 18 miles northeast of Downtown, East Side and Canyon Road* ☎ *505/982–4429 general info, 505/983–9155 snow report* ⊕ *www.skisantafe.com.*

DAY TRIPS FROM
SANTA FE

Updated
by Andrew
Collins

SANTA FE MAKES A GREAT base for exploring the entire North-central Rio Grande Valley, a region rich in Spanish-colonial and Native American heritage and abounding with scenic drives, dazzling geographical formations, colorful villages, and important historic sites. Every community and attraction covered *in this chapter* could be visited as a day trip, but consider planning overnight excursions, too—you'll find a handful of wonderfully distinctive accommodations in these smaller villages.

It's also practical to embark on some of these trips en route to Albuquerque or Taos. For example, you could drive the Turquoise Trail or visit Tent Rock National Monument on the way to Albuquerque. The side trips to points north—such as the High Road, Bandelier and Los Alamos, and Abiquiú and Georgia O'Keeffe Country—are worth investigating on your way to Taos.

THE TURQUOISE TRAIL

★ Fodor's Choice The most prominent side trip south of the city is along the fabled Turquoise Trail, an excellent—and leisurely—alternative route from Santa Fe to Albuquerque that's far more interesting than Interstate 25. Etched out in the early 1970s, the scenic Turquoise Trail (or more prosaically, NM 14) is a National Scenic Byway that's dotted with ghost towns now popular with writers, artists, and other urban refugees. This 70 miles of piñon-studded mountain back road along the eastern flank of the sacred Sandia Mountains is a gentle roller coaster that also affords panoramic views of the Ortiz, Jémez, and Sangre de Cristo mountains. It's believed that 2,000 years ago Native Americans mined turquoise in these hills. The Spanish took up turquoise mining in the 16th century, and the practice continued into the early 20th century, with Tiffany & Co. removing a fair share of the semiprecious stone. In addition, gold, silver, tin, lead, and coal have been mined here. There's plenty of opportunity for picture taking and picnicking along the way. You can drive this loop in three hours with minimal stops, or make a full day of it, if you stop to explore the main attractions along the way and make the side excursion up to Sandia Crest, which overlooks Albuquerque. You'll find plenty of great information online at ⊕ *www.turquoisetrail.org.*

MADRID

28 miles southwest of Santa Fe and 4 miles southwest of Cerrillos on NM 14.

Abandoned when its coal mine closed in the 1950s, Madrid (locals put the emphasis on the first syllable: *mah*-drid) has gradually been rebuilt and is now—to the dismay of some longtime locals—actually a bit trendy. The entire town was offered for sale for $250,000 back in the '50s, but there were no takers. Finally, in the early 1970s, a few artists fleeing big cities settled in and began restoration. Weathered houses and old company stores have been repaired and turned into boutiques and galleries, some of them selling high-quality furniture, paintings, and crafts. Big events here include the CrawDaddy Blues Fest in mid-May, the Madrid and Cerrillos Studio Tour in early October, and Madrid Christmas Open House, held weekends in December, when galleries and studios are open and the famous Madrid Christmas lights twinkle brightly.

As you continue south down NM 14 from Madrid, after about 11 miles you pass through the sleepy village of **Golden,** the site of the first gold rush (in 1825) west of the Mississippi. It has a rock shop and a mercantile store. The rustic adobe church and graveyard are popular with photographers.

WHERE TO EAT

$ ✕ **The Hollar.** *Southern.* Stop by this funky restaurant set inside a converted freight car for well-prepared Southern and Southwestern comfort food, from fried green tomatoes to crispy-shrimp and grits. There's a good-size patio from which you can watch the colorful parade of tourists and art buyers strolling through town. **Known for:** biscuits with pulled pork; live music on the patio many days; good selection of local beers. Ⓢ *Average main: $12* ✉ *2849 NM 14* ☏ *505/471–4821* ⊕ *www.thehollar.com* ⊙ *Limited hrs Jan.–Mar. (call to confirm).*

$ ✕ **Java Junction.** *Café.* Aged hippies, youthful hipsters, and everyone in between congregate at Java Junction for lattes, chai, sandwiches, breakfast burritos, bagels, pastries, and other toothsome treats. You can also pick up a number of house-made gourmet goods, from hot sauces to jalapeño-raspberry preserves. **Known for:** hip crowd; upstairs room for rent. Ⓢ *Average main: $6* ✉ *2855 NM 14* ☏ *505/438–2772* ⊕ *www.java-junction.com* ⊙ *No dinner.*

8

★ Fodor's Choice 🍴 **Mineshaft Tavern.** *Southwestern.* A rollicking
$ old bar and restaurant adjacent to the Old Coal Mine Museum, this boisterous place—there's live music many nights—was a miners' commissary back in the day. Today it serves what many people consider the best green-chile cheeseburger (available with beef, wagyu, buffalo, or mushroom-veggie) in New Mexico, along with plenty of ice-cold beers on tap and a selection of other pub favorites and comfort foods. **Known for:** green-chile cheeseburgers; live music; fried green-chile appetizer. [$] *Average main: $12* ✉ *2846 NM 14* ☎ *505/473–0743* 🌐 *www.themineshafttavern.com.*

SANDIA PARK

24 miles southwest of Madrid and 22 miles northeast of Albuquerque on NM 14.

The southern stretch of the Turquoise Trail, as you continue from Golden and begin encountering upscale housing developments around Paa-Ko Ridge Golf Club, is more densely populated than the northern section—it's almost suburban in character, with the towns of Sandia Park (population 260), Cedar Crest (population 1,000), and several smaller nearby communities considered part of metro Albuquerque. The Turquoise Trail meanders along the eastern flanks of the Sandia Mountains before intersecting with Interstate 40, which leads east for the final 10 miles into Albuquerque proper.

EXPLORING

Sandia Crest. For awesome views of Albuquerque and half of New Mexico, take NM 536 up the back side of the Sandia Mountains through Cibola National Forest to Sandia Crest. At the 10,378-foot summit, explore the foot trails along the rim (particularly in summer) and take in the breathtaking views of Albuquerque down below, and of the so-called Steel Forest—the nearby cluster of radio and television towers. Always bring an extra layer of clothing, even in summer—the temperature at the crest can be anywhere from 15 to 25 degrees cooler than down in Albuquerque. ✉ *NM 536.*

★ Fodor's Choice **Tinkertown Museum.** It may take months for this
FAMILY odyssey of a place to completely sink in: quirky and utterly fascinating, Tinkertown Museum contains a world of miniature carved-wood characters. The museum's late founder, Ross Ward, spent more than 40 years carving and collecting

the hundreds of figures that populate this cheerfully bizarre museum, including an animated miniature Western village, a Boot Hill cemetery, and a 1940s circus exhibit. Ragtime piano music, a 40-foot sailboat, and a life-size general store are other highlights. The walls surrounding this 22-room museum have been fashioned out of more than 50,000 glass bottles pressed into cement. This homage to folk art, found art, and eccentric kitsch tends to strike a chord with people of all ages. As you might expect, the gift shop offers plenty of fun oddities. ✉ *121 Sandia Crest Rd. (NM 536)* ☎ *505/281–5233* 🌐 *www.tinkertown.com* 🎟 *$3.75* ⏲ *Closed Nov.–Mar.*

WHERE TO STAY

$ 🏨 **Elaine's, A Bed and Breakfast.** *B&B/Inn.* This antiques-filled three-story log-and-stone home is set in the evergreen folds of the Sandia Mountain foothills. **Pros:** astounding views of the Sangre de Cristos; delicious breakfasts. **Cons:** somewhat remote location. [$] *Rooms from: $109* ✉ *Snowline Estates, 72 Snowline Rd.* ☎ *505/281–2467* 🌐 *www.elainesbnb.com* 🛏 *5 rooms* 🍴 *Breakfast.*

CERRILLOS

FAMILY **Casa Grande.** This 28-room adobe (several rooms of which are part of a shop), has a small mining museum ($2) with a display of early mining exhibits. There's also a clean and neat, but oddly out-of-place petting zoo ($2 for food to feed the critters) with about 20 animals, and a genuinely scenic overlook. ✉ *17 Waldo St.* ☎ *505/438–3008.*

Cerrillos Hills State Park. One of New Mexico's newest state parks, this patch of undulating hills dotted with piñon and juniper contains 5 miles of hiking trails, some of them leading to historic mines, as well as interpretative signs related to the 1,100 years of mining history along the Turquoise Trail. The park itself is just north of the village center of Cerrillos, where you'll find a small visitor center (at 37 Main Street, open daily 2–4 pm or by appointment) with further exhibits and information on the park. ✉ *NM 59, ½ mile north of downtown (follow signs)* ☎ *505/474–0196* 🌐 *www.emnrd.state.nm.us/spd/cerrilloshillsstatepark.html* 🎟 *$5 per vehicle* ⏲ *Visitor center closed Tues. and Wed.*

8

KASHA-KATUWE TENT ROCKS NATIONAL MONUMENT

46 miles west of Santa Fe.

Hoodoos and slot canyons form an enchanted hiking get-away that can be accessed from Interstate 25 on the drive between Albuquerque and Santa Fe. If you have time for just one hike, this is an excellent choice.

EXPLORING

★ Fodor's Choice **Kasha-Katuwe Tent Rocks National Monument.** The
FAMILY sandstone rock formations here resemble stacked tents in a stark, water- and wind-eroded box canyon. Tent Rocks offers superb hiking year-round, although it can get hot in summer, when you should bring extra water. The drive to this magical landscape offers its own delights, as the road heads west toward Cochiti Dam and through the cotton-wood groves around the pueblo. It's a good hike for kids. The round-trip hiking distance is only 2 miles, about 1½ leisurely hours, but it's the kind of place where you'll want to hang out for a while. Take a camera, but leave your pets at home—no dogs are allowed. There are no facilities here, just a small parking area with a posted trail map and a self-pay admission box; you can get gas and pick up picnic supplies and bottled water at Pueblo de Cochiti Convenience Store. ✉ *BIA 92, off NM 22 (follow signs along well-paved road to trail parking area), Cochiti Lake* ☎ *505/331–6259* ⊕ *www.blm.gov/visit/kktr* 🎫 *$5 per vehicle.*

THE SANTA FE TRAIL

In the mid-19th century, this vast tract of grasslands and prairies, along with the eastern foothills of the Sangre de Cristo range, became the gateway to New Mexico for American settlers headed here from the Midwest. Towns along the Santa Fe Trail's modern offspring, Interstate 25—notably Las Vegas but also Raton up near the Colorado border—remain popular stops for road-tripping fans of Old West history.

PECOS NATIONAL HISTORIC SITE

30 miles southeast of Santa Fe via I–25 and NM 63.

Pecos was the last major encampment that travelers on the Santa Fe Trail reached before Santa Fe. Today the little

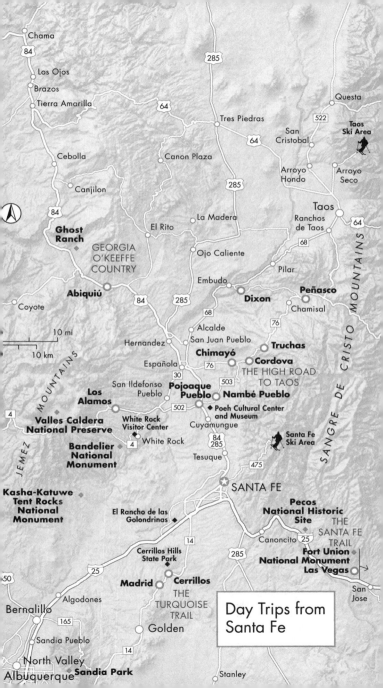

Day Trips from
Santa Fe

village is mostly a starting point for exploring the Pecos National Historic Park.

EXPLORING

Pecos National Historic Park. The centerpiece of this national park is the ruins of Pecos, once a major pueblo village with more than 1,100 rooms. About 2,500 people are thought to have lived in this structure, as high as five stories in places. Pecos, in a fertile valley between the Great Plains and the Rio Grande Valley, was a trading center centuries before the Spanish conquistadors visited in about 1540. The Spanish later returned to build two missions. The pueblo was abandoned in 1838, and its 17 surviving occupants moved to the Jémez Pueblo. Anglo travelers on the Santa Fe Trail observed the mission ruins with a great sense of fascination. You can view the mission ruins and the excavated pueblo on a 1¼-mile self-guided tour, a Civil War battlefield on a 2½-mile trail, and the small but outstanding visitor center museum containing photos, pottery, and artifacts from the pueblo. ⊠ *NM 63, off I–25 at Exit 299 or 307, Pecos* 📷 *505/757–7241* ⊕ *www.nps.gov/peco* 🗺 *Free.*

LAS VEGAS

67 miles northeast of Santa Fe and 42 miles northeast of Pecos National Historic Site via I–25.

The antithesis of its Nevada namesake, Las Vegas, elevation 6,470 feet, is a town of about 13,000 that time appears to have passed by. For decades, Las Vegas was actually two towns divided by Rio Gallinas: West Las Vegas, the Hispanic community anchored by the Spanish-style plaza, and East Las Vegas, where German Jews and Midwesterners established themselves around a proper town square. Once an oasis for stagecoach passengers en route to Santa Fe, it became—for a brief period after the railroad arrived in the late 19th century—New Mexico's major center of commerce, and its largest town, where more than a million dollars in goods and services were traded annually.

The seat of San Miguel County, Las Vegas lies where the Sangre de Cristo Mountains meet the high plains of New Mexico, and its name, meaning "the meadows," reflects its scenic setting. A smattering of intriguing antiques shops, galleries, and genial cafés line the Old Town Plaza and the main drag, Bridge Street. More than 900 structures here are listed on the National Register of Historic Places, and the town has nine historic districts, many with homes and commercial buildings of ornate Italianate design. Strolling around this very walkable town gives a sense of the area's rough-and-tumble history—Butch Cassidy is rumored to have tended bar here, and miscreants with names like Dirty-Face Mike, Rattlesnake Sam, and Web-Fingered Billy—not to mention Billy the Kid—once roamed the streets. You may also recognize some of the streets and facades from movies; Las Vegas is where scenes from *Wyatt Earp, No Country for Old Men,* and *All the Pretty Horses* were filmed and where Tom Mix shot his vintage Westerns.

EXPLORING

Las Vegas Chamber of Commerce Visitors Center. To gain an appreciation of the town's architecture, follow the walking tours described in free brochures available at the Las Vegas Chamber of Commerce Visitors Center. Best bets include Stone Architecture of Las Vegas; the Carnegie Park Historic District, with the Carnegie Library; and the Business District of Douglas–6th Street and Railroad Avenue. The latter includes the Mission Revival La Casteneda, a former hotel from the famed Harvey House railroad chain, with a well-preserved grand lobby and dining room. ✉ *500 Railroad Ave., Las Vegas* ☎ *505/425-3707, 800/832-5947* ⊕ *www.visitlasvegasnm.com.*

Las Vegas City Museum & Rough Rider Memorial Collection. The exhibits here include historical photos, medals, uniforms, and memorabilia from the Spanish-American War, documents pertaining to the city's history, and Native American artifacts. Theodore Roosevelt recruited many of his Rough Riders—the men the future president led into battle in Cuba in 1898—from northeastern New Mexico, and their first reunion was held here in 1899. ✉ *727 Grand Ave., Las Vegas* ☎ *505/426-3205* ⊕ *www.lasvegasmuseum.org* ✎ *Free* ⊙ *Closed Sun. and Mon.*

FAMILY **Las Vegas National Wildlife Refuge.** More than 250 known species—including eagles, sandhill cranes, hawks, and prairie falcons—travel the Central Flyway to this 8,672-acre area of marshes, native grasslands, and forested canyons. Here, where the Sangre de Cristo Mountains meet the Great Plains, the 1¾-mile-long Gallinas Nature Trail winds beside sandstone cliffs and ruins, and an 8-mile auto tour loops through the most picturesque habitats of the refuge (four-wheel-drive can be necessary following rain or snow). The visitor center leaves out free maps and bird species guides for visitors at all times. ✉ *NM 281, 1½ miles east of Las*

Vegas on NM 104, then 4½ miles south on NM 281, Las Vegas ☎ 505/425–3581 🌐 www.fws.gov/refuge/las_vegas 🎟 Free ⏲ Visitor center closed weekends.

Montezuma Castle/United World College of the USA. About 5 miles northwest of downtown in the village of Montezuma, students from around the world study language and culture at the Montezuma Castle/United World College of the USA (UWC-USA). Looming over the school property is the fantastically ornate, vaguely Queen Anne–inspired Montezuma Castle, a former resort hotel developed by the famed Fred Harvey Company and the Santa Fe Railroad, and designed by the famous Chicago firm of Burnham and Root. The structure that stands today was the third incarnation of the Montezuma Hotel, which opened in 1886. Student-led tours of the castle are available on certain Saturdays throughout the school year (call ahead or check the website). Check in at the Moore Welcome Center when you arrive.

Continue another ½ mile past the campus turnoff on NM 65 to reach signs (on the right) for the **hot springs** that inspired Montezuma's tourist boom in the 1880s. Soaking in these relaxing, lithium-laced pools is free, as long as you follow basic rules: no nude bathing, no alcohol, and bathing only between 5 am and midnight. If crowds allow, try soaking in all three different pools; temperatures vary significantly but the views of the castle and the creek are lovely from each pool. ✉ *NM 65, Montezuma* ☎ *505/454–4200* 🌐 *www.uwc-usa.org* 🎟 *Free.*

WHERE TO EAT

$ FAMILY 🍴 **Charlie's Spic & Span Bakery & Café.** *Mexican.* Huevos rancheros and burritos smothered with spicy salsa top the list in this large, simply furnished room that rings with friendly greetings among locals and is a good bet for either breakfast or lunch (or a very early dinner—it's open until 6 most days, and 3 on Sundays). You can also pick up cookies, doughnuts, and pastries from the on-site bakery, or a stack of freshly made corn tortillas from the *tortilleria*. **Known for:** decadent doughnuts and sweets; stuffed sopaipillas smothered in green and red chile. [$] *Average main: $8* ✉ *715 Douglas Ave., Las Vegas* ☎ *505/426–1921* ⏲ *No dinner.*

WHERE TO STAY

★ Fodor's Choice [H] **Plaza Hotel.** *Hotel.* Rooms at this three-story
$ Italianate hotel, which has hosted the likes of Doc Holliday and Jesse James, balance the old and the new—they're not overly fancy, but they and the hotel's common areas, restaurant, and bar have been steadily undergoing a renovation since new owners purchased the property in 2014. **Pros:** distinctive and affordable rooms; captures the vibe of the Old West; many shops and eateries within walking distance. **Cons:** moderate street noise; an old property with plenty of quirks. [$] *Rooms from: $99* ✉ *230 Plaza, Las Vegas* ☎ *505/425-3591* 🌐 *www.plazahotel-nm.com* 🛏 *71 rooms* 🍴 *No meals.*

FORT UNION NATIONAL MONUMENT

30 miles north of Las Vegas via I–25 and NM 161.

The ruins of New Mexico's largest American frontier–era fort sit on an empty windswept plain. The site still echoes with the isolation surely felt by the soldiers stationed here between 1851 and 1890, when the fort was established to protect travelers and settlers along the Santa Fe Trail. It eventually became a military supply depot for the Southwest, but was abandoned with the taming of the West. Today you can walk among the extensive ruins on your own or on a ranger tour (they're given throughout the year, more often during the busier spring–fall season). Admission to the park is free.

8

EXPLORING

FAMILY **Fort Union Visitor Center.** The Fort Union Visitor Center provides historical background about the fort and the Santa Fe Trail; guided tours and interpretive talks are also given by staff and volunteers. ✉ *Off NM 161, Exit 364 from I–25, Watrous* ☎ *505/425-8025* 🌐 *www.nps.gov/foun* 🎟 *Free.*

BANDELIER AND LOS ALAMOS

In the Jémez region, the 1,000-year-old Ancestral Puebloan ruins at Bandelier National Monument present a vivid contrast to nearby Los Alamos National Laboratory, birthplace of the atomic bomb. The surrounding town of Los Alamos has a number of worthy museums.

LOS ALAMOS

35 miles north of Santa Fe via U.S. 285/84 and NM 502 west.

Look at old books on New Mexico and you rarely find a mention of Los Alamos, now a busy town of about 18,000 that has the highest per capita income in the state. Like so many other Southwestern communities, Los Alamos was created expressly as a company town; only here the workers weren't mining iron, manning freight trains, or hauling lumber—they were busy toiling at America's foremost nuclear research facility, Los Alamos National Laboratory (LANL). The facility still employs some 10,000 full-time workers.

A few miles from ancient cave dwellings, scientists led by J. Robert Oppenheimer built Fat Man and Little Boy, the atom bombs that in August 1945 decimated Hiroshima and Nagasaki, respectively. LANL was created in 1943 under the auspices of the intensely covert Manhattan Project, whose express purpose it was to expedite an Allied victory during World War II. Indeed, Japan surrendered—but a full-blown Cold War between Russia and the United States ensued for another four and a half decades.

EXPLORING

FAMILY **Bradbury Science Museum.** Los Alamos National Laboratory's public showcase, the Bradbury provides a balanced and provocative examination of such topics as atomic weapons and nuclear power. You can experiment with lasers; witness research in solar, geothermal, fission, and fusion energy; learn about DNA fingerprinting; and view fascinating exhibits about World War II's Project Y (the Manhattan Project, whose participants developed the atomic bomb). ✉ *1350 Central Ave.* ☎ *505/667–7000* ⊕ *www.lanl. gov/museum* 🎫 *Free.*

Fuller Lodge Art Center. New Mexican architect John Gaw Meem designed Fuller Lodge, a short drive up Central Avenue from the Bradbury Science Museum. The massive log building was erected in 1928 as a dining and recreation hall for a small private boys' school. In 1942 the federal government purchased the school and made it the base of operations for the Manhattan Project. Part of the lodge contains an art center that shows the works of northern New Mexican artists; there's a gorgeous rose garden on the grounds. This is a bustling center with drop-in art classes, nine art shows per year, and an outstanding gallery gift shop featuring works by nearly 100 local artisans. ✉ *2132 Central Ave.* ☎ *505/662–9331* 🌐 *www.fullerlodgeartcenter.com* 🎟 *Free* 🕒 *Closed Sun.*

Los Alamos History Museum. A small campus behind the Fuller Lodge links succinct, informative indoor and outdoor exhibits tracing the history of human activity on the site of The Atomic City, from a 13th-century Ancestral Pueblo, to a Boy Scout–influenced prep school for young men from prominent families (including Gore Vidal and William S. Burroughs), to the Manhattan Project and beyond. Permanent exhibits in the Ranch School's former guesthouse set the scene. Steps away, the Hans Bethe House re-creates home life for the top-level scientists working on the atomic bomb. The house next door, home to project coordinator J. Robert Oppenheimer, remains a private residence, but can be viewed from the outside. ✉ *1050 Bathtub Row* 🌐 *www.losalamoshistory.org* 🎟 *$5.*

★ Fodor'sChoice **Pajarito Environmental Education Center at the Los**
FAMILY **Alamos Nature Center.** Built in 2015, the sleek, angular Los Alamos Nature Center, operated by the Pajarito Environmental Education Center, stands out as much for its dramatic design as for the engaging exhibits within. Families appreciate the interactive Children's Discovery Area and the giant scale model of the Pajarito Plateau that kids are encouraged to play on. There's also a high-tech planetarium with astronomy shows or films most weekends, nature trails, wildlife and conservation exhibits, and gardens with local flora and plenty of visiting birdlife. ✉ *2600 Canyon Rd.* ☎ *505/662–0460* 🌐 *www.peecnature.org* 🎟 *Free* 🕒 *Closed Thurs.*

8

WHERE TO EAT

$$ ✕ **Blue Window Bistro.** *American.* Despite its relative wealth, Los Alamos has never cultivated much of a dining scene, which makes this brightly colored and elegant restaurant all the more welcome. The kitchen turns out a mix of New Mexican, American, and Continental dishes, from first-rate salads to traditional filet mignon to shredded-chicken blue-corn enchiladas. **Known for:** filet mignon and New York strip steaks; one of the best cocktail, wine, and beer selections in town. [$] *Average main: $20* ✉ *1789 Central Ave.* ☎ *505/662–6305* 🌐 *www.labluewindowbistro.com* 🕒 *Closed Sun. No lunch Sat.*

BANDELIER NATIONAL MONUMENT

10 miles south of Los Alamos via NM 501 and NM 4, 44 miles northwest of Santa Fe via U.S. 285/84 and NM 502 to NM 4.

Seven centuries before the Declaration of Independence was signed, compact city-states existed in the Southwest. Remnants of one of the most impressive examples can be seen at Frijoles Canyon in Bandelier National Monument. At the canyon's base, near a gurgling stream, the remains of cave dwellings, ancient ceremonial kivas, and other stone structures stretch out for more than a mile beneath the sheer walls of the canyon's tree-fringed rim. For hundreds of years the Ancestral Puebloan people, relatives of today's Rio Grande Pueblo Indians, thrived on wild game, corn, and beans. Suddenly, for reasons still undetermined, the settlements were abandoned.

EXPLORING

★ Fodor'sChoice **Bandelier National Monument.** Along a paved, self-
FAMILY guided trail, steep wooden ladders and narrow doorways lead to a series of cave dwellings and cell-like rooms. There is one kiva in the cliff wall that is large, and tall enough to stand in. Bandelier National Monument, named after author and ethnologist Adolph Bandelier (his novel *The Delight Makers* is set in Frijoles Canyon), contains 33,000 acres of backcountry wilderness, waterfalls, and wildlife. Some 70 miles of trails traverse the park. A small museum in the visitor center focuses on the area's prehistoric and contemporary Native American cultures, with displays of artifacts from 1200 to modern times.

Note that from mid-May to mid-October, visitors arriving by car between 9 am and 3 pm must park at the White Rock Visitor Center 10 miles east on NM 4 and take a free shuttle bus into the park. ✉ *15 Entrance Rd., off NM 4, Los Alamos* ☎ *505/672–0343* ⊕ *www.nps.gov/band* ☑ *$20 per vehicle, good for 7 days.*

White Rock Visitor Center. This sleek, eco-friendly building is a one-stop for finding out about the many things to see and do in the area, from Bandelier and Los Alamos to the Jémez Mountain Trail National Scenic Byway, the hiking at nearby White Rock Overlook, and Valles Caldera National Preserve. You can also catch free shuttle buses into Bandelier (in fact, you can only visit the park in this way from mid-May to mid-October, daily 9–3) and downtown Los

Alamos. The region's nicest chain hotel, the Hampton Inn & Suites Los Alamos, is next door. Discover Los Alamos operates a second visitor center in Los Alamos at 109 Central Park Square. ✉ *115 NM 4, White Rock* ☎ *505/672–3183, 800/444–0707* 🌐 *www.visitlosalamos.org* 🎫 *Free.*

WHERE TO EAT

$ 🍴 **Pig + Fig.** *American.* Your best bet before or after visiting Bandelier for anything from a light snack to a substantial lunch or early dinner, this cheerful bakery and café features the farm-to-table cuisine and tempting desserts (be sure to try a macaron or two) of gifted chef Laura Crucet. Share plates of tapas, dig into a hearty bowl of beef bourguignon, or savor one of the outstanding sandwiches, such as the signature "hot pig + fig" with honey-cured ham, spinach, Brie, and fig jam. **Known for:** meat-cheese-olive plates; lemon tarts; a reasonably priced and well-curated list of wines by the glass. [$] *Average main: $10* ✉ *35 Rover Blvd., Suite G, White Rock* ☎ *505/672–2742* 🌐 *www.pigandfig-cafe.com* ⏰ *Closed Sun. and Mon.*

VALLES CALDERA NATIONAL PRESERVE

20 miles northwest of Bandelier National Monument on NM 4.

A high-forest drive brings you to the awe-inspiring Valles Grande, which at 14 miles in diameter is one of the world's largest calderas and which became Valles (*vah*-yes) Caldera National Preserve in 2000.

8

EXPLORING

★ Fodor's Choice **Valles Caldera National Preserve.** The caldera resulted from the eruption and collapse of a 14,000-foot peak over 1.25 million years ago; the flow out the bottom created the Pajarito Plateau and the ash from the eruption spread as far east as Kansas. You can't imagine the volcanic crater's immensity until you spot what look like specks of dust on the lush meadow floor and realize they're elk. The Valles Caldera Trust manages this 89,000-acre multiuse preserve with the aim to "protect and preserve the scientific, scenic, geologic, watershed, fish, wildlife, historic, cultural, and recreational values of the Preserve, and to provide for multiple use and sustained yield of renewable resources within the Preserve."

The preserve is open to visitors for hiking, cross-country skiing, horseback riding, horse-drawn carriage rides, van wildlife photography tours, mountain-bike tours, bird-watching, fly-fishing, and may other outdoorsy endeavors. ⊠ *NM 4, mile marker 39.2, 10 miles west of junction with NM 501, Jemez Springs* ☎ *575/829–4100* ⊕ *www. nps.gov/vall* 🖃 *$20 per vehicle, good for 7 days* ☉ *Visitor center closed Sun.*

GEORGIA O'KEEFFE COUNTRY

It's a 20-minute drive north of Santa Fe to reach the Española Valley, where you head northwest to the striking mesas, cliffs, and valleys that so inspired the artist Georgia O'Keeffe—she lived in this area for the final 50 years of her life. Passing through the small, workaday city of Española, U.S. 84 continues to the sleepy village of Abiquiú and eventually up past Ghost Ranch, areas where O'Keeffe both lived and worked. Other notable communities in this area are tiny Ojo Caliente, famous for its hot-springs spa retreat, and Los Ojos and Chama, known respectively for their weaving collective and scenic railroad.

ABIQUIÚ

50 miles northwest of Santa Fe on U.S. 84.

This tiny, very traditional Hispanic village was originally home to freed *genizaros,* indigenous and mixed-blood slaves who served as house servants, shepherds, and other key roles in Spanish, Mexican, and American households well into the 1880s. Many descendants of original families still live in the area, although since the late 1980s Abiquiú and its surrounding countryside have become a nesting ground for those fleeing big-city life, among them actresses Marsha Mason and Shirley MacLaine. Abiquiú—along with parts of the nearby Española Valley—is also a hotbed of organic farming, with many of the operations here selling their goods at the Santa Fe Farmers' Market and to restaurants throughout the Rio Grande Valley.

EXPLORING

Abiquiú Studio Tour. A number of artists live in Abiquiú, and several studios showing traditional Hispanic art, as well as contemporary works and pottery, are open regularly to the public; many others open each year over Columbus Day weekend (second weekend of October) for the annual Abiquiú Studio Tour. ⊠ *Abiquiu* ☎ *505/257–0866* ⊕ *www. abiquiustudiotour.org.*

Bode's. Bode's, pronounced *boh*-dees, across from the Abiquiú post office, is much more than a gas station. It's a popular stop for newspapers, quirky gifts, locally made arts and crafts, cold drinks, supplies, fishing gear (including licenses), amazing breakfast burritos, hearty green-chile stew, sandwiches, and other short-order fare. The friendly, busy station serves as general store and exchange post for news and gossip. ✉ *21196 U.S. 84, look for Phillips 66 gas station sign* ☎ *505/685–4422* 🌐 *bodes.com* 🎫 *Free.*

★ Fodor's Choice **Georgia O'Keeffe Home & Studio.** In 1945 Georgia O'Keeffe bought a large, dilapidated late-18th-century Spanish-colonial adobe compound just off the plaza. Upon the 1946 death of her husband, photographer Alfred Stieglitz, she left New York City and began dividing her time permanently between this home, which figured prominently in many of her works, and the one in nearby Ghost Ranch. The patio is featured in *Black Patio Door* (1955) and *Patio with Cloud* (1956). O'Keeffe died in 1986 at the age of 98 and left provisions in her will to ensure that the property's houses would never be public monuments.

Highly engaging one-hour tours are available by advance reservation through Santa Fe's Georgia O'Keeffe Museum, which owns the house and operates the tours Tuesday–Saturday from early March through late November (call for hours); the cost is $35–$45 depending on the day and season (summer Saturdays are most expensive). Tours depart by shuttle bus from the tour office (a new, expanded visitor center will open at this location in mid-2018), which is next to the Abiquiu Inn. Book well ahead in summer, as these tours fill up quickly. ✉ *21120 U.S. 84* ☎ *505/946–1098* 🌐 *www.okeeffemuseum.org/tickets-and-tours* 🎫 *$35–$45* ⏲ *Closed Sun. and Mon. and late Nov.–early Mar.*

8

WHERE TO EAT

$$ 🍴 **Café Abiquiú.** *Eclectic.* This inviting, art-filled restaurant at the Abiquiu Inn (which is also the departure point for tours of the nearby O'Keeffe Home & Studio) serves tasty New Mexican, Italian, and American fare, including blue-corn tacos stuffed with grilled trout and red-chile rib-eye steaks. Be sure to peek inside the adjoining art gallery featuring local work, and take a stroll through the graceful gardens. **Known for:** Copper Canyon eggs Benedict with corn cakes and red-chile mornay sauce; fresh fruit cobblers. [$] *Average main: $19* ✉ *21120 U.S. 84* ☎ *505/685–4378* 🌐 *www.abiquiuinn.com.*

★ Fodor'sChoice ✕ **El Paragua Restaurant.** *Mexican.* With a dark,
$$ intimate atmosphere of wood and stone, this historic place
started out as a lemonade-cum-taco stand in the late 1950s
but is now known for some of the state's most authentic
New Mexican and regional Mexican cuisine. Steaks and
fish are grilled over a mesquite-wood fire; other specialties
include chorizo enchiladas, panfried breaded trout aman-
dine, and menudo. **Known for:** authentic regional cuisine;
exceptional service. Ⓢ *Average main: $20* ✉ *603 Santa Cruz
Rd., NM 76 just east of NM 68, Española* ☎ *505/753–3211,
800/929–8226* ⊕ *www.elparagua.com.*

WHERE TO STAY

$$$ ⌬ **Abiquiu Inn.** *B&B/Inn.* Deep in the Chama Valley, this
inn has a secluded vibe amid the red-rock geography that
inspired Georgia O'Keeffe. **Pros:** good base for exploring
O'Keeffe Country; breathtaking high-desert scenery. **Cons:**
service is friendly but fairly hands-off; rooms at the front
of the inn get noise from the road. Ⓢ *Rooms from: $189*
✉ *21120 U.S. 84* ☎ *505/685–4378* ⊕ *www.abiquiuinn.com*
↩ *25 rooms* ⦿*No meals.*

★ Fodor'sChoice ⌬ **Ojo Caliente Mineral Springs Resort & Spa.** *Resort.*
$$ Set in a remote village in the vicinity of the red rocks and
rugged mountains of Abiquiú, this fabled hot springs
resort fits the tastes and budget of all sorts of travelers,
from spiritually minded adventurers on a modest budget
to romance-seekers wanting an upscale yet secluded spa
getaway (it's a favorite of celebs filming movies in New
Mexico). **Pros:** very reasonably priced (for the simplest
rooms); relaxing and serene setting; unpretentious and
friendly vibe. **Cons:** a little funky and New Age-y for some
tastes; remote. Ⓢ *Rooms from: $169* ✉ *50 Los Baños Dr.,
Ojo Caliente* ☎ *505/583–2233, 800/222–9162* ⊕ *www.
ojocaliente.ojospa.com* ↩ *49 units* ⦿*No meals.*

GHOST RANCH

15 miles north of Abiquiú on U.S. 84.

For art historians, the name Ghost Ranch brings to mind
Georgia O'Keeffe, who lived on a small parcel of this
22,000-acre dude and cattle ranch. The ranch's owner
in the 1930s—conservationist and publisher of *Nature
Magazine*, Arthur Pack—first invited O'Keeffe here to
visit in 1934; Pack soon sold the artist the 7-acre plot on
which she lived summer through fall for most of the rest of
her life. In 1955 Pack donated the rest of the ranch to the
Presbyterian Church, which continues to use Pack's origi-

nal structures and part of the land as a conference center, but Ghost Ranch is also open to visitors for tours, hikes, workshops, and all sorts of other activities.

If you have the time, consider continuing north another 30 miles along gorgeous U.S. 84 to the tiny weaving village of Los Ojos and 12 more miles to Chama, a forested town near the Colorado border that's famous as the terminus of the scenic Cumbres & Toltec Railroad. From Los Ojos, in summer (this route is closed from fall through spring because of snow) you can cut across to Taos (80 miles away) via U.S. 64, crossing one of the prettiest mountain passes in the state.

EXPLORING

★ Fodor's Choice **Cumbres & Toltec Scenic Railroad.** In the lush and
FAMILY densely wooded town of Chama, nestled at the base of 10,000-foot Cumbre Pass, the railroad has played a vital role since the 1880s, when workers piled into town to construct the Denver & Rio Grande Railroad. You can get a sense of this history strolling along the town's main drag, Terrace Avenue, which has a handful of cute shops, cafés, and B&Bs, and by taking a ride on the historic Cumbres & Toltec Scenic Railroad, the nation's longest (and highest) narrow-gauge train excursion. Passengers are transported by handsomely restored, 1920s coal-driven steam engines and 19th-century parlor cars, passing over 10,200-foot Cumbres Pass and through the rugged San Juan Mountains. You chug over ancient trestles, around breathtaking bends, and high above the Los Pinos River—if the terrain looks at all familiar, you may have seen this railroad's "performance" in *Indiana Jones and the Last Crusade.* Midway through the trip you break for lunch and can switch to a waiting Colorado-based train to complete the 64 miles to Antonito, Colorado (from which you'll be shuttled back by bus), or return from this point on the same train. Themed dinner and sunset rides as well as kids'-oriented "Cinder Bear Express" excursions are offered throughout the season. ✉ *15 Terrace Ave., Chama* ☎ *575/741–3126, 888/286–2737* ⊕ *www.cumbrestoltec.com* 🖃 *$99–$196* ☺ *Closed mid.-Oct.–late May.*

★ Fodor's Choice **Ghost Ranch Education & Retreat Center.** Open to
FAMILY the public year-round, this sprawling, stunningly situated ranch is busiest in summer, when the majority of workshops take place, and when visitors drive up having toured the O'Keeffe home in nearby Abiquiú. Now a retreat center, the

ranch offers a wealth of interesting activities for day visitors, including two different guided Georgia O'Keeffe tours across the landscape she painted during the five decades that she summered here. Her original house is not part of the tour and is closed to the public. Other guided hikes amid the property's dramatic rock formations touch on archaeology and paleontology, history, and the several movies that have been filmed here (*Cowboys and Aliens, City Slickers, Wyatt Earp,* and a few others). Visitors can tour the **Florence Hawley Ellis Museum of Anthropology,** which contains Native American tools, pottery, and other artifacts excavated from the Ghost Ranch Gallina digs, and the adjacent **Ruth Hall Museum of Paleontology.** Workshops, which touch on everything from photography and poetry to yoga and wellness, are offered throughout the year—guests camp or stay in semi-rustic cottages or casitas. And you can also sign up for guided trail rides, hikes (guided or on your own), massages, and more. When you arrive, drop by the welcome center, which also houses a trading post stocked with books, art, O'Keeffe ephemera, and a basic coffee station (there's also a dining hall serving cafeteria-style meals throughout the day). ⊠ *U.S. 84, between mile markers 224 and 225, about 13 miles north of Abiquiú village, Abiquiu* ☎ *505/685–1000, 877/804–4678* ⊕ *www.ghostranch.org.*

★ Fodor'sChoice **Tierra Wools.** Bordering the Rio Chama, U.S. 84 works its way north through monumental red rocks and golden sandstone spires that inspired Georgia O'Keeffe's vivid paintings of creased mountains, stark crosses, bleached animal skulls, and adobe architecture. Just beyond the rugged town of Tierra Amarilla sits Los Ojos, a tiny village that's become a model of successful rural economic development by having tapped into its ancient roots—the raising of Churro sheep (the original breed brought over by the Spanish, prized for its wool) and weaving. Tierra Wools cooperative produces some of the finest original weavings in the Southwest. Designs are based on the old Rio Grande styles, and weavers make rugs and capes of superb craftsmanship entirely by hand, using old-style looms (they're happy to provide visitors with demonstrations). Weaving workshops are offered. You'll also find a smattering of artists' studios nearby, most of them in rustic buildings with corrugated metal roofs. ⊠ *91 Main St., Los Ojos* ☎ *575/588–7231* ⊕ *www.handweavers.com* 🖾 *Free* ☺ *Closed Dec.–mid-Apr.*

THE HIGH ROAD TO TAOS

★ **Fodor's**Choice The main route to Taos (NM 68, the so-called "Low Road") is a quite dramatic drive if you've got limited time, but by far the most spectacular way is via what's known as the High Road. Towering peaks, lush hillsides, orchards, and meadows surround tiny, ancient Hispanic villages that are as picturesque as they are historically fascinating. The well-signed High Road follows U.S. 285/84 north to NM 503 (a right turn just past Pojoaque toward Nambé), to County Road 98 (a left toward Chimayó), to NM 76 northeast to NM 75 east, to NM 518 north. The drive takes you through the badlands of stark, weathered rock—where numerous Westerns have been filmed—quickly into rolling foothills, lush canyons, and finally into pine forests. Although most of these insular, traditional Hispanic communities offer little in the way of shopping and dining, the region has become a haven for artists.

★ **Fodor's**Choice **High Road Art Tour.** From Chimayó to Peñasco, you can find mostly low-key but often high-quality art galleries, many of them run out of the owners' homes. During the final two weekends in September each year, more than three dozen artists show their work in the High Road Art Tour; for a studio map, or plenty of useful information on galleries open not just during the tour but year-round, visit the website. ✉ *Chimayo* 🕮⊕ *www.highroadnewmexico.com.*

8

Depending on when you make this drive, you're in for some of the state's most radiant scenery. In mid-April the orchards are in blossom; summer turns the valleys into lush green oases; and in fall the smell of piñon adds to the sensual overload of golden leaves and red-chile ristras hanging from the houses. In winter the fields are covered with quilts of snow, and the lines of homes, fences, and trees stand out like bold pen-and-ink drawings against the sky. But the roads can be icy and treacherous—if in doubt, stick with the Low Road to Taos. ■TIP→ **If you decide to take the High Road just one way between Santa Fe and Taos, you might want to save it for the return journey—the scenery is even more stunning when traveling north to south.**

POJOAQUE AND NAMBÉ PUEBLOS

17 miles north of Santa Fe on U.S. 285/84.

EXPLORING

Nambé Falls and Nambé Lake. There's a shady picnic area and a large fishing lake that's open April through October at this scenic and popular hiking area along the High Road, just east of Pojoaque (the cost is $15 per carload for a day pass). The waterfalls are about a 15-minute hike in from the parking and picnic area along a rocky, clearly marked path. The water pours over a rock precipice—a loud and dramatic sight given the river's modest size. ✉ *Off NM 503 and NP Hwy. 102, Nambe* ☎ *505/455–2304* 🌐 *www.nambepueblo.org* 🎟 *$15* ⏲ *Closed Mon.–Wed.*

Poeh Cultural Center and Museum. Situated just off U.S. 285/84 at Pojoaque Pueblo, this impressive complex of traditional adobe buildings, including the three-story Sun Tower, makes an engaging first stop as you begin a drive north of Santa Fe toward Taos; the facility comprises a museum, a cultural center, and artists' studios. The museum holds some 10,000 photographs, including many by esteemed early-20th-century photographer Edward S. Curtis, as well as more than 600 works of both traditional and contemporary pottery, jewelry, textiles, and sculpture. ✉ *78 Cities of Gold Rd., North Side* ☎ *505/455–5041* 🌐 *www.poehcenter.org* 🎟 *Donation suggested* ⏲ *Closed Sun.*

WHERE TO STAY

$$$ 🏨 **Buffalo Thunder Resort & Casino.** *Resort.* Managed by Hilton, this expansive, upscale gaming and golfing getaway is the closest full-service resort to Downtown—it's 15 miles north of the Plaza, just off a freeway but with spectacular views of the mountains and Rio Grande Valley. **Pros:** snazzy rooms with plenty of amenities; convenient to opera and Low and High roads to Taos; panoramic mountain and mesa views. **Cons:** rates can be a bit steep, especially when there are events on property; lobby is noisy and crowded with gamers on many evenings; a 15-minute drive from the Plaza. [$] *Rooms from: $219* ✉ *30 Buffalo Thunder Trail, off U.S. 285/84, Exit 177, North Side* ☎ *505/455–5555, 877/455–7775* 🌐 *www.buffalothunderresort.com* 🛏 *375 rooms* 🍴 *No meals.*

CHIMAYÓ

28 miles north of Santa Fe and 12 miles northeast of Nambé/Pojoaque on NM 76.

From U.S. 285/84 north of Pojoaque, scenic NM 503 winds past horse paddocks and orchards in the narrow Nambé Valley, then ascends into the red-sandstone canyons with a view of Truchas Peaks to the northeast before dropping into the bucolic village of Chimayó. Nestled into hillsides where gnarled piñons seem to grow from bare bedrock, Chimayó is famed for its weaving, its red chiles, and its two chapels, particularly El Santuario de Chimayó.

EXPLORING

★ Fodor'sChoice **El Santuario de Chimayó.** This small, frontier, adobe church has a fantastically carved and painted reredos (altar screen) and is built on the site where, believers say, a mysterious light came from the ground on Good Friday in 1810 leading to the discovery of a large wooden crucifix beneath the earth. The chapel sits above a sacred *pozito* (a small hole), the dirt from which is believed to have miraculous healing properties. Dozens of abandoned crutches and braces placed in the anteroom—along with many notes, letters, and photos—testify to this. The Santuario draws a steady stream of worshippers year-round—Chimayó is considered the Lourdes of the Southwest. During Holy Week as many as 50,000 pilgrims come here. The shrine is a National Historic Landmark. It's surrounded by small adobe shops selling every kind of religious curio imaginable and some very fine traditional Hispanic work from local artists. ⊠ *15 Santuario Dr., signed lane off CR 98, Chimayo* ☎ *505/351–9961* ⊕ *www.holychimayo.us* ⊠ *Free.*

Santo Niño de Atocha. A smaller chapel 200 yards from El Santuario was built in 1857 and dedicated to Santo Niño de Atocha. As at the more famous Santuario, the dirt at Santo Niño de Atocha's chapel is said to have healing properties in the place where the *Santo Niño* was first placed. The little boy saint was brought here from Mexico by Severiano Medina, who claimed Santo Niño de Atocha had healed him of rheumatism. Tales of the boy saint's losing one of his shoes as he wandered through the countryside helping those in trouble endeared him to the people of northern New Mexico. It became a tradition to place shoes at the foot of the statue as an offering. Many soldiers who survived the Bataan Death March during World War II credit Santo Niño for saving them, adding to his beloved status

8

in this state where the percentage of young people who enlist in the military remains quite high. ✉ *CR 94A, off CR 98, Chimayo* 🎟 *Free.*

WHERE TO EAT

$ 🍴 **Rancho de Chimayó.** *Mexican.* In a century-old adobe hacienda tucked into the mountains, with whitewashed walls, hand-stripped vigas, and cozy dining rooms, the Rancho de Chimayó is still owned and operated by the family that first occupied the house. There's a fireplace in winter and, in summer, a terraced patio shaded by catalpa trees. **Known for:** the Chimayó Cocktail with apple cider, lemon juice, premium tequila, and crème de cassis; green-chile stew; a gorgeous terraced back patio. [$] *Average main: $17* ✉ *300 Juan Medina Rd. (Country Rd. 98), Chimayo* ☎ *505/351–4444* 🌐 *www.ranchodechimayo.com* ⊗ *Nov.–Apr., closed Mon.*

WHERE TO STAY

$$ 🏨 **Casa Escondida.** *B&B/Inn.* Intimate and peaceful, this adobe inn has sweeping views of the Sangre de Cristo range. **Pros:** very good value, with gracious hosts and in beautiful surroundings; no TVs. **Cons:** remote setting means you need a car to get places. [$] *Rooms from: $149* ✉ *CR 0100, off NM 76, Chimayo* ☎ *505/351–4805* 🌐 *www.casaescondida.com* 🛏 *8 rooms* 🍽 *Breakfast.*

★ Fodor's Choice 🏨 **Rancho Manzana B&B.** *B&B/Inn.* A great base
$ if you're making an overnight adventure of the High Road, or an affordable and charming lodging option that's an easy and scenic 30-minute drive from Downtown Santa Fe, this distinctive, eco-conscious retreat facing Plaza del Cerro, one of the state's best-preserved Spanish-colonial plazas, is an easy walk to the attractions and shops in historic Chimayó. **Pros:** totally secluded yet convenient to area attractions; beautiful setting; very reasonable rates. **Cons:** some of the rooms are a bit on the cozy side. [$] *Rooms from: $79* ✉ *26 Camino de Mision, Chimayo* ☎ *505/351–2227, 888/505–2227* 🌐 *www.ranchomanzana.com* 💳 *No credit cards* 🛏 *4 rooms* 🍽 *Breakfast.*

SHOPPING

★ Fodor's Choice **Centinela Traditional Arts.** The Trujillo family weaving tradition, which started in northern New Mexico more than seven generations ago, is carried out in this colorful, inviting gallery. Irvin Trujillo and his wife, Lisa, are both gifted, renowned master weavers, creating Rio Grande–style tapestry blankets and rugs, many of them with natural dyes that authentically replicate early weavings. Most designs are historically based, but the Trujillos are never shy about innovating and their original works are as breathtaking as the traditional ones. ⊠ *946 NM 76, Chimayo* ☎ *505/351–2180* ⊕ *www.chimayoweavers.com.*

Oviedo Carvings & Bronze. Long-acclaimed artist Marco Oviedo has earned a reputation for his sometimes whimsical, sometimes inspirational bronze carvings, which depict everything from Native figures to regional wildlife. Most of these are no more than a foot tall, and prices are quite reasonable. ⊠ *NM 76, 1 mile east of CR 98, Chimayo* ☎ *505/351–2280* ⊕ *www.oviedoart.us.*

CORDOVA

5 miles east of Chimayó via NM 76.

You'll have to turn south off NM 76 to get down into the narrow, steep valley cradling this lovely village, but you'll be happy you did. A picturesque mountain town with a small central plaza, a school, a post office, and a church, Cordova is the center of the centuries-old regional wood-carving industry. The town supports a slew of full-time and part-time carvers. Many of them are descendants of José Dolores López, who in the 1920s created the village's signature unpainted "Cordova style" of carving. A few of the *santeros* (makers of religious images) have signs outside their homes indicating that santos are for sale. Many pieces are fairly expensive, a reflection of the hard work and fine craftsmanship involved—ranging from several hundred dollars for small ones to several thousand for larger figures—but there are also affordable and delightful small carvings of animals and birds.

TRUCHAS

4 miles northeast of Cordova via NM 76.

Truchas (Spanish for "trout") is where Robert Redford shot the movie *The Milagro Beanfield War* (based on the novel written by Taos author John Nichols). This pastoral village is perched dramatically on the rim of a deep canyon beneath the towering Truchas Peaks, mountains high enough to be almost perpetually capped with snow. The tallest of the Truchas Peaks is 13,102 feet, the second-highest point in New Mexico. Truchas has been gaining appeal with artsy, independent-minded transplants from Santa Fe and Taos, who have come for the cheaper real estate and the breathtaking setting. There are several excellent galleries in town.

Continue 7 miles north on NM 76, toward Peñasco, and you come to the marvelous San José de Gracia Church in the village of Trampas. It dates from circa 1760.

SHOPPING

★ Fodor's Choice **Cardona-Hine Gallery.** With highly impressive, museum-quality artwork that might have you thinking this gallery was plucked out of Manhattan, Cardona-Hine opened in a red-roofed adobe house in the historic center of Truchas back in 1988, helping to spur the community's growth as a serious gallery destination. Inside you'll find oil paintings by the talented founders, Barbara McCauley and her late husband, Alvaro Cardona-Hine, as well as works by sculptor Marcia McEachron. ⊠ *82 County Rd. 75* ☎ *505/689–2253* ⊕ *www.cardonahinegallery.com.*

PEÑASCO

15 miles north of Truchas and 25 miles southeast of Taos on NM 76.

Although still a modest-size community, Peñasco is one of the "larger" villages along the High Road and a good bet if you need to fill your tank with gas or pick up a snack at a convenience store. The village is also home to a growing number of fine galleries as well as one of the most celebrated small-town restaurants in northern New Mexico, Sugar Nymphs Bistro.

WHERE TO EAT

★ Fodor's Choice ✕ **Sugar Nymphs Bistro.** *American.* You can't
$$ miss the vivid murals on the building in sleepy Peñasco that houses both a vintage theater and an intimate restaurant where acclaimed chef-owners Kai Harper Leah and Ki Holste serve up tantalizing farm-to-table fare, from bountiful salads and creatively topped pizzas to triple-layer chocolate cake. This is hands down the best restaurant on the High Road. **Known for:** juicy bacon cheeseburgers; Sunday brunch; decadent organic carrot cake and other fabulous desserts. ⓢ *Average main: $18* ⊠ *15046 NM 75* ☎ *575/587–0311* ⊕ *www.sugarnymphs.com* ☉ *Reduced hrs in winter (call first).*

SHOPPING

Gaucho Blue Gallery. Nearly across the street from the wonderful Sugar Nymphs Bistro, this eclectic gallery (open spring–fall) carries a great mix of paintings and other pieces by local artists—notably Nick Beason's edgy monotypes and copper etchings and Lise Poulsen's felted kimonos and striking fiberworks. You'll find both contemporary and traditional works here. ⊠ *14148 NM 75* ☎ *575/587–1076* ⊕ *www.gauchoblue.com.*

DIXON

13 miles west of Peñasco, 47 miles north of Santa Fe, and 25 miles south of Taos on NM 75.

The small village of Dixon is home to a number of artists as well as a couple of the wineries that are helping put the northern Rio Grande Valley on the map among oenophiles. Artistic sensitivity, as well as generations of dedicated farmers, account for the community's well-tended fields, pretty gardens, and fruit trees—a source of produce for restaurants and farmers' markets throughout the region. It's simple to find your way around; there's only one main road.

If you're driving the High Road, Dixon is a slight detour from Peñasco. You can either return the way you come and continue from Peñasco over the mountains into Taos, or from Dixon you can pick up NM 68, the Low Road, and continue north to Taos through the scenic Rio Grande Gorge.

8

EXPLORING

Dixon Studio Tour. During the first full weekend in November, area artists open up their home studios to the public, drawing folks from throughout the region to one of the state's top small art towns. ⊠ *Dixon* ⊕ *www.dixonarts.org.*

La Chiripada Winery. Nestled under mature shade trees down a dirt lane in Dixon's quaint village center, this producer of first-rate wines is the oldest vintner in the northern part of the state. La Chiripada's Viogner, Special Reserve Riesling, and Dolcetto have all earned considerable acclaim. There's also a nicely crafted New Mexico Port, which pairs well with dessert. There's a small art gallery, and the winery also has a tasting room in Taos at 103 Bent Street. ⊠ *NM 75, 3 miles east of NM 68* ☎ *505/579–4437* ⊕ *www. lachiripada.com.*

Vivac Winery. "Vivac" means "high-altitude refuge," and that's a fitting name for this hip winery located right at the turnoff on NM 68 (the Low Road) to NM 75 (which leads to the High Road). Owned and run by brothers Jesse and Chris Padberg and their wives Michele and Liliana, the vineyards and charming tasting room, with an adjacent patio, are set deep in the Rio Grande gorge surrounded by sheer cliffs. It's a dramatic setting for sampling these elegant, generally dry wines, which feature a mix of grapes, including Italian Dolcetto, Spanish Tempranillo, French Cabernet Sauvignon, and German off-dry Riesling. The Tasting Room also sells artisan (and local) Ek.chuah Chocolates, house-made cheeses, and jewelry; there's a second tasting room at the farmers' market building in Santa Fe. ⊠ *2075 NM 68* ☎ *505/579–4441* ⊕ *www.vivacwinery.com.*

WHERE TO EAT

$ ✕ **Zuly's Cafe.** *Southwestern.* This simple, cheerful spot serving authentic New Mexico fare in the village center is good to know about if you've built up an appetite tasting vino at the several wineries nearby. You might start your day off with a stick-to-your-ribs breakfast of chile-smothered huevos rancheros. **Known for:** hearty breakfast burritos; green-chile cheeseburgers. Ⓢ *Average main: $9* ⊠ *234 NM 75* ☎ *505/579–4001* ☉ *Closed Sun. and Mon. No dinner Tues.–Thurs.*

ALBUQUERQUE

Updated
by Lynne
Arany

TODAY'S SMART TRAVELER KNOWS SOMETHING special is afoot in this wonderfully diverse and charmingly quirky historic town hard by the Rio Grande. You'll want to plan on spending at least a day or more before venturing beyond. Perfectly set as the gateway to other New Mexico wonders like Zuni, El Morro, and Chaco Canyon, Albuquerque's own rich history and dramatic terrain—desert volcanoes, unique cottonwood bosque along the broad banks of the river that flows through its very center, and a striking confluence of mountain ranges—have long captured the imagination of folks en route from here to there. Today, vibrant art galleries, growers' markets, a coffee and microbrewery scene, and its world-class museums as well as superb nature trails and spectacular topography—and, absolutely, the seemingly endless blue sky and the joyous hot-air balloons that decorate it—make it a worthy destination of its own.

Centuries-old traces of Native American populations past and present abound throughout the Rio Grande Valley, and Albuquerque is no exception. Their trade routes are what drew the Spanish here; sections of what became their Camino Real are still intact. The little farming settlement was proclaimed "Alburquerque," after the Viceroy of New Spain—the 10th Duke of Alburquerque—in 1706. By the time Anglo traders arrived in the 1800s, that first "r" had been dropped, but that settlement, now known as Old Town, was still the heart of town. By the 1880s, with the railroad in place, the center of town moved east to meet it, in the Downtown we know today. Remnants of all linger still—and may readily be seen in the soft aging adobes in the North and South Valley, or the old Rail Yard buildings in Barelas.

In the spirit of one of the earliest local proponents of preserving our natural heritage, Aldo Leopold, Albuquerque is committed to protecting its exquisite bosque lands—and the waterfowl, porcupines, and other wildlife that call them home. A network of bicycle trails has been extended from there throughout the city. A noted Public Art program, a developing innovation economy, a remarkably diverse population, and a surprisingly eclectic range of architecture further set this city apart.

A bit of quiet attention reveals Albuquerque's subtle beauty—a flock of sandhill cranes overhead; a hot-air balloon, seemingly within reach; vintage art deco buildings and

TOP REASONS TO GO

Dazzling views, dramatic topography. An outdoors-lover's dream—mountains to volcanoes, and the Rio Grande between. Walking and biking trails abound, and you can paddle the Rio as well.

Arts, heritage & history, from ancient adobes to Route 66's motor-court neon, from early rail days to the Manhattan Project story and Bill Gates's first moves, flamenco to ¡Globalquerque!...and galleries and museums that cover it all.

Farm-fresh dining, piquant and traditional northern New

Mexican specialties, vibrant growers' markets, and luxe B&Bs and inns.

Microbreweries (coffee and wine, too). Award-winning brews and a pub, café, or winery for every mood.

Roadways to ruins (and pueblos today). Explore nearby Petroglyph National Monument, and, a bit farther out, Acoma, Jémez, Santa Ana, and Sandia pueblos, and onward to Chaco Canyon.

Balloons, of course, and the 360 days a year of blue sky in which to enjoy them.

motel signs along old Route 66; Pueblo Revival details on the university campus; the fabulous facade of the KiMo theater; a sudden glimpse across the western desert to a 100-mile-distant snowcapped Mt. Taylor; and the Sandia Mountains lit pink by the fading sun.

ORIENTATION AND PLANNING

GETTING ORIENTED

On first take, Albuquerque's sprawl may appear intimidating, but navigating it is usually fast, and as simple as understanding how it got built up back in the day: there's the historic Rio Grande corridor (north–south) and the east–west Route 66 (or, Central Avenue) corridor, which came along with the automobile. Rio Grande neighborhoods (North Valley and Barelas/South Valley) are most enjoyed by sticking to local backroads. From Old Town east through Downtown/EDo to UNM/Nob Hill and beyond, local is still good, but if you're high-tailing it, Interstate 40 will be your primary route. Street addresses indicate the city's cardinal quadrants, with the railroad tracks dividing west from east, and Central Avenue splitting north from south. Visitors seeking a deeper sense of Albuquerque's rich culture and heritage—and retreat-like luxe accommodations—will want to allow travel time along the Rio Grande routes; those seeking museums, shopping, hotels, and more dining options, too, might settle in the Old-Town–Nob Hill zone. Outlying neighborhoods have their specific charms as well.

ALBUQUERQUE NEIGHBORHOODS

Old Town. A step back in time to the Spanish settlement on which Albuquerque was founded, Old Town's shops and galleries reflect the Native American population that preceded it. The adobe buildings here date as far back as 1706. The adjacent Sawmill district extends the historic spirit, building on the old lumber-milling industry, with a growing enclave of hotels, dining, and shops.

Downtown/EDo. With the stunning Pueblo Deco Kimo Theatre as its centerpiece, Downtown supports a small but world-class group of art galleries, eye-dazzling murals, and a lively coffee and microbrew scene, and has managed to preserve enough remnants of its railroad-era architecture to reward anyone walking this way. Head east to EDo and find great dining and lodging options, and a surprisingly Victorian residential neighborhood.

Barelas/South Valley. Historic Barelas is home to the acclaimed National Hispanic Cultural Center and the emerging Rail Yard market developments. The low-lying enclave, centered on 4th Street SW, gradually gives way to the rural South Valley.

UNM/Nob Hill. Rich with an extensive arts complex on campus, and an exemplary jazz venue—Outpost Performance Space—just off, the neighborhood that stretches from south of UNM east into art deco–influenced Nob Hill is spotted throughout with dining upscale and down, quaint shops and galleries, microbreweries, and the city's venerable indie cinema, The Guild.

Los Ranchos/North Valley. Along the Rio Grande Valley, where first Pueblo peoples, then generations of Hispanic and Anglo families, have resided, lies the city's agrarian heart. Notable for farm-fresh dining and some very special accommodations, its cottonwood-lined bosque trails offer a shaded respite, as well as a perfect jump-off to points farther north along the backroads, including the charming village of Corrales and down-home Bernalillo, Santa Ana, and Jémez pueblos, and even Chaco Canyon or Santa Fe. (Los Ranchos de Albuquerque is a small village within the greater extent of Albuquerque's North Valley.)

Uptown/Northeast Heights. Barely developed until the 1970s, this booming residential area north of Interstate 40 begins with Uptown (the city's shopping center nexus) and rises steadily east into the Heights and the Sandia foothills, where there's great hiking and a breathtaking aerial tram to the top of the peak.

East Side. Home to the must-see National Museum of Nuclear Science & History, and a somewhat seedy stretch of old Route 66 with vintage motor court signs along the way.

Airport. The mesa-top area just north of the airport has several hotels and is a short drive from town.

West Side. Head west on the lovely Montaño bridge over the Rio Grande and discover the fascinating sandhill crane flyway and nesting ground at the Open Space Visitor Center, plus memorable Petroglyph National Monument.

PLANNER

WHEN TO GO

Albuquerque is sunny year-round. Fall is by far the most popular time to visit. On just about any day in late-August through November, big balloons sail across the sharp blue sky and the scent of freshly roasting green chiles permeates the air. Balloon Fiesta brings enormous crowds for nearly two weeks in early October (book hotels at this time as far in advance as possible). Shortly after, the weather's still great and hotel prices plummet. Albuquerque's winter days (usually 10°F warmer than those in Santa Fe) are usually mild enough for hiking, biking, and golf, or simply strolling around Old Town or Nob Hill. The occasional frigid spike usually thaws by morning. Spring brings winds, though plenty of sunshine, too, and rates stay low until the summer crowds flock in. Hot but dry temps in mid-May through mid-July stay well below Phoenix-like extremes, but can hit the high 90s and hover there a bit, especially in June. This is followed by roughly six to eight weeks of cooler temperatures, a bit more humidity, and the spectacular late-afternoon cloud formations that herald the brief "monsoon" season.

9

GETTING HERE AND AROUND

AIR TRAVEL
Albuquerque International Sunport (*ABQ*). The major gateway to New Mexico is Albuquerque International Sunport, a well-designed and attractive art-filled facility that's just 5 miles southeast of Downtown and 3 miles south of UNM/ Nob Hill. There's a free ABQ Ride bus shuttle service on weekdays from the airport to Downtown's Alvarado Transportation Center, where you can connect with Rail Runner service. ✉ *2200 Sunport Blvd. SE* ☎ *505/244–7700* ⊕ *abqsunport.com.*

BIKE SHARE
Rental stands are scattered about Downtown and Old Town, but expansion to other neighborhoods is inevitable. A smartphone is required to charge a bike. For a 24-hour pass, there's a one-time member fee ($3), then trips under 90 minutes are free; after that it's $3/hour and up to $30 max per ride. Monthly and annual passes are available as well.

Contact Bike Share. ⊕ *bike.zagster.com/abq.*

BUS TRAVEL
If you're not planning to explore much beyond Old Town, Downtown, and Nob Hill, the city's public bus system, ABQ Ride, is a practical option. Rapid Ride lines ply Central Avenue every seven to eight minutes from early to midnight or 1 am; one-, two-, and three-day passes ($2–$6) are available on the bus or online. In the works, but not yet operational as of this writing, the electric ART (Albuquerque Rapid Transit) will eventually replace Rapid Rides along Central Avenue; ART tickets will need to be purchased in advance. You can download trip-planning apps or obtain a customized trip plan at the city's public bus website, ABQ Ride.

The Alvarado Transportation Center Downtown is ABQ Ride's central hub and offers direct connections to the NM Rail Runner Express train service north to Santa Fe and to the South Valley suburbs. Buses accept bicycles at no additional charge, although space is limited. Service is free on the Downtown D-RIDE shuttle route (available only on weekdays), or if you are transferring (to any route) from the Rail Runner; otherwise, the fare is $1 (bills or coins, exact change only). Bus stops are well marked. *See also Bus Travel in the Travel Smart chapter.*

Bus Contact ABQ Ride. ☎ *505/243–7433* ⊕ *www.cabq.gov/transit.*

CAR TRAVEL

While a bus might suffice for destinations along the Route 66/Central Avenue corridor, to get a real feel for the Duke City's many treasures, a car is necessary. Getting around town is not difficult, and local roads are often quickest. The main highways through the city, north–south Interstate 25 and east–west Interstate 40, converge just northeast of Downtown and generally offer the speediest access to outlying neighborhoods and the airport. Rush-hour jams are common in the mornings and late afternoons, but they're still far less severe than in most big U.S. cities. All the major car-rental agencies are represented at Albuquerque's Sunport airport.

Because it's a driving city, most businesses and hotels have free or inexpensive off-street parking, and it's easy to find metered street parking in many neighborhoods as well as affordable garages Downtown. Problems usually arise only when there's a major event in town, such as a concert near the University of New Mexico or a festival Downtown or in Old Town, when you may want to arrive on the early side to get a space.

TAXI TRAVEL

Taxis are metered in Albuquerque, and service is around-the-clock. Given the considerable distances around town, cabbing it can be expensive; figure about $9 from Downtown to Nob Hill, and about $20 from the airport to Downtown or EDo. There's also a $1 airport fee. The Uber/Lyft phenomenon has severely cut back taxi options in town and it is advisable to call ahead and always reconfirm taxi trips.

Taxi Contacts Yellow-Checker Cab. ☎ *505/247–8888, 505/243–7777* ⊕ *www.yellowcabnm.com.*

TRAIN TRAVEL

The New Mexico Rail Runner Express, a commuter-train line, provides a picturesque, hassle-free way to make a day trip to Santa Fe. These sleek bi-level trains with large windows run south for about 35 miles to the suburb of Belén (stopping in Isleta Pueblo and Los Lunas), and north about 65 miles on a scenic run right into the historic heart of Santa Fe, with stops in Bernalillo, Kewa Pueblo (Santo Domingo), and a few other spots. Albuquerque stops are Downtown, at the Alvarado Transportation Center (where ABQ Ride offers free bus service to the airport), and at

9

the north end of town at Journal Center/Los Ranchos. On weekdays, the trains run about eight or nine times per day, from about 6 am until 9 pm. Four trains usually run on Saturdays and three usually run on Sundays. Fares are zone-based (one-way from $2 to $8), but day passes are just $1 more; all are discounted with an online purchase, and bicycles always ride free. Free connections to local bus service are available at most stations—keep your train ticket to get on. *For information on Amtrak service, see Train Travel in the Travel Smart chapter.*

Train Contact New Mexico Rail Runner Express. ✉ *809 Copper Ave. NW* ☎ *866/795-7245* ⊕ *www.riometro.org.*

VISITOR INFORMATION

The Albuquerque Convention and Visitors Bureau (Visit Albuquerque) operates tourism information kiosks at the airport (on the baggage-claim level) and at 303 Romero Street in Old Town, set back on Plaza Don Luis, near the northwest corner of the main plaza and San Felipe de Neri church. To see what's going on by date, go to ⊕ *www.abq365.com.*

Contact Visit Albuquerque. ✉ *Downtown* ☎ *505/222-4357, 800/284-2282* ⊕ *www.visitalbuquerque.org.*

GUIDED TOURS

ABQ Trolley Co. (*AT&SF Productions*). These narrated rides on open-air trolleys go to unique areas—join them on a Best of ABQ City Tour, or one that hits only *Breaking Bad* shooting locations. There are brew cruise trolley tours too, or try the pedal-it-yourself version. Tour trollies depart year-round from Hotel Albuquerque (Old Town); brew excursions start from Downtown (*219 Central Ave. NW*). ✉ *Hotel Albuquerque, 800 Rio Grande NW* ☎ *505/200-2642* ⊕ *www.abqtrolley.com.*

Albuquerque Historical Society. Downtown architecture—the full gamut from the railroad era to mission to modernist—is the focus of these free Saturday morning tours (10 am–11:30 am) run by the Albuquerque Historical Society; they depart from in front of Tucanos restaurant at the corner of 1st Street and Central Avenue SW. Call to confirm or arrange an alternate time. ☎ *505/289-0586* ⊕ *albuqhistsoc.org.*

Albuquerque Museum of Art and History. With paid museum admission, the Albuquerque Museum of Art and History leads free, hour-long historical walks through Old Town, beginning at 11 am Tuesday through Sunday, mid-March through November. They also offer excellent tours of Casa San Ysidro in Corrales (February–November; call for info). ✉ *2000 Mountain Rd. NW* ☎ *505/243–7255* ⊕ *albuquer-quemuseum.org.*

NM Jeep Tours. Respected backcountry and local-history experts, NM Jeep Tours offers guided trips that start from Albuquerque and go as far as time and permits allow. Itineraries (ruins, ghost towns, rock formations, petroglyphs) are tailored to your interests and time frame. ☎ *505/633–0383* ⊕ *nmjeeptours.com.*

Public Art. Albuquerque's Public Art program, started in 1978, is one of the oldest in the country, and the city is strewn with its wonders. Download a growing stock of self-guided brochures and apps for locating the 650-piece collection. ✉ *Albuquerque Convention Center, 2 Civic Plaza NW, West Lobby foyer* ☎ *505/768–3833* ⊕ *www.cabq. gov/publicart.*

Tours of Old Town. Tours of Old Town offers guided walking strolls around Old Town. The standard tour lasts about 75 minutes and is offered Friday through Wednesday, four times daily. Longer ghost-hunting and moonlight tours are also offered on occasion—check for times. ✉ *303 Romero St. NW, Plaza Don Luis N-120* ☎ *505/246–8687* ⊕ *www. toursofoldtown.com.*

PLANNING YOUR TIME

While some of the spots on your local agenda will likely require car travel, Albuquerque does contain a handful of neighborhoods well suited to exploring on foot. In both Downtown and Old Town, you'll find plenty of parking (garages, lots, and street; but be prepared to feed street meters on weekends), and good areas to get out of the car and walk. The same is true of Nob Hill and the adjoining UNM neighborhood. For a short visit to the city, focusing your time on these two areas is amply rewarding; allow at least a half day for each. If hiking or biking appeal—and Old Town is a ready departure point for that—at least another half day or so is warranted.

Farther-afield spots require an average of 20 minutes via car to get to. A helpful strategy is to bunch together more outlying attractions that interest you, perhaps hitting Gruet Winery and the Balloon Museum the same day you go out to Petroglyph National Monument or ride the Sandia Peak Tram.

9

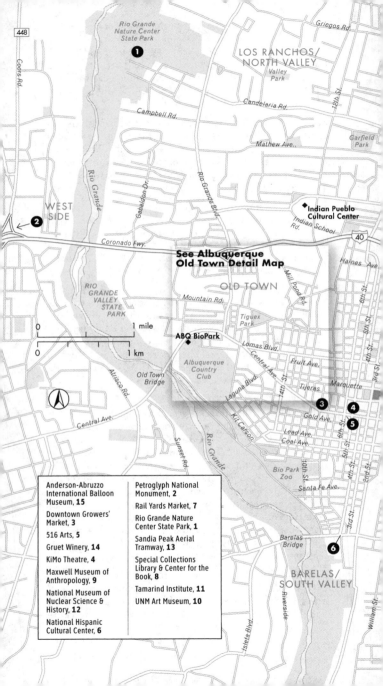

448

Griegos Rd.

Rio Grande
Nature Center
State Park

1

LOS RANCHOS/
NORTH VALLEY

Valley
Park

18th St.

Campbell Rd.

Candelaria Rd.

Mathew Ave..

Garfield
Park

Rio Grande

Rio Grande Blvd.

Gabaldon Dr.

Indian Pueblo
Cultural Center

WEST
SIDE

2

Indian School Rd.

40

Coronado Fwy.

See Albuquerque
Old Town Detail Map

Haines Ave.

RIO
GRANDE
VALLEY
STATE
PARK

OLD TOWN

Mountain Rd.

Mill Pond Rd.

6th St.

5th St.

Tiguex
Park

0   1 mile

0   1 km

ABQ BioPark

Lomas Blvd.

Fruit Ave.

4th St.

3rd St.

Albuquerque
Country
Club

Central Ave.

14th St.

Laguna Blvd.

Tijeras

Marquette

3

4

Atrisco Rd.

Old Town
Bridge

Gold Ave.

5

Central Ave.

Sunset Rd.

Rio Grande

Kit Carson

Lead Ave.

Coal Ave.

10th St.

5th St.

6th St.

4th St.

3rd St.

Bio Park
Zoo

Santa Fe Ave.

Barelas
Bridge

6

Riverside

BARELAS/
SOUTH VALLEY

Isleta Blvd.

William St.

Anderson-Abruzzo International Balloon Museum, **15**	Petroglyph National Monument, **2**
Downtown Growers' Market, **3**	Rail Yards Market, **7**
516 Arts, **5**	Rio Grande Nature Center State Park, **1**
Gruet Winery, **14**	Sandia Peak Aerial Tramway, **13**
KiMo Theatre, **4**	Special Collections Library & Center for the Book, **8**
Maxwell Museum of Anthropology, **9**	Tamarind Institute, **11**
National Museum of Nuclear Science & History, **12**	UNM Art Museum, **10**
National Hispanic Cultural Center, **6**	

EXPLORING

Albuquerque's terrain is diverse. Along the river in the North and South valleys, the elevation hovers at about 4,800 feet. East of the river, the land rises gently to the foothills of the Sandia Mountains, which climb to over 6,000 feet; the 10,378-foot summit is a grand spot from which to view the city below. West of the Rio Grande, where Albuquerque is growing most aggressively, the terrain rises abruptly in a string of mesas topped by five volcanic cones. The changes in elevation from one part of the city to another result in corresponding changes in temperature, as much as 10°F at any time. It's not uncommon for snow or rain to fall on one part of town but for it to remain dry and sunny in another, and because temperatures can shift considerably throughout the day and evening, it's a good idea to bring along a couple of layers when exploring large areas or for several hours.

OLD TOWN

Albuquerque's social and commercial anchor since the settlement was established in 1706, Old Town and the surrounding blocks contain the wealth of the city's top cultural attractions, including several excellent museums. The action extends from the historic Old Town Plaza for several blocks in all directions—most of the museums are north and east of the plaza. In this area you'll also find a number of restaurants and scads of shops. The artsy Saw Mill and Wells Park/Mountain Road neighborhoods extend just east of Old Town's museum row; the Los Duranes section, where the Indian Pueblo Cultural Center commands attention, is just a bit beyond walking distance to the northeast of Old Town.

However, the IPCC runs an hourly courtesy shuttle (☎ *505/843–7270* ⊕ *www.indianpueblo.org*) from June through October on Fridays through Sundays, making for a pleasant 15-minute journey between Old Town and the museum.

From Old Town to Downtown, it's a quick 1¼-mile bike ride, bus ride, walk, or drive southeast along Central Avenue.

TOP ATTRACTIONS

★ Fodor'sChoice **ABQ BioPark.** The city's foremost outdoor attrac-
FAMILY tion and nature center, the park comprises Tingley Beach
(and its trout-stocked ponds) as well as three distinct attractions: Aquarium, Botanic Garden, and Zoo. The garden
and aquarium are located together (admission gets you
into both facilities), just west of Old Town, off Central
Avenue; the zoo is a short drive southeast, off 10th Street.
You can also ride the scenic Rio Line vintage narrow-gauge
railroad between the zoo and gardens and the aquarium
complex; rides are free if you purchase a combination
ticket to all of the park's facilities. ⊠ *903 10th St. SW, Old
Town* ☎ *505/764–6200* ⊕ *www.abqbiopark.com* ☞ *Tingley
Beach and grounds free, Aquarium and Botanic Garden
$14.50, Zoo $14.50, Zoo train ticket $3, combination
ticket for all attractions, including unlimited train tickets,
$22* ☉ *Aquarium, botanic garden, and zoo closed weekends
June–Aug. No trains Mon.*

★ Fodor'sChoice **Albuquerque Museum of Art and History.** This
light-filled modern structure, designed by noted architect Antoine Predock, serves up a brilliantly curated
selection of contemporary art, from the museum's own
Southwestern artists–centric collections and world-class
touring shows. Additional exhibits display a collection of
Spanish-colonial artifacts, the largest in the nation. The
Common Ground galleries represent an important permanent collection of primarily 20th-century paintings, all by
world-renowned artists with a New Mexico connection.
The sculpture garden contains more than 50 contemporary works by Southwestern artists that include Glenna
Goodacre, Michael Naranjo, and Luis Jiménez. Slate at
the Museum, a casual eatery operated by Downtown's
Slate Street Cafe, serves soups, salads, espresso drinks,
desserts, and other tasty light fare. ⊠ *2000 Mountain Rd.
NW, Old Town* ☎ *505/243–7255 museum, 505/242–0434
shop, 505/242–5316 café* ⊕ *www.albuquerquemuseum.
com* ☞ *$4; free Sun. 9–1 and all day 1st Wed. each month*
☉ *Closed Mon.*

FAMILY **¡Explora!** This imaginatively executed science museum—
its driving concept is "Ideas You Can Touch"—is right
across from the New Mexico Museum of Natural History
and Science. ¡Explora! bills itself as an all-ages attraction
(and enthralled adults abound), but there's no question
that many of the innovative hands-on exhibits such as a
high-wire bicycle and a kinetic sculpture display are geared

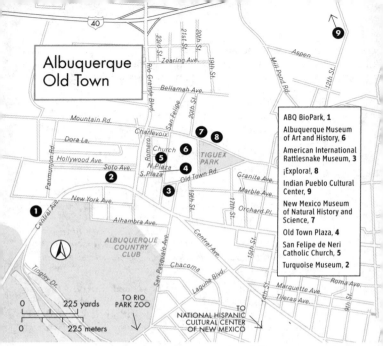

ABQ BioPark, 1

Albuquerque Museum
of Art and History, 6

American International
Rattlesnake Museum, 3

¡Explora!, 8

Indian Pueblo Cultural
Center, 9

New Mexico Museum
of Natural History and
Science, 7

Old Town Plaza, 4

San Felipe de Neri
Catholic Church, 5

Turquoise Museum, 2

to children. They offer big fun in addition to big science (and a good dose of art as well). While its colorful Bucky dome is immediately noticeable from the street, ¡Explora! also features a playground, theater, and a freestanding staircase that appears to "float" between floors. ✉ *1701 Mountain Rd. NW, Old Town* ☎ *505/224–8300* ⊕ *www. explora.us* 🎟 *$8.*

FAMILY **Indian Pueblo Cultural Center.** The multilevel semicircular layout of this museum was inspired by Pueblo Bonito, the prehistoric ruin in northwestern New Mexico. Start by visiting their permanent exhibit space "We Are of This Place: The Pueblo Story," which interprets the Pueblo peoples' legacy through carried-down traditions and remarkable pieces from their renowned holdings of fine Native American pottery, textiles, baskets, and other masterworks. Changing exhibits may feature close-ups of a particular artist, such as the gorgeously composed and colored copper-plate prints of Santa Clara Pueblo painter Helen Hardin. Mural Discovery Tours are offered on Fridays at 1 pm and ceremonial dances are performed year-round on weekends; there are often arts-and-crafts demonstrations as well. The museum gift shop, Shumakolowa, provides a fine overview of current Pueblo arts. The **Pueblo Harvest Café** is a tasty spot for breakfast, lunch, or dinner. Note: The museum lies a bit northeast of Old Town, in the Los Duranes neighborhood—a five-minute drive away. ⊠ *2401 12th St. NW, Los Duranes* ☎ *505/843–7270, 866/855–7902* ⊕ *www.indianpueblo.org* ⌚ *$8.40.*

FAMILY **New Mexico Museum of Natural History and Science.** The wonders at Albuquerque's most popular museum include a simulated volcano (with a river of bubbling hot lava flowing beneath the see-through glass floor), the frigid Ice Age cave, and "Dawn of the Dinosaurs." The only Triassic exhibit in North America, this permanent hall features some of the state's own rare finds. The Evolution Elevator (aka the Evolator) uses video, sound, and motion to whisk you through 35 million years of New Mexico's geological history. The Paul Allen–funded "Start-Up!" galleries explore the silicon age, detailing the birth of the PC right here in the Duke City (bet you didn't know that Seattle was the *second* stop for Allen and a very young Bill Gates). These exhibitions are a fascinating tour through the early garage days of many such start-ups, including the Apple side of the story. Also here is the LodeStar Science Center; the state-of-the-art planetarium is home to the wildly popular First Friday Fractals show (tickets available online only). ⊠ *1801 Mountain Rd. NW, Old Town* ☎ *505/841–2800* ⊕ *www.nmnaturalhistory.org* ⌚ *Museum $8, DynaTheater $7, planetarium $7.*

FAMILY **Old Town Plaza.** Tranquil, with the lovely 1793 San Felipe de Neri Catholic Church still presiding along the north side, Old Town Plaza is a pleasant place to sit on wrought-iron benches under shade trees. Roughly 200 shops, restaurants, cafés, galleries, and several cultural sites in *placitas* (small plazas) and lanes surround the plaza. During fiestas Old Town comes alive with mariachi bands and dancing señoritas; at Christmas time it is lit with luminarias (the votive candles in paper bag lanterns known as *farolitos* up in Santa Fe). Mostly dating back to the late 1800s, styles from Queen Anne to Territorial and Pueblo Revival, and even Mediterranean, are apparent in the one- and two-story (almost all adobe) structures. ■TIP→ **An abundance of guided walks through Old Town are available** (*see Albuquerque Planner, Guided Tours*). ⊠ *Old Town.*

9

WORTH NOTING

FAMILY **American International Rattlesnake Museum.** Included in the largest collection of different species of living rattlers in the world are such rare and unusual specimens as an albino western diamondback. From the outside the museum looks for all the world like a plain old shop, but inside, the museum's exhibits, its engaging staff, and a video supply visitors with the lowdown on these venomous creatures—for instance, that they can't hear their own rattles and that the human death rate from rattlesnake bites is less than 1%. The mission here is to educate the public on the many positive benefits of rattlesnakes, and to contribute to their conservation. ✉ *202 San Felipe St. NW, just off southeast corner of Plaza, Old Town* ☎ *505/242–6569* ⊕ *www.rattlesnakes.com* 🎫 *$6.*

FAMILY **San Felipe de Neri Catholic Church.** Well over two centuries after it first welcomed worshippers, this structure, erected in 1793, is still active (mass is offered daily). The building, which replaced Albuquerque's first Catholic church, has been expanded several times, but its adobe walls and other original features remain. Small gardens front and flank the church; the inside is a respite from the tourism bustle beyond its doorstep—the painting and iconography is simple, authentic, and lovely, the atmosphere hushed. Next to it is a shop and small museum that displays relics—vestments, paintings, carvings—dating from the 17th century. ■TIP→ **There's a hidden treasure behind the church: inside the gnarled tree is a statue that some speculate depicts the Virgin Mary.** ✉ *2005 Plaza NW, Old Town* ☎ *505/243–4628* ⊕ *www.sanfelipedeneri.org* ☉ *Museum and gift shop closed Sun.*

FAMILY **Turquoise Museum.** Just west of the hubbub of Old Town, this museum may be inside a small strip mall, but visitors will forget that once they focus on the beauty, mythology, and physical properties of turquoise, a semiprecious but adored gemstone that many people associate with the color of New Mexico's skies. A guided 45-minute tour begins by entering via a simulated mine shaft (albeit a shallow, low-tech one), and leads to one-of-a-kind showpieces and examples from more than 65 mines on four continents. Displays show how turquoise forms, the importance of individual mines, and uses of the stone by Native Americans in prehistoric times. At the education center you can learn to distinguish the real McCoy from plastic. The museum's proprietors are a multigenerational family of longtime traders, and know whereof they speak; if you retain nothing else, do remember that only turquoise specified as "natural" is the desirable, unadulterated stuff. There is an active silversmith's shop adjacent to the display area; a small gift shop sells historic and contemporary pieces. ⊠ *2107 Central Ave. NW, Old Town* ☎ *505/247–8650* ⊕ *www.turquoisemuseum.com* 🖻 *$9.55* ⊗ *Closed Sun.* ☞ *Tour reservations recommended.*

DOWNTOWN/EDO

Although Downtown doesn't have many formal attractions short of its anchoring arts scene, this neighborhood rewards those who take a closer look. Along Central Avenue and the parallel Gold Avenue there's a trail of architectural detail, from the Simms Building to the Venetian Gothic Revival Occidental Insurance Building, and the federal courthouse's Spanish Mission pile. Hints of Albuquerque's 1880s railroad-era and Route 66 past abound; contemporary murals and a strong public art presence add to the appeal.

TOP ATTRACTIONS

★ **Fodor's**Choice **516 Arts.** 516 Arts holds a special place in the New Mexico art scene. World-class contemporary art dominates the changing shows at this multilevel nonprofit. Visually compelling collaborations with an international set of museums and artists cross media boundaries, and often explore issues that are not only dear to the hearts and minds of this multicultural, environmentally diverse state, but resonate globally. The installations here are always top-notch, the works displayed are of the highest quality, the ideas—whether expressed in video, prints, sculpture, diodes, or paint—provocative. ⊠ *516 Central Ave. SW, Downtown* ☎ *505/242–1445* ⊕ *www.516arts.org* ⊗ *Closed Sun. and Mon.*

★ **Fodor's**Choice **KiMo Theatre.** Decorated with light fixtures made from buffalo skulls (the eye sockets glow amber in the dark), Navajo symbols, and nine spectacular Western-themed wall murals by Carl Von Hassler, the KiMo represents Pueblo Deco at its apex. It's one of the few notable early-20th-century structures remaining in Downtown Albuquerque. The self-guided tour is fantastic (guided tours can also be arranged by appointment), or catch a film or a live performance. ⊠ *423 Central Ave. NW, at 5th St., Downtown* ☎ *505/768–3522 theater, 505/768–3544 event info* ⊕ *www.cabq.gov/kimo* 🖻 *Free self-guided tours* ⊗ *Closed Sun. and Mon.*

9

★ Fodor'sChoice **Rail Yards Market.** The Sunday market here
FAMILY (May–October, 10–2) is a fine excuse to explore this
wondrous, light-filled, almost cathedral-like space, said
to have been the largest steam locomotive repair facility
in the country in its heyday. Dating back to the early
20th century, the Atchison, Topeka & Santa Fe buildings
here, built on the Atlantic & Pacific originals from the
1880s, put you at the center of how Downtown (or New
Town, as it was then known)—and modern Albuquerque—came to be. The market, vibrant with growers and
makers, occupies the 1917 Blacksmith Shop. ⊠ *777 1st
St. SW, Barelas* ☎ *505/600–1109* ⊕ *railyardsmarket.org*
⊘ *Closed Nov.–Apr.*

WORTH NOTING

FAMILY **Downtown Growers' Market.** Toe-tapping music and the fresh-
est of fresh produce—and surely the delicious shade created
by the towering cottonwoods here in Robinson Park—have
folks gathering every Saturday morning from April through
mid-November. This sweet respite on the western fringe of
Downtown also hosts city crafts makers; high-quality wares
range from fine block-printed linens to small-batch soaps.
Get a blueberry muffin from Bosque Baking Co. and a hot
brew from Java Joe's, and enjoy a stroll. ⊠ *Robinson Park,
Central Ave. at 8th St. NW, Downtown* ⊕ *www.downtown-
growers.com* ⊘ *Closed late Nov.–mid Mar.*

Special Collections Library & Center for the Book. Designed by
Arthur Rossiter in 1925 in a Spanish–Pueblo Revival style,
this was the main Albuquerque library for some 50 years
(renowned Santa Fe woodblock artist Gustav Baumann
contributed the lovely interior embellishments). Repur-
posed as the Special Collections division in 1975, the old
library now houses an important genealogy center as well
as a small museum comprised of historic printing presses
and related ephemera, known as the Center for the Book.
Changing exhibits in the dramatic double-story, viga-lined,
main reading room are always well presented. ⊠ *423 Central Ave. NE, at Edith Blvd., Downtown* ☎ *505/848–1376*
⊕ *www.abqlibrary.org/centerforthebook* ▣ *Free* ⊘ *Closed
Sun. and Mon.*

BARELAS/SOUTH VALLEY

The historic Barelas neighborhood, to the south of Old Town and Downtown, features the must-see National Hispanic Cultural Center. Otherwise it's mostly a residential neighborhood; bounded by the bosque trails and a revitalizing rail yard, it gradually gives way to the broad South Valley, a rough-around-the-edges area that contains modest homes in some sections, and farmlands or light industry in others.

TOP ATTRACTIONS

★ Fodor'sChoice **National Hispanic Cultural Center.** A showpiece
FAMILY for the city, and a showcase for Hispanic culture in Albuquerque's historic Barelas neighborhood, this beautifully designed space contains a vibrant art museum, multiple performance venues, a restaurant, a fresco-lined torreon (freestanding windowless tower) depicting the span of Hispanic (and pre-Hispanic) history, a 10,000-volume genealogical research center and library, and an education center. Its stunning and acoustically superb Roy E. Disney Center for Performing Arts and smaller Albuquerque Journal Theatre host ballet, flamenco dancing, bilingual theater, traditional Spanish and New Mexican music, the famous world music festival ¡Globalquerque!, and many other performances. Exhibits at its first-rate museum include dynamic displays of photography, paintings, sculpture, and traditional and contemporary craftwork by local artists as well as internationally known names. A vintage WPA-era school contains the library and **La Fonda del Bosque** restaurant ($, no dinner), which features Latin fusion fare indoors and out on the patio. ⊠ *1701 4th St. SW, at Avenida César Chavez (Bridge Blvd.), Barelas* ☎ *505/246–2261 museum, 505/724–4771 box office* ⊕ *www.nhccnm.org* ᴨ *$6* ⊙ *Closed Mon., restaurant closed Sun. and Mon.*

9

UNM/NOB HILL

Established in 1889, the University of New Mexico (UNM) is the state's leading institution of higher education. Its many outstanding galleries and museums are open to the public free of charge. The university's Pueblo Revival–style architecture is noteworthy, particularly the beautifully preserved 1938 west wing of Zimmerman Library, which houses the superb Center for Southwest Research and changing historical exhibits, and the Alumni Chapel, both designed by John Gaw Meem, a Santa Fe–based architect whose mid-20th-century work became a template for new campus buildings for years to come. Newer structures such as Antoine Predock's George Pearl Hall tip their hat to Meem, but are distinctive in their own right. Federico Muelas's mesmerizing 2012 "Flor Azul/Blue Flower" artwork, the 900-square-foot LED-and-sound installation on the outside of George Pearl Hall, is best seen at night. It joins the numerous contemporary sculptures that make this campus worth a stroll; Bruce Nauman's 1988 "The Center of the Universe" is a destination in itself. Stop at the campus Welcome Center (☎ *505/277–1989* ⊕ *www. unm.edu*) to pick up self-guided campus art and architecture tour maps.

The campus's easterly spread leads directly into the heart of Nob Hill and a quintessential assortment of Route 66 and art deco–era remnants. Vintage motels and gas stations with neon signage house cool galleries, microbreweries, cafés, upscale furnishing shops, and more. The circa-1947 Nob Hill Business Center sits right on old Route 66 (Central Avenue), sandwiched between Carlisle Boulevard and Amherst Drive SE, and is still the heart of this neighborhood. Anchored by the wonderful Mariposa Gallery and IMEC, Amherst Drive (just the one sweet block between Central and Silver) is the primo side street by far. Other noteworthy businesses—from some of the city's best restaurants, to offbeat shops, the Guild indie cinema, and a good mix of professional and student hangouts—run along Central, both a few blocks east of Carlisle, and to the west, back to UNM.

TOP ATTRACTIONS

Maxwell Museum of Anthropology. Tapping a vast collection of sublime Southwestern artifacts and archival photos, the Maxwell's superb shows encompass three fascinating fields: archaeology, cultural anthropology, and evolutionary anthropology. As the first public museum in Albuquerque (established in 1932), its influence has grown over the years, but its compact space ensures that exhibits are scaled to the essentials. A viewer—whether of a permanent exhibit on peoples of the Southwest, or a temporary one (such as 2017–8's "Entering Standing Rock")—will be intrigued and informed, but not overwhelmed. Of special note is their rare and substantial collection of Mimbres pottery from AD 800–1000. The museum's gift shop is well worth a look for its selection of reliably vetted Native

American crafts. ⊠ *University of New Mexico, 500 University Blvd. NE, at northwest end of campus, University of New Mexico* ☎ *505/277–4405* ⊕ *maxwellmuseum.unm. edu* 🖃 *Free* ⊘ *Closed Sun. and Mon.* ☞ *Parking permits available inside museum.*

Tamarind Institute. This world-famous institution played a major role in reviving the fine art of lithographic printing, which involves working with plates of traditional stone and modern metal. Tamarind certification is to a printer what a degree from Juilliard is to a musician. A small gallery within the modern facility exhibits prints and lithographs by well-known masters like Jim Dine, Kiki Smith, and Ed Ruscha, as well as up-and-comers in the craft. Guided tours (reservations essential) are conducted on the first Friday of each month at 1:30. ⊠ *2500 Central Ave. SE, University of New Mexico* ☎ *505/277–3901* ⊕ *tamarind.unm.edu* 🖃 *Free* ⊘ *Closed Sat.–Mon.*

★ Fodor'sChoice **UNM Art Museum.** University Art Museum features magnificent 20th- and 21st-century prints, as well as photos and paintings that rival the finest collections throughout the Southwest. Changing exhibits cull from more than 30,000 archived pieces, which include groundbreaking works by modernist giants such as Bridget Riley, Richard Diebenkorn, and Elaine DeKooning. Photography—Ansel Adams, Beaumont Newhall—is a particular strength, and provocative shows have featured immense prints, complemented with video projections and a range of mixed-media installations. Transcendentalist master Raymond Jonson's work, as well as other landmark acquisitions he made, are displayed. Having celebrated its 50th anniversary in 2013, the museum's vision is to allow yet more of their impressive holdings—a Picasso print, an O'Keeffe painting—to be seen regularly. Lectures and symposia, gallery talks, and guided tours are regularly scheduled. ⊠ *University of New Mexico Center for the Arts, 1 University of New Mexico, University of New Mexico* ☎ *505/277–4001* ⊕ *artmuseum.unm.edu* 🖃 *$5 donation suggested* ⊘ *Closed Sun. and Mon.*

LOS RANCHOS/NORTH VALLEY

Many attractions lie north of Downtown, Old Town, and the University of New Mexico. Quite a few, including the Casa Rondeña winery and the Rio Grande Nature Center, are clustered in a contiguous stretch that comprises two of the city's longest-settled areas: the lush cottonwood-lined North Valley and Los Ranchos de Albuquerque, along the Rio Grande. Early Spanish settlers made their homes here, building on top of even earlier Pueblo homesteads. Historic adobe houses abound. The Montaño Road Bridge crosses through the area, making a sublime gateway to the West Side.

TOP ATTRACTIONS

FAMILY **Anderson-Abruzzo International Balloon Museum.** This dramatic museum celebrates the city's legacy as the hot-air ballooning capital of the world. Albuquerque's high altitude, mild climate, and a fortuitous wind pattern known as the Albuquerque Box make it an ideal destination for ballooning. The dashing, massive facility is named for Maxie Anderson and Ben Abruzzo, who pioneered ballooning here and were part of a team of three aviators who made the first manned hot-air balloon crossing of the Atlantic Ocean in 1978. Filling the airy museum space are several fully inflated historic balloons, and both large- and small-scale replicas of gas balloons and zeppelins. You'll also see vintage balloon baskets, china and flatware from the ill-fated *Hindenburg* and an engaging display on that tragic craft, and dynamic exhibits that trace the history of the sport, dating back to the first balloon ride, in 1783. Interactive stations are set up so kids can design their own balloons. ⊠ *9201 Balloon Museum Dr. NE, off Alameda Blvd., North Valley* ☎ *505/768–6020* ⊕ *www.balloonmuseum.com* ☜ *$4, free Sun. 9–1 and 1st Fri. every month (except Oct.)* ⊙ *Closed Mon.* ⌁ *No food sold on-site.*

★ **Fodor's** Choice **Rio Grande Nature Center State Park.** Along the
FAMILY banks of the Rio Grande, this 270-acre refuge in an especially tranquil portion of the bosque (about midway up on the Paseo del Bosque trail) is the nation's largest cottonwood forest. There are numerous walking and biking trails that wind into the 53-acre Aldo Leopold Forest and down to the river. Bird-watchers come to view all manner of migratory waterfowl. Constructed half aboveground and half below the edge of a pond, the park's interpretive center has viewing windows and speakers that broadcast the sounds of the birds you're watching. You may see sandhill cranes, frogs, ducks, and turtles. The park has active programs for adults and children. ⊠ *2901 Candelaria Rd. NW, North Valley* ☎ *505/344–7240* ⊕ *www.rgnc.org, www.nmparks.com* ☜ *$3 per vehicle, grounds free.*

UPTOWN/NORTHEAST HEIGHTS

In the Northeast Heights you are approaching the foot-hills of the Sandia Mountains, in upscale neighborhoods that surprise with the sudden appearance of piñon and ponderosa. Trips to this area can easily be combined with more north-central venues like the Balloon Museum and local microbreweries, or the National Museum of Nuclear Science & History, which, once you've made it into the foothills, is due south.

TOP ATTRACTIONS

Gruet Winery. First-time visitors may be forgiven for pausing as they approach Gruet's redbrick chalet-style building, set down as it is hard by the highway in a transitional industrial area. Inside, however, is one of the nation's most acclaimed producers of sparkling wines (to see its actual vineyards you'll have to head south to Elephant Butte). Gruet (pronounced *grew*-ay) had been famous in France since the 1950s for its Champagnes. In New Mexico, the Gruet family has been producing wine since 1984, and it's earned nationwide kudos for its Methode Champenoise (employing traditional Champagne-making methods for its sparkling wine), as well as for impressive Pinot Noirs, Rosés, and Chardonnays. Most of the state's top restaurants carry Gruet vintages, as do leading wine cellars around the country. ✉ *8400 Pan American Freeway NE (I–25), off the northbound I–25 frontage road, between Paseo del Norte and Alameda Blvd., Northeast Heights* ☎ *505/821–0055* ⊕ *www.gruetwinery. com* ✇ *Winery free, 5-wine tasting $12–$15.*

★ Fodors Choice **Sandia Peak Aerial Tramway.** Tramway cars climb
FAMILY 2.7 miles up the steep western face of the Sandias, giving you a close-up view of red rocks and tall trees—it's the world's longest aerial tramway. From the observation deck at the 10,378-foot summit you can see Santa Fe to the northeast and Los Alamos to the northwest—about 11,000 square miles of spectacular scenery. Tram cars leave from the base at regular intervals for the 15-minute ride to the top. You may see birds of prey soaring above or mountain lions roaming the cliff sides. An exhibit room at the top surveys the wildlife and landscape of the mountain. ■TIP→ **It's much colder and windier at the summit than at the tram's base, so pack a jacket.** You can also use the tram as a way to reach the Sandia Peak ski and mountain-biking area. ✉ *10 Tramway Loop NE, Far Northeast Heights* ☎ *505/856–7325* ⊕ *www.sandiapeak.com* ✇ *$25.*

9

EAST SIDE

South of Interstate 40 and the Northeast Heights, the East Side bridges the older and historic parts of Route 66 with pockets of newer development of an upscale nature. Bicyclists frequent the nearby Tramway trails, and you might continue on into the mountains, but the area's charms are otherwise sparse—though you will want to make time for the destination-worthy National Museum of Nuclear Science & History.

TOP ATTRACTIONS

★ Fodor'sChoice **National Museum of Nuclear Science & History.** Previously known simply as the National Atomic Museum, this brilliant Smithsonian affiliate traces the history of the atomic age and how nuclear science has dramatically influenced the course of modern history. Exhibits include replicas of Little Boy and Fat Man (the bombs dropped on Japan at the end of World War II), a compelling display about the difficult decision to drop atomic bombs, and a look at how atomic culture has dovetailed with pop culture. There are also children's programs and an exhibit about X-ray technology. The campus also contains the 9-acre Heritage Park, which has a B-29 and other mega-airships, plus rockets, missiles, cannons, and even a nuclear sub sail. One highlight is the restored 1942 Plymouth that was used to transport the plutonium core of "the Gadget" (as that first weapon was known) down from Los Alamos to the Trinity Site for testing. ⊠ *601 Eubank Blvd. SE, a few blocks south of I–40, East Side* ☎ *505/245–2137* ⊕ *www. nuclearmuseum.org* ⊡ *$12.*

FAMILY

WEST SIDE

The fastest-growing part of Albuquerque lies on a broad mesa high above the Rio Grande Valley. The West Side is primarily the domain of new suburban housing developments and strip malls, some designed more attractively than others. Somewhat controversially, growth on the West Side has seemed to occur below, above, and virtually all around the archaeologically critical Petroglyph National Monument. Allow a 20-minute drive from Old Town and the North Valley to reach the monument.

TOP ATTRACTIONS

FAMILY **Petroglyph National Monument.** Beneath the stumps of five extinct volcanoes, this park encompasses more than 25,000 ancient Native American rock drawings inscribed on the 17-mile-long West Mesa escarpment overlooking the Rio Grande Valley. For centuries, Native American hunting parties camped at the base, chipping and scribbling away. Archaeologists believe most of the petroglyphs were carved on the lava formations between 1100 and 1600, but some images at the park may date back as far as 1000 BC. A paved trail at **Boca Negra Canyon** (north of the visitor center on Unser Boulevard, beyond Montaño Road) leads past several dozen petroglyphs. A tad more remote is the sandy **Piedras Marcadas Canyon** trail, a few miles farther north. The trail at **Rinconado Canyon** (south of the visitor center on Unser) is unpaved. The rangers at the visitor center will supply maps and help you determine which trail is best for the time you have. ✉ *Visitor center, 6001 Unser Blvd. NW, at Western Trail Rd., 3 miles north of I–40 Exit 154, West Side* ☎ *505/899–0205* ⊕ *www.nps.gov/ petr* 🖾 *Free* ☞ *Parking $1 weekdays, $2 weekends; parking at Boca Negra Canyon is $2 all days.*

WHERE TO EAT

The Duke City has long been a place for hearty home-style cooking in big portions, and to this day it's easy to find great steak-and-chops houses, retro diners, and authentic New Mexican restaurants. The trick is finding them amid Albuquerque's miles of chain options and legions of dives, but if you look, you'll be rewarded with innovative food, and generally at prices much lower than in Santa Fe or other major Southwestern cities.

In Nob Hill, Downtown, and Old Town many notable new restaurants have opened, offering swank decor and complex and artful variations on modern Southwest, Mediterranean, Asian, and other globally inspired cuisine. A significant Vietnamese population has made that cuisine a star, but Indian, Japanese, Thai, and South American traditions all have a presence, making this New Mexico's best destination for ethnic fare.

9

	WHAT IT COSTS			
	$	$$	$$$	$$$$
Restaurants	under $18	$18–$24	$25–$30	over $30

Prices in the restaurant reviews are the average cost of a main course at dinner or, if dinner is not served, at lunch.

Restaurant reviews have been shortened. For full information, visit Fodors.com.

OLD TOWN

$$$$ ✕**Antiquity.** *American.* Within the thick adobe walls of this darkly lighted, romantic space off the plaza in Old Town, patrons have been feasting on rich, elegantly prepared American classics for more than 50 years. This isn't the edgy, contemporary restaurant to bring an adventuresome foodie—Antiquity specializes in classics, from starters of French onion soup and Alaskan King crab cakes with a perfectly piquant remoulade sauce to main courses like Chicken Madagascar, Australian lobster tail with drawn butter, and black Angus New York strip-loin steak with horseradish sauce. **Known for:** old world–style service; timeless menu; congenial buzz. Ⓢ *Average main: $45* ✉ *112 Romero St. NW, Old Town* ☎ *505/247–3545* ⊕ *www.antiquityrestaurant.com* ⊘ *No lunch.*

$$ ✕**Church Street Café.** *Mexican.* This spacious, traditional adobe eatery remains as authentic as its menu, which features family recipes spanning four generations, with fresh, local ingredients and spirits employed to satiate streams of hungry tourists and locals. Request the courtyard for alfresco dining amid trellises of sweet grapes and flowers, to the occasional accompaniment of a classical and flamenco guitarist. **Known for:** charming nooks; historic tile and tin decorations; flower-filled courtyard seating. Ⓢ *Average main: $21* ✉ *2111 Church St. NW, Old Town* ☎ *505/247–8522* ⊕ *www.churchstreetcafe.com* ⊘ *No dinner Sun.*

★ Fodor'sChoice ✕**Duran Central Pharmacy.** *Mexican.* A favorite
$ of old-timers who know their way around a blue-corn
FAMILY enchilada (and know that the red is the chile to pick for it), this lunch counter serves fine, freshly made and warm flour tortillas, too. Duran's harkens to the days when every drugstore had a soda fountain; it's got a full kitchen now, with your choice of counter stools, cozy table, or the little shaded patio right off old Route 66. **Known for:** friendly

but fast service; relaxed, cozy atmosphere; retro charm. [$] *Average main: $9* ✉ *1815 Central Ave. NW, Old Town* ☎ *505/247–4141 Ext. 4* 🌐 *www.duransrx.com.*

$ 🍴 **Golden Crown Panaderia.** *Bakery.* On the eastern fringe FAMILY of Old Town, this aromatic, down-home-style bakery is especially well known for two things: its hearty green-chile bread and its hand-tossed (or thin-crust) pizzas made with blue corn, peasant, or green-chile dough. You can also order hot cocoa, cappuccino, an award-winning local IPA or lager (or wine), some *biscochito* (the official state cookie), fruit-filled empanadas, plenty of other sweets, and sandwiches (ask what bread is fresh and hot), and a nationally renowned coffee milk shake. **Known for:** innovative pizza doughs; green-chile bread; a (free) biscochito for all. [$] *Average main: $12* ✉ *1103 Mountain Rd. NW, Old Town* ☎ *505/243–2424* 🌐 *www.goldencrown.biz* ⏲ *Closed Mon.*

$ 🍴 **La Crêpe Michel.** *French.* When red-or-green chile overload sets in, Old Town offers an antidote: this tiny, French creperie tucked down a side alley, in what feels like a secret garden. Salads, steak frites, and a lovely dessert selection act as foils for the nicely presented crepes, both *salées* (with salmon and asparagus) and *sucrées* (with chocolate); the vegetable sides, though, while pretty in presentation, can be somewhat sparse. **Known for:** peaceful setting; crème caramel; attentive service. [$] *Average main: $13* ✉ *400 San Felipe St. NW, Old Town* ☎ *505/242–1251* 🌐 *www.lacrepemichel.com* ⏲ *Closed Mon.*

$$$ 🍴 **Seasons Rotisserie & Grill.** *American.* Upbeat and elegant, Seasons's pleasing arches, soothing palette, and open-kitchen plan draw diners for business lunches and dinner dates; oenophiles revel in its well-chosen cellar. Innovative wood-fueled grills and pastas dominate the seasonally changing roster of dishes with tangy sauces (Atlantic salmon has a lemon-thyme beurre blanc; vegetable and mozzarella crostada is brightened with a smoked ancho coulis; braised Iowa pork shank comes with a coal-roasted pear jus); great starters include autumn squash griddle cakes with dried tart cherry chutney. **Known for:** wood-grilled dishes; strong vegetarian options; extra-lively rooftop scene. [$] *Average main: $25* ✉ *2031 Mountain Rd. NW, Old Town* ☎ *505/766–5100* 🌐 *www.seasonsabq.com* ⏲ *No lunch weekends.*

$$ 🍴 **Vinaigrette.** *American.* Salads are the thing at Vinaigrette, just as they are at owner Erin Wade's immensely popular original outpost in Santa Fe. Fresh, local greens are featured, but heartier add-ons (from seared tuna and panko-crusted goat cheese to hibiscus-cured duck confit and

9

flank steak) will satisfy the hungriest in your party. **Known for:** bright and inviting contemporary space; robust servings; patio dining in season. [$] *Average main: $18* ✉ *1828 Central Ave. SW, Old Town* ☎ *505/842–5507* 🌐 *www.vinaigretteonline.com.*

DOWNTOWN/EDO

★ Fodor's Choice ✕ **Farina Pizzeria & Wine Bar** (*Farina Downtown*).
$ *Pizza.* A stellar spot for truly artisanal thin-crust pizza, Farina draws loyal crowds inside an ancient former EDo grocery store with hardwood floors, exposed-brick walls, a pressed-tin ceiling, and simple rows of wooden tables along with a long bar. This spirited place serves up exceptional pizzas with blistering-hot crusts and imaginative toppings; the Salsiccia, with sweet-fennel sausage, roasted onions, and mozzarella, has plenty of fans. **Known for:** a consistent run of awards won; contemporary art-filled atmosphere; creative pizza toppings. [$] *Average main: $17* ✉ *510 Central Ave. SE* ☎ *505/243–0130* 🌐 *www.farinapizzeria.com* ⏲ *No lunch Sun.*

★ Fodor's Choice ✕ **The Grove Café & Market.** *Café.* This airy, modern
$ EDo neighborhood favorite features locally grown, seasonal specials at reasonable prices. Enjoy such fresh, quality treats as Grove Pancakes with fresh fruit, crème fraîche, local honey, and real maple syrup; a Farmers Salad with roasted golden beets, Marcona almonds, goat cheese, and lemon-basil vinaigrette; or an aged Genoa salami sandwich with olive tapenade, arugula, and provolone on an artisanal sourdough bread. **Known for:** committment to local growers; prettily plated food; quick-moving line to order. [$] *Average main: $11* ✉ *600 Central Ave. SE* ☎ *505/248–9800* 🌐 *www.thegrovecafemarket.com* ⏲ *Closed Mon. No dinner.*

$$ ✕ **Slate Street Cafe.** *Eclectic.* A high-energy, high-ceilinged dining room with a semicircular, central wine bar and modern lighting, this stylish restaurant sits amid pawn shops and bail-bond outposts on a quiet, unprepossessing side street Downtown. Once inside, you'll find a sophisticated, colorful space serving memorable, modern renditions of classic road fare, such as chicken fried steak, a beet-and-feta burger, and brown bag fish-and-chips. **Known for:** tastings in their wine loft; fish-and-chips; sleek business meeting spot. [$] *Average main: $20* ✉ *515 Slate St. NW, Downtown* ☎ *505/243–2210* 🌐 *www.slatestreetcafe.com* ⏲ *No dinner Sun. and Mon.*

$ ×**Standard Diner.** *American.* Set in the heart of EDo, the Stan-
FAMILY dard occupies a 1930s Texaco station with high ceilings and
massive plate-glass windows and offers better-than-stan-
dard takes on diner standbys. The extensive menu dabbles
in meal-size salads (try the Southwestern Cobb), burgers
(including a terrific one topped with maple-bourbon butter),
sandwiches, and traditional diner entrées given surprise
flourishes (country-fried ahi tuna with wasabi guacamole,
bacon-wrapped meat loaf). **Known for:** breakfast served
till 3 pm; cozy booths; beer/wine happy hour. Ⓢ *Average
main: $15* ⊠ *320 Central Ave. SE* ☎ *505/243–1440* ⊕ *www.
standarddiner.com.*

BARELAS/SOUTH VALLEY

$ ×**Barelas Coffee House.** *Mexican.* Barelas may look like a set
FAMILY in search of a script, but it's the real deal: diners come from
all over the city to sup in this old-fashioned chile parlor in a
historic Route 66 neighborhood south of Downtown. You
may notice looks of quiet contentment on the faces of the
many dedicated chile eaters as they dive into their bowls of
Barelas's potent red. **Known for:** local hangout; old-fashioned hospitality; chicharrones and the huevos rancheros
supreme. Ⓢ *Average main: $8* ⊠ *1502 4th St. SW, Barelas*
☎ *505/843–7577* ⊗ *Closed Sun. No dinner.*

UNM/NOB HILL

$ ×**Flying Star Cafe.** *Café.* Flying Star is a staple here, and
each outpost of this locally owned order-at-the-counter-
first café suits its neighborhood. At the original spot in
Nob Hill, the university crowd crunches into a snug space
to dig into a mix of creative American and New Mexican dishes (plus several types of wine and beer). **Known
for:** late-night dessert; bottomless coffee and Wi-Fi; creative menu with solid basics at heart. Ⓢ *Average main:
$11* ⊠ *3416 Central Ave. SE, Nob Hill* ☎ *505/255–6633*
⊕ *www.flyingstarcafe.com.*

$$$ ×**Frenchish.** *Bistro.* Innovative, flavorful, fun, and, indeed,
French-ish. In 2016, Nob Hill welcomed the return of the
renowned culinary team of Nelle Bauer and James Beard
award semifinalist, Jennifer James, and this coolly modern
spot with its refreshing bistro menu. **Known for:** twists on
French classics; reservations recommended; walk-ins may
sit at congenial chef's counter. Ⓢ *Average main: $27* ⊠ *3509
Central Ave. NE, Nob Hill* ☎ *505/433–5911* ⊕ *www.fren-
chish.co* ⊗ *Closed Sun. and Mon. No lunch.*

$ 🍴 **Frontier Restaurant.** *Café.* This definitive student hangout—it's directly across from UNM—is open seven days from 5 am till the wee hours, and hits the spot for inexpensive diner-style American and New Mexican chow. A notch up from a fast-food joint, the chile's good (vegetarian and non), the breakfast burritos are fine (the burgers are, too), and who can resist a hot, melty oversize Frontier sweet roll? **Known for:** hours to suit both early birds and night owls; succulent cinnamon buns; roadside attraction–style decor. [$] *Average main: $7* ✉ *2400 Central Ave. SE, at Cornell Dr. SE, University of New Mexico* ☎ *505/266–0550* 🌐 *www.frontierrestaurant.com.*

FAMILY

★ Fodor's Choice 🍴 **Model Pharmacy.** *American.* Real-deal 1940s soda fountain, check; dependable grilled-to-order sandwiches (the standards, from tuna to bagels and burgers, all updated with crisp fresh ingredients), check; friendly, speedy service, check. Model first opened across the street in 1947, and it's still got the spirit, and the goods: milk shakes, egg creams, rickeys, and fresh fruit cobblers. **Known for:** retro setting; ice cream treats; old school, gracious service. [$] *Average main: $10* ✉ *3636 Monte Vista Blvd. NE, Nob Hill* ☎ *505/255–8686* 🌐 *modelpharmacy.com* ⏲ *Closed Sun. No dinner.*

$ FAMILY

$ 🍴 **Range Café.** *American.* A local standby for any meal, the Range Cafe has a high comfort quotient with hearty dishes like their Chimayo grilled-chicken sandwich with bacon and blue-cheese spread, fresh-spinach enchiladas with black beans and arroz verde, Matt's Hoosier Tenderloin Plate, and the generously plated salmon-berry salad; chipotle barbecue beer-battered onion rings work great as a side, whether supporting burgers or standard New Mexican plates. Breakfast, served until 3 pm, has fans for its house-made green-chile turkey sausage and huevos rancheros. **Known for:** exemplary New Mexican classics; colorful, funky decor; strong local roots. [$] *Average main: $13* ✉ *2200 Menaul Blvd. NE, University of New Mexico* ☎ *505/888–1660* 🌐 *www.rangecafe.com.*

FAMILY

$ 🍴 **Viet Taste.** *Vietnamese.* Excellent, authentic Vietnamese food is served up in this compact, modern, bamboo-accented restaurant (once inside, it's easy to ignore the fact that it's within one of Albuquerque's ubiquitous strip malls). Consider the popular *pho* (noodle soup) variations, order the tofu (or chicken or shrimp) spring rolls with tangy peanut sauce, dig into the spicy lemongrass with chicken, and all will be well. **Known for:** authentic Vietnamese dishes; gracious, accommodating service; well-matched beer and wine list. $ *Average main: $10* ✉ *5721 Menaul Blvd. NE, University of New Mexico* ☎ *505/888–0101* ⊘ *Closed Sun.*

$ ✕ **Zacatecas.** *Mexican.* With the vibrant Zacatecas, The Compound's Mark Kiffin introduced that rare bird to Albuquerque's dining scene: a restaurant inspired by the taquerias in *old*Mexico. Creative (and nontraditional) offerings—*empanada de hongos* with *queso fresca* (tortillas with fresh mushrooms and cheese), tacos of slow-braised cochinita de pibil, serrano-spiked shrimp, and a complex chicken mole come to mind—are complemented by a range of tequilas, mezcals, bourbons, and beer not readily found elsewhere in the state. **Known for:** tacos, tequila, and bourbon; lively open space, especially in summer; nontraditional twists on Mexican taqueria fare. $ *Average main: $16* ✉ *3423 Central Ave. NE, Nob Hill* ☎ *505/255–8226* ⊕ *zacatecastacos.com* ⊘ *Closed Mon. No lunch Tues.–Thurs.*

$$$ ✕ **Zinc Wine Bar & Bistro.** *Contemporary.* A snazzy spot in Nob Hill, Zinc captures the essence of a San Francisco neighborhood bistro with its high ceilings, hardwood floors, lovely zinc-clad bar, and table-seating replete with white tablecloths and dark-wood straight-back café chairs. Consider the starter of crispy duck-confit eggrolls with curry-chile-lime dipping sauce, or the main dish of seared scallops with wild-rice–cranberry pilaf and a tarragon-crayfish beurre blanc—then select a matching vintage from the extensive wine list. **Known for:** seasonal, organic fare; vegan-friendly; special-event-worthy atmosphere. $ *Average main: $28* ✉ *3009 Central Ave. NE, Nob Hill* ☎ *505/254–9462* ⊕ *www.zincabq.com* ⊘ *No brunch weekdays.*

LOS RANCHOS/NORTH VALLEY

9

$$$ ✕ **Campo.** *American.* Pink light rising on the Sandias, lavender fields aglow; dining at Los Poblanos—its menu wholly committed to finely prepared dishes made from organic and locally grown ingredients—can be a transcendent experience in the sprawling farmlands of Albuquerque's historic North Valley. Dishes range from a superb farm salad (currants, pepita, and feta join the freshest greens), to ahi tuna, to a lovely apple cake, and are complemented with wine and microbrew selections both local—Milagro Vineyards' best, from Corrales—and regional. **Known for:** reservations a must; brilliant architectural touches from renowned New Mexico historic sites; year-round view. $ *Average main: $27* ✉ *Los Poblanos Historic Inn & Organic Farm, 4803 Rio Grande Blvd. NW, Los Ranchos de Albuquerque*

☎ *505/338–1615* ⊕ *www.lospoblanos.com* ⊘ *No lunch. No dinner Mon. and Tues.*

$ ✕**Casa de Benavidez.** *Mexican.* The fajitas at this welcoming local favorite with a romantic patio are among the best in town (the shrimp or vegetable renditions are both generous and especially memorable), and the *carne adovada* is faultless; the burger wrapped inside a sopaipilla is another specialty, as are the chimichangas packed with beef. As always, all diners can choose from red and green chile; vegetarians will want to ask the kind waitstaff to serve it green. **Known for:** shaded patio seating; live Spanish guitar music; attentive service. Ⓢ *Average main: $13* ✉ *8032 4th St. NW, Los Ranchos de Albuquerque* ☎ *505/898–3311* ⊕ *www.casadebenavidez.com* ⊘ *No dinner Sun.*

$$$ ✕**Farm & Table.** *American.* Set in the rural far-north end of town, yet all of 15 minutes from Downtown, you will find this much-reported friend-of-farmers dining spot. Its menu reflects the deep connection its owner shares with this long-farmed land, and is best experienced with dishes like a rustic quinoa salad, pan-roasted quail, or beef tenderloin with a red chile hollandaise. **Known for:** reservations critical (a week or more ahead); commitment to local growers; attractive farm setting. Ⓢ *Average main: $30* ✉ *8917 4th St. NW, North Valley* ☎ *505/503–7124* ⊕ *www.farmand-tablenm.com* ⊘ *No dinner Sun. and Mon. No brunch/ lunch weekdays.*

$ ✕**Mary & Tito's.** *Mexican.* Run by the same family since
FAMILY   it opened in 1963, Mary & Tito's is casual, friendly, and the real deal. Grab a booth and try the carne adovada–stuffed sopaipilla, the rellenos, or anything with the red (even the James Beard Foundation commented on it in its 2010 America's Classics award, but we say the original old family recipe trumps the meatless version they whip up on request). **Known for:** down-home no-frills family spot; award-winning red chile; early closing times. Ⓢ *Average main: $9* ✉ *2711 4th St. NW, North Valley* ☎ *505/344–6266* ⊘ *Closed Sun. No dinner after 6 pm Mon.–Thurs.*

WHERE TO STAY

With a few notable independently owned exceptions—Hotel Albuquerque, Hotel Andaluz, and Hotel Parq Central—Albuquerque's lodging options fall into two categories: modern chain hotels and motels, and distinctive and typically historic inns and B&Bs.

If you are seeking charm and history, both Los Poblanos Inn in the North Valley and the Hotel Parq Central in EDo are top choices. In Old Town, the Best Western Rio Grande Inn has a real Southwest feel and is very fairly priced to boot. And the Nativo Lodge makes a stay along the chain-strewn north Interstate 25 corridor a more memorable experience. If you need to be near the airport, there's no shortage of economical, plain-Jane, franchise hotels there, though the Sheraton Airport is by far the nicest of the lot. But keep in mind that it's barely a 15-minute ride from the airport to the more interesting neighborhoods and lodging opportunities covered here. And, wherever you stay in Albuquerque, you can generally count on finding rates considerably lower than the national average, and much cheaper than those in Santa Fe.

WHAT IT COSTS

	$	$$	$$$	$$$$
Hotels	under $110	$110–$180	$181–$260	over $260

Prices are for two people in a standard double room in high season, excluding 12%–13% tax.

Hotel reviews have been shortened. For full information, visit Fodors.com.

OLD TOWN

$$ **Best Western Plus Rio Grande Inn.** *Hotel.* This contemporary
FAMILY four-story low-rise—a short 10-minute walk from Old Town's main plaza *and* conveniently just off Interstate 40—has attractive Southwestern design and furnishings and the usual modern touches, like reliable and fast Wi-Fi. **Pros:** free shuttle to airport and around town within 1-mile radius; secure, free parking; year-round pool; dog-friendly rooms available. **Cons:** can be a hike from the rear rooms to the front desk; possible traffic noise; breakfast meal plan costs extra. $ *Rooms from: $130* ✉ *1015 Rio Grande Blvd. NW, Old Town* ☎ *505/843–9500, 800/780–7234 reservations only* 🌐 *www.riograndeinn.com* 🛏 *173 rooms* 🍴 *No meals.*

$$ **Böttger Mansion of Old Town.** *B&B/Inn.* A National Register property built in 1912 in the American Foursquare style, Böttger Mansion offers thoughtfully refurbished rooms incorporating fine woodwork and other period details—a claw-foot tub, a lovely mural by the original owner's grandson, or a pressed-tin ceiling. **Pros:** in the

9

Where to Eat and Stay in Albuquerque

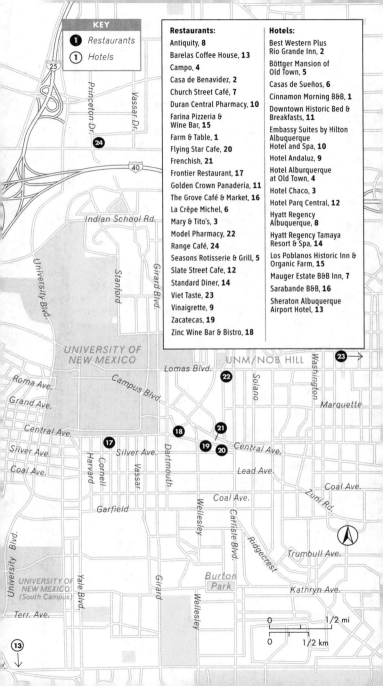

KEY

- **1** Restaurants
- **①** Hotels

Restaurants:

Antiquity, **8**

Barelas Coffee House, **13**

Campo, **4**

Casa de Benavidez, **2**

Church Street Café, **7**

Duran Central Pharmacy, **10**

Farina Pizzeria & Wine Bar, **15**

Farm & Table, **1**

Flying Star Cafe, **20**

Frenchish, **21**

Frontier Restaurant, **17**

Golden Crown Panaderia, **11**

The Grove Café & Market, **16**

La Crêpe Michel, **6**

Mary & Tito's, **3**

Model Pharmacy, **22**

Range Café, **24**

Seasons Rotisserie & Grill, **5**

Slate Street Cafe, **12**

Standard Diner, **14**

Viet Taste, **23**

Vinaigrette, **9**

Zacatecas, **19**

Zinc Wine Bar & Bistro, **18**

Hotels:

Best Western Plus Rio Grande Inn, **2**

Böttger Mansion of Old Town, **5**

Casas de Sueños, **6**

Cinnamon Morning B&B, **1**

Downtown Historic Bed & Breakfasts, **11**

Embassy Suites by Hilton Albuquerque Hotel and Spa, **10**

Hotel Andaluz, **9**

Hotel Alburquerque at Old Town, **4**

Hotel Chaco, **3**

Hotel Parq Central, **12**

Hyatt Regency Albuquerque, **8**

Hyatt Regency Tamaya Resort & Spa, **14**

Los Poblanos Historic Inn & Organic Farm, **15**

Mauger Estate B&B Inn, **7**

Sarabande B&B, **16**

Sheraton Albuquerque Airport Hotel, **13**

heart of Old Town, close to dining and attractions; architectural interest; tour packages available; resident cats. **Cons:** stair-access only to the upper rooms; wood floors may creak; resident cats. $ *Rooms from: $150* ✉ *110 San Felipe St. NW, Old Town* ☎ *505/243–3639* 🌐 *www.bottger.com* 🛏 *7 rooms* 🍴 *Breakfast.*

$$ 🏨 **Casas de Sueños.** *B&B/Inn.* This historic compound (it's a National Register property) of 1930s- and '40s-era adobe casitas is perfect if you're seeking seclusion and quiet, yet desire proximity to museums, restaurants, and shops. **Pros:** charming, quirky, and tucked away; some private patios. **Cons:** units vary in ambience and age—some are more enchanting than others; some high beds, claw baths, and tall steps—ask about accessibility. $ *Rooms from: $139* ✉ *310 Rio Grande Blvd. SW, on the south side of Central Ave., Old Town* ☎ *505/767–1000, 800/665–7002* 🌐 *www.casasdesuenos.com* 🛏 *21 casitas* 🍴 *Breakfast.*

$$$ 🏨 **Hotel Albuquerque at Old Town.** *Hotel.* At this 11-story Southwestern-style Heritage Hotels & Resorts property overlooking Old Town, attention is paid throughout to New Mexican artisan craftwork, from Nambe Pueblo–designed metalwork to Navajo rugs. **Pros:** comfy Territorial-style lobby; lovely gardens and pool patio out back. **Cons:** no seating provided for the room balconies; air-conditioning units can be loud. $ *Rooms from: $189* ✉ *800 Rio Grande Blvd. NW, Old Town* ☎ *505/843–6300, 877/901–7666* 🌐 *www.hhandr.com/albuquerque* 🛏 *188 rooms* 🍴 *No meals.*

$$$ 🏨 **Hotel Chaco.** *Hotel.* Heritage Hotels & Resorts, Inc.'s, special commitment to New Mexico shines through in their fastidious study of Chaco Canyon as an inspiration for their latest Albuquerque hotel. Designed by the Gensler firm, the hotel uses materials meant to evoke the fine stone chinking that comprise most of the 9th- to 12th-century structures found at that not-to be-missed ancient Puebloan site. **Pros:** thoughtful interior decor; contemplative outdoor lounge space; cool emerging Sawmill location. **Cons:** fortress-like entrance; fitness center not 24/7; $30 resort fee (included in price). $ *Rooms from: $259* ✉ *2000 Bellamah Ave. NW, Old Town* ☎ *505/246–9989, 866/505–7829 for reservations only* 🌐 *www.hotelchaco.com* 🛏 *118 rooms* 🍴 *No meals.*

DOWNTOWN/EDO

$$ ⌧ **Downtown Historic Bed & Breakfasts.** *B&B/Inn*. Comprising a pair of grand early-20th-century homes as well as a private carriage house and one other cottage in the Huning Highland Historic District, this property exudes romance… and intrigue. **Pros:** plush period furnishings; ample privacy; prime EDo location. **Cons:** cozy decor may be a bit overstuffed for some. $ *Rooms from: $129* ✉ *207 High St., Downtown* ☎ *505/842–0223* ⊕ *downtownhistoric.com* ⇨ *10 rooms* ⦿ *Breakfast* ☞ *Free parking.*

$$ ⌧ **Embassy Suites by Hilton Albuquerque Hotel and Spa.** *Hotel*.
FAMILY This all-suites high-rise with a striking contemporary design sits on a bluff alongside Interstate 25, affording guests fabulous views of the Downtown skyline and vast desert mesas to the west, and the Sandia Mountains to the east. **Pros:** convenient location adjacent to Interstate 25, near the Interstate 40 interchange; congenial staff; on-site spa. **Cons:** suites attract families in addition to business travelers; rooms starting to show age; views limited on lower floors. $ *Rooms from: $180* ✉ *1000 Woodward Pl. NE, Downtown* ☎ *505/245–7100, 800/362–2779* ⊕ *www. embassysuitesalbuquerque.com* ⇨ *261 suites* ⦿ *Breakfast.*

$$ ⌧ **Hotel Andaluz.** *Hotel*. Opened in 1939 by Conrad Hilton and now on the National Register of Historic Places, this impressive 10-story period structure is now an independently owned high-end boutique hotel. **Pros:** grand historic aesthetic but with plenty of modern perks. **Cons:** street noise can carry into rooms; may be too dark and moody for some; fitness center access is across street. $ *Rooms from: $180* ✉ *125 2nd St. NW, Downtown* ☎ *505/388–0088* ⊕ *www.hotelandaluz.com* ⇨ *114 rooms* ⦿ *No meals.*

★ **Fodor's**Choice ⌧ **Hotel Parq Central.** *Hotel*. A decidedly imag-
$$ inative adaptation of a disused building, the landmark Parq Central occupies a striking tile-trimmed three-story former AT& SF Railroad employees' hospital that dates to 1926. **Pros:** wonderfully landscaped, historic building; smartly designed rooms with sound-blocking windows; free shuttle to airport and within 3 miles of hotel; walk to fine EDo restaurants. **Cons:** desks in rooms are quite small (though hotel will provide a larger one on request); parking (free) can be sparse when Apothecary Lounge is hopping; noise might travel to rooms nearest the Lounge. $ *Rooms from: $150* ✉ *806 Central Ave. SE, Downtown* ☎ *505/242–0040, 888/796-7277* ⊕ *www.hotelparqcentral. com* ⇨ *74 rooms* ⦿ *Breakfast.*

9

$$ 🏨 **Hyatt Regency Albuquerque.** *Hotel.* In the heart of Downtown this Hyatt high-rise comprises a pair of desert-color towers that figure prominently in the city's skyline. **Pros:** easy walk to the KiMo Theatre and Downtown art galleries/coffee shops; saltwater lap pool, 24/7 fitness center; Civic Plaza and Convention Center are adjacent. **Cons:** mazelike layout till you get your bearings; no views on lower floors. [$] *Rooms from: $180* ✉ *330 Tijeras Ave. NW, Downtown* ☎ *505/842–1234* 🌐 *albuquerque.regency.hyatt.com/en/hotel/home.html* 🛏 *382 rooms* 🍴 *No meals.*

★ Fodor's Choice 🏨 **Mauger Estate B&B Inn.** *B&B/Inn.* This well-
$$ run B&B has retained many of its original 1897 Queen Anne–style architectural elements, including oval windows with beveled and "feather-pattern" glass, hardwood floors, high ceilings, a redbrick exterior, and a sweet veranda. **Pros:** pleasant common room to indulge in an afternoon cookies-and-wine spread; responsive and informed innkeeper; delicious breakfast (which they can pack to go). **Cons:** at night it can feel a bit sketchy for walking, but parking is secure. [$] *Rooms from: $119* ✉ *701 Roma Ave. NW, Downtown* ☎ *505/242–8755, 800/719–9189* 🌐 *www.maugerbb.com* 🛏 *10 rooms* 🍴 *Breakfast.*

LOS RANCHOS/NORTH VALLEY

$$ 🏨 **Cinnamon Morning B&B.** *B&B/Inn.* A beautifully maintained hideaway, this Southwestern-style adobe compound is barely a 10-minute drive north of Old Town; set just south of Rio Grande Nature Center State Park, it is a perfect roost for exploring local trails as well as the backroads north, or hopping back into town. **Pros:** grounds are a shady oasis in summer heat; near the Rio Grande trails and local shops; delightful host is well informed—ask for help with travel plans; on-site snacks 24/7. **Cons:** host's two small dogs roam public areas; guests' pets are limited to rooms not in the main house; location is inconvenient without a car. [$] *Rooms from: $135* ✉ *2700 Rio Grande Blvd. NW, North Valley* ☎ *505/345–3541* 🌐 *www.cinnamonmorning.com* 🛏 *7 rooms* 🍴 *Breakfast.*

★ Fodor's Choice 🏨 **Hyatt Regency Tamaya Resort and Spa.** *Resort.*
$$$ Set spectacularly on 550 pristine acres on the Santa Ana Pueblo (just north of Albuquerque, near Bernalillo), Tamaya awaits those seeking a culturally rich and even spiritually revivifying respite. **Pros:** cultural activities and horseback riding; perfect backroads drive from historic Albuquerque and Corrales; convenient base from which to explore the north route to Chaco Canyon. **Cons:** pet policy limited

to dogs; additional daily resort fee. Ⓢ *Rooms from: $219* ✉ *1300 Tuyuna Trail, Santa Ana Pueblo* ☎ *505/867–1234* ⊕ *tamaya.regency.hyatt.com/en/hotel/home.html* ⚘. *Twin Warriors Golf Course and Santa Ana Golf Club* ⌒ *350 rooms* ⦿ *No meals.*

★ Fodor'sChoice ⌖ **Los Poblanos Historic Inn & Organic Farm.** *B&B/* $$$ *Inn.* Designed in the 1930s by the renowned Pueblo Revival FAMILY architect John Gaw Meem for a local political power couple, Los Poblanos stands today as a quintessential element of Albuquerque's North Valley and its pastoral soul. **Pros:** seasonal farm-to-fork dining; fine bedding and linens; in-room massage available; set on a lavender farm. **Cons:** peacocks startle (and consequently screech) occasionally; full spa services off-site. Ⓢ *Rooms from: $230* ✉ *4803 Rio Grande Blvd. NW, Los Ranchos de Albuquerque* ☎ *505/344–9297* ⊕ *www.lospoblanos.com* ⌒ *50 rooms* ⦿ *Breakfast.*

$$$ ⌖ **Sarabande B & B.** *B&B/Inn.* While the name of this soothing, Modernist compound is inherited from the prior owners, the current setup now blends a respect for its Southwestern roots with a refreshing commitment to a— rare for these parts—high-end mid-century modern aesthetic. **Pros:** casita-like feel; delicious breakfast; pastoral hideaway. **Cons:** five-day cancel notice required (longer at Balloon Fiesta); property manager reachable by phone/text, but not on-site 24/7; pay half up front. Ⓢ *Rooms from: $185* ✉ *5637 Rio Grande Blvd. NW, Los Ranchos de Albuquerque* ☎ *505/348–5593* ⊕ *www.sarabandebnb.com* ⌒ *5 rooms* ⦿ *Breakfast.*

AIRPORT

9

$$ ⌖ **Sheraton Albuquerque Airport Hotel.** *Hotel.* Only 200 yards from the airport, this 15-story Sheraton sits up high on a mesa with wide-open views of the Sandia Mountains to the east and Downtown Albuquerque and the desert beyond to the northwest. **Pros:** short walk from airport (free shuttle service offered, too); resources for the business traveler. **Cons:** scant services or shopping nearby; hotel management and service can be weak; only program members get free Wi-Fi. Ⓢ *Rooms from: $110* ✉ *2910 Yale Blvd. SE, Airport* ☎ *505/843–7000, 888/625–4937* ⊕ *sheratonalbuquerqueairport.com* ⌒ *278 rooms* ⦿ *No meals.*

NIGHTLIFE AND PERFORMING ARTS

For the 411 on arts and nightlife, consult the freebie weekly Alibi (⊕ *www.alibi.com*), out on Thursdays. For highlights on some of the best live music programming in town, go to ⊕ *ampconcerts.org*. The *Albuquerque Journal*'s (⊕ *www.abqjournal.com*) Friday "Venue" section provides listings as well.

NIGHTLIFE

BARS AND LOUNGES

Effex Night Club. Albuquerque's sizable gay and lesbian community—and anyone else seeking a jumping dance scene—flocks to Effex, a vibrant, centrally located, two-level nightclub with a huge rooftop bar and an even larger downstairs dance floor. ✉ *420 Central St. SW, Downtown* ☎ *505/842–8870* ⊕ *www.effexabq.com.*

O'Niell's Pub. O'Niell's serves up the Irish comfort food you'd expect, along with a touch of Cajun and Mexican for variety, and presents an eclectic mix of local music, from jazz to jug band, western swing, and more. The expansive patio is perfect for afternoon beer and snacks. ✉ *4310 Central Ave. SE, Nob Hill* ☎ *505/255–6782* ⊕ *www.oniells.com.*

BREWPUBS

The art of craft beer brewing is hardly new to Albuquerque—credit relative long-timers like Marble Brewery, Tractor Brewing, and Chama River Brewing for setting the bar. Award-winners abound, and the area now has well over a dozen microbreweries. Big, hoppy IPAs represent about 50% of the lot, but half the fun is trying out the seasonal beers. In addition to an annual bounty of brew fests (⊕ *www.nmbeer.org*), a few favored hangouts include:

Bosque Brewing Co. Public House. Striking nature photographs line this hugely popular, modernly rustic pub, which offers a memorable Scotia Scotch Ale and Brewers' Boot Amber Ale year round as well as seasonal specialties like Doppelbier, a double German ale—and savory repasts to accompany them. Their brewmaster has made them multi-time National IPA Challenge Champions. ✉ *106 Girard Blvd. SE, Suite B, Nob Hill* ☎ *505/508–5967* ⊕ *www.bosquebrewing.com.*

Canteen Brewhouse. Music, beer, and eats (bratwurst to veggie wrap)—not necessarily in that order—are generously offered here. Picture cutoffs, casual picnic seating, and a sweet choice of IPAs, a good red ale, or a briskly cold

2016 World Beer Cup–winning High Plains Pils. ✉ *2381 Aztec Rd. NE, University of New Mexico* ☎ *505/881–2737* ⊕ *canteenbrewhouse.com.*

★ **Fodor's**Choice **La Cumbre Brewing Co.** La Cumbre's Elevated IPA took home gold in the 2011 Great American Brew Fest and Bronze in the 2012 World Beer Cup; its A Slice of Hefen is a traditional Bavarian wonder year-round, as is its lush Red Ryeot. Food trucks await outside the convivial taproom. ✉ *3313 Girard Blvd. NE, University of New Mexico* ☎ *505/872–0225* ⊕ *www.lacumbrebrewing.com.*

Marble Brewery. Distinctive craft brews like hoppy Imperial Red and rich Oatmeal Stout draw fans of artisan beer to Downtown's Marble Brewery. The homey pub, with an expansive outdoor patio, contains a beautiful 40-foot bar and serves tasty apps and sandwiches—there's live music some evenings, and a growing dynasty of locations here and in Santa Fe. ✉ *111 Marble Ave. NW, Downtown* ☎ *505/243–2739* ⊕ *www.marblebrewery.com.*

LIVE MUSIC

★ **Fodor's**Choice **¡Globalquerque!** Held at the National Hispanic
FAMILY Cultural Center, ¡Globalquerque! is a dazzling two-day world-music festival that puts Albuquerque on the global music map. In addition to three evening performances, a full day is devoted to (free) kids programming. The festival's producer AMP Concerts is also the organization that lures acts like Lucinda Williams, Vieux Farka Toure, David Byrne, Philip Glass, and Richard Thompson to intimate venues all around town. ✉ *Albuquerque* ⊕ *www. globalquerque.com.*

9

Outpost Performance Space. Outpost Performance Space programs an inspired, eclectic slate, from local *nuevo*-folk to techno, jazz, and traveling East Indian ethnic. Some big names—especially in the jazz world—show up at this special small venue, which is a key player in bringing the stellar New Mexico Jazz Festival to the state every July. ✉ *210 Yale Blvd. SE, University of New Mexico* ☎ *505/268–0044* ⊕ *www.outpostspace.org.*

Tablao Flamenco. Flamenco music and dance speak to something in Albuquerque's soul, and for folks new to the tradition or yearning for a taste, this venue—with tapas and vinos to match—is the perfect spot to kindle that flame. In an intimate, appropriately dark sultry setting, small plates created by Mark Miller (of Santa Fe's Coyote Cafe fame), and the right cavas to complement them are served. Make reservations (shows are Friday–Sunday), arrive early, and be dazzled by the world-class artists performing here. ✉ *Hotel Albuquerque at Old Town, 800 Rio Grande Blvd. NW, Old Town* ☎ *505/222–8797* ⊕ *www.tablaoflamenco.org.*

PERFORMING ARTS

Albuquerque has a remarkable wealth of local talent, but it also draws a surprising number of world-class stage performers from just about every discipline imaginable. Check the listings mentioned at the introduction to this section for everything from poetry readings, impromptu chamber music recitals, folk, jazz, and blues festivals, and formal symphony performances to film festivals, Flamenco Internacional, and theater.

MUSIC

★ Fodor'sChoice **Chatter Sunday.** Holding sway at 10:30 am Sunday mornings, the Chatter chamber ensemble's classical-to-modern music program draws a devoted crowd of regulars. Free cappuccino and a spoken-word performance round out the one-hour shows. Expect the crème of local and guest performers—Santa Fe Opera stars often pop in during the season. Arrive early—the seating is open and limited; best to buy tickets ahead (online). ✉ *Las Puertas, 1512 1st St. NW, Downtown* ⊕ *www.chatterabq.org* ▣ *$15.*

New Mexico Philharmonic. The highly respected New Mexico Philharmonic dips deeply into the full realm of classical repertoire, including, at Christmas, Handel's *Messiah.* Most performances are at 2,000-seat Popejoy Hall or the National Hispanic Cultural Center's Roy E. Disney Hall; in summer they occasionally suit up for outdoor performances at the ABQ BioPark. ✉ *Albuquerque* ☎ *505/323–4343* ⊕ *www.nmso.org.*

PERFORMING ARTS CENTERS

KiMo Theatre. The stunning KiMo Theatre, an extravagantly ornamented 650-seat Pueblo Deco movie palace, is one of the best places in town to see any type of show. Jazz, dance, blues, film—everything from traveling road shows to an inspired city-sponsored film series (Hitchcock pre-Hollywood, for example)—might turn up here. Former Albuquerque resident Vivian Vance of *I Love Lucy* fame once performed on the stage; today you're more likely to see Laurie Anderson, Wilco, or a film-festival screening. ✉ *423 Central Ave. NW, Downtown* ☎ *505/768–3544* ⊕ *www.cabq.gov/kimo.*

Popejoy Hall. Popejoy Hall presents blockbuster Broadway touring shows, dance performances, concerts from rock and pop to mariachi and classical, comedy acts, and lectures. **Rodey Theatre**, a smaller, 400-seat house in the same complex, stages experimental and niche works throughout the year. **Keller Hall**, also in the Center for the Arts, is a small venue with fine acoustics, a perfect home for the university's excellent chamber music program. ✉ *University of New Mexico Center for the Arts, 203 Cornell Dr. NE, University of New Mexico* ✛ *Enter from Central Ave. SE* ☎ *505/925–5858, 877/664–8661* ⊕ *www.popejoypresents.com* ☞ *Free parking at remote lots includes shuttle service to venue.*

THEATER

Albuquerque Little Theatre. Albuquerque Little Theatre is a nonprofit community troupe that's been going strong since 1930. Its staff of professionals teams up with local volunteer talent to produce comedies, dramas, musicals, and mysteries. The company theater, across the street from Old Town, was built in 1936 and designed by John Gaw Meem. It contains an art gallery, a large lobby, and a cocktail lounge. ✉ *224 San Pasquale Ave. SW, Old Town* ☎ *505/242–4750* ⊕ *www.albuquerquelittletheatre.org.*

Tricklock Company. In January and February, theater fans of the fresh and new flock to the Revolutions International Theatre Festival, presented by the Tricklock Company. Recognized internationally, Tricklock mounts productions throughout the year and emphasizes works that take it— and the audience—to the edge of theatrical possibility. ✉ *110 Gold Ave. SW, Downtown* ☎ *505/414–3738* ⊕ *www. tricklock.com.*

9

SHOPPING

Albuquerque's shopping strengths include a handful of cool retail districts, such as Nob Hill, Old Town, Downtown/ EDo, and the North Valley. These are good neighborhoods for galleries; antiques; Native American arts; Old West finds and apparel; Mexican crafts; textiles, jewelry, pottery, glass, and other fine handicrafts by nationally acclaimed local artists; home-furnishing shops; bookstores; and offbeat gift shops. Indoor flea markets are quite popular all around town, and everyone knows that museum gift shops are always worth a look-see—Albuquerque's are no exception.

Uptown. The Uptown neighborhood is Albuquerque's hub of chains and mall shopping. The older traditional mall is Coronado (at Louisiana Boulevard NE and Menaul Boulevard NE), which has a Barnes & Noble, Macy's, and a Sephora. Upscale ABQ Uptown is an attractive outdoor village containing an Apple Store, Pottery Barn, MAC cosmetics, and Williams-Sonoma. The Winrock center is anchored by Dillards; a Target and Trader Joe's are nearby. ⊠ *Louisiana Blvd. NE, between I–40 and Menaul Blvd. NE, Uptown.*

ANTIQUES

Old Town Antiques. Take a moment in this neat and quiet shop to appreciate the very particular eye of its owner, Connie Fulwyler, who, while not at all intrusive, will gladly fill in the backstory of any piece here. Her offerings center on 19th- and 20th-century art and history (Anglo, Mexican, and Native American), with a touch of "odd science" and politics: find a winsome piggy bank rendered in 1940s–50s Tlaquepaque glazeware, an original Harrison Begay gouache painting, vintage Taxco sombrero cufflinks, 1813 political engravings, early 20th-century Santo Domingo bowls, a Gilbert Atencio serigraph used for a menu cover, rare books and paper ephemera, and more. ⊠ *416 Romero St. NW, Old Town* ☎ *505/842–6657* ⊕ *oldtownantiquesabq.com.*

ART GALLERIES

In addition to 516 Arts *(see Downtown section in Exploring Albuquerque, above)*, and Tamarind Institute at UNM *(see UNM/Nob Hill section in Exploring Albuquerque, above)*, Albuquerque has a solid and growing gallery scene. For comprehensive gallery listings, turn to the *Collector's Guide* (⊕ *www.collectorsguide.com*); Albuquerque ARTScrawl listings are online (⊕ *artscrawlabq.org*) as well as in the *abqARTS* monthly.

Central Features Contemporary Art. Enter this brightly lit gallery space and be wowed by the very smart, obviously thoughtful selection of works presented by the excellent and particular eye of founder Nancy Zastudil. Known for topical themes, the contemporary work shown here—often large scale—is carefully placed to immerse the viewer, as the artist intended. Environmentally informed drawings by Nina Elder, the fabulously colored real/surreal paintings of Jennifer Nehrbass, and provocative 3-D pieces by Corey Pickett that explore current gun laws are typical of the exhibitions that make a visit here worthwhile. ⊠ *514 Central Ave. SW, 2nd fl., Downtown* ☎ *505/252–9983* ⊕ *www.centralfeatures.com.*

Harwood Art Center. Harwood Art Center, on the fringe of Downtown and Old Town in the historic Sawmill/Wells Park neighborhood, is a remarkable city resource for its working-artist studios, classes, and as a gallery in its own right. Shows—predominantly of New Mexico–based artists working in nontraditional forms—take place in their historic brick school building and change monthly. ⊠ *1114 7th St. NW, off Mountain Rd., Old Town* ☎ *505/242–6367* ⊕ *www.harwoodartcenter.org.*

IMEC. A sliver of a shop that's really a gallery, IMEC (International Metalsmith Exhibition Center) carries a superb range of work by a nationally renowned group of metal- and glass-work artisans. Many are New Mexico based, like Luis Mojica, who does stunning work in sterling, resin, and mother-of-pearl, and Mary Kanda, whose intricate glass-bead pieces are richly colored. ⊠ *101 Amherst Dr. SE, Nob Hill* ☎ *505/265–8352* ⊕ *www.shopimec.com.*

Mariposa Gallery. Mariposa Gallery sells contemporary fine crafts, including jewelry, sculptural glass, works in mixed media and clay, and fiber arts. The changing exhibits focus on established and upcoming artists; its buyer's sharp eyes can result in real finds for the serious browser. ⊠ *3500 Central Ave. SE, Nob Hill* ☎ *505/268–6828* ⊕ *www.mariposa-gallery.com.*

9

Richard Levy Gallery. A stellar roster of artists with an international following show at this shoebox-shaped gallery that would be right at home on either coast. Its clean lines are perfect for displaying pieces from photographers (Natsumi Hayashi, Hiroshi Sugimoto), multimedia artists (Eric Tillinghast, John Baldessari), and printmakers (Alex Katz, Ed Ruscha), as well as works from global initiatives like ISEA 2012: Machine Wilderness and 2009's LAND/ART New Mexico. ⊠ *514 Central Ave. SW, Downtown* ☎ *505/766–9888* ⊕ *www.levygallery.com.*

Sanitary Tortilla Factory (*SCA Contemporary Art @ the Sanitary Tortilla Factory*). At a nexus of Downtown's coffee-beer-arts scene, Sanitary Tortilla is an exemplary Downtown adaptive reuse project. Now housing artist studios and gallery space, the onetime tortilla and chile go-to for politicos and locals of all stripes provides a cleverly curated counterpoint to the 516 Arts–Central Features–Richard Levy arts nexus down on Central. Occasional outdoor installations (Pastel FD's Botanical mural project, a collaboration with 516) complement the intriguing shows inside. ⊠ *401–403 2nd St. SW, Downtown* ☎ *505 /228–3749* ⊕ *sanitarytortillafactory.org* ⊗ *Closed Sat.–Thurs. except for events or by appointment.*

Weyrich Gallery. Weyrich Gallery carries distinctive jewelry, fine art, Japanese tea bowls, woodblocks, hand-colored photography, and other largely Asian-inspired pieces, all at prices that are very reasonable. ⊠ *2935-D Louisiana Blvd. NE, East Side* ☎ *505/883–7410* ⊕ *www.weyrichgallery.com.*

BOOKS

★ Fodor'sChoice **Bookworks.** This North Valley stalwart has been reviving readers' spirits for many a year in a cozy neighborhood setting. A superb independent, Bookworks fairly prides itself on service, and book lovers from all corners flock here for its fine stock of regional coffee-table books, a well-culled selection of modern fiction and nonfiction, architecture and design titles, well-chosen CDs, calendars, and cards, and a (small) playground's worth of kids' books. Regular signings and readings draw some very big guns to this tiny treasure. ⊠ *4022 Rio Grande Blvd. NW, Los Ranchos de Albuquerque* ☎ *505/344–8139* ⊕ *www.bkwrks.com.*

Page 1 Books. Page 1, one of the great independent bookstores in Albuquerque, is a singular find for its mix of rare and used books shelved to entice the serious browser, while also offering a deep selection of literature, fiction and nonfiction, print ephemera, books for kids, gifts for the book lover, and even textbooks. Count on astute staff recommendations, as well as a regular roster of book signings, poetry readings, and children's events. ⊠ *5850 Eubank Blvd. NE, Northeast Heights* ☎ *505/294–2026* ⊕ *www. page1book.com.*

CLOTHING AND ACCESSORIES

★ Fodor'sChoice **The Man's Hat Shop.** The Man's Hat Shop has been a mainstay on Central Avenue since 1946. Anyone, man or woman, who needs just the right hat, with just the right fit, will find what they're looking for—fedora, porkpie, Cossack-style, coonskin, and of course top-of-the-line

Western felt or straw. Owner Stuart Dunlap clearly loves his business and will help guide you among some 4,000 styles to a new chapeau that suits, or modify one you already have. ✉ *511 Central Ave. NW, Downtown* ☎ *505/247–9605* ⊕ *www.themanshatshop.com.*

GIFTS, FOOD, AND TOYS

★ Fodor'sChoice **The Farm Shop at Los Poblanos.** The Farm Shop at
FAMILY Los Poblanos, beside the beautiful country inn of the same name, carries books, culinary gadgets, the same house-made lavender lotions and soaps inn guests receive, and a considerable variety of artisan jams, vinegars, sauces, and gourmet goodies. ✉ *4803 Rio Grande Blvd. NW, Los Ranchos de Albuquerque* ☎ *505/344–9297, 866/344–9297* ⊕ *www.lospoblanos.com.*

Kei & Molly Textiles. With joyful designs composed in the spirit of traditional woodblock prints, whimsical and artful pure cotton flour-sack dish towels—and yardage, napkins, potholders, and more—roll off the silk-screen presses. View the process from their retail shop, where you will also find an irresistible selection of hand-hewn products from other local makers with keen eyes for design, like Baby Blastoff (baby and kids apparel) and Live Clay (small bowls), as well as South Valley Soaps and more. ✉ *4400 Silver Ave. SE, Suite A, Nob Hill* ☎ *505/268–4400* ⊕ *www. keiandmolly.com.*

Spur Line Supply Co. A hop across the street from the Albuquerque Museum and at the frontline of Sawmill District development, Spur Line sets a tone with its clever juxtaposition of vendors across a swath of New Mexico makers. Check out vinyl from Hi-Phy records (there's even a modern version of a listening booth), cards and sundries from Power and Light Press (a Silver City letterpress shop), or a darn good apple fritter or chocolate ganache donut from the Bristol Doughnut Co. ✉ *800 20th St. NW, Suite B, Old Town* ☎ *505 /242–6858* ⊕ *www.spurlinesupplyco.com.*

Theobroma Chocolatier. Theobroma Chocolatier carries beautiful, handcrafted, high-quality chocolates, truffles, and candies (most of them made on the premises), as well as Taos Cow ice cream. ✉ *12611 Montgomery Blvd. NE, Northeast Heights* ☎ *505/293–6545* ⊕ *www.theobroma-chocolatier.com.*

HISPANIC IMPORTS AND TRADITIONS

Casa Talavera. Peruse a wide selection of hand-painted Mexican Talavera tiles at this Old Town stalwart that's been in business since 1970. Prices are reasonable, making the colorful geometrics, florals, mural patterns, and solids close to irresistible. Tin lighting fixtures as well as ceramic sink and cabinet knobs fill in the rest of the space in this DIY-inspiring shop (yes, they ship). ⊠ *621 Rio Grande Blvd., Old Town* ☎ *505/243–2413* ⊕ *www.casatalavera.com.*

Jackalope. Jackalope, a longtime Southwestern-style furniture and bric-a-brac shop, is still a good browse for folk art and rug imports, but it shines brightest in its garden pottery and outdoor decor selection. ⊠ *6400 San Mateo Blvd. NE, Northeast Heights* ☎ *505/349–0955* ⊕ *www.jackalope.com.*

NATIVE AMERICAN ARTS AND CRAFTS

Bien Mur Indian Market Center. The Sandia Pueblo–run Bien Mur Indian Market Center showcases the best of regional Native American rugs, jewelry, and crafts of all kinds. It is a great place to get familiar with the distinct styles found across the 19 pueblos, and you can feel secure about purchases made here. ⊠ *100 Bien Mur Dr. NE, off Tramway Rd. NE east of I–25, Northeast Heights* ☎ *505/821–5400, 800/365–5400* ⊕ *www.bienmurindianmarket.com.*

Grey Dog Trading. Grey Dog carries a very special selection of fetishes, contemporary and historic, from both Zuni and Cochiti Pueblo artisans, along with kachina dolls, baskets, and a small grouping of vintage and contemporary Native American jewelry and pottery, for the beginning and seasoned collector. Gorgeous hand-carved Ye'i figures by Navajo artist Sheldon Harvey are also on display, as are his paintings. This shop's owners are well respected in this field, and present work from all 19 pueblos as well as Hopi and Navajo pieces. ⊠ *400 San Felipe St. NW, Suite 8, Old Town* ☎ *505/243–0414, 877/606–0543* ⊕ *www. greydogtrading.com.*

SPORTS AND THE OUTDOORS

Albuquerque is blessed with an exceptional setting for outdoor sports, backed by a favorable, if sometimes unpredictable, climate. Biking and hiking are year-round activities here. Usually 10°F warmer than Santa Fe's, Albuquerque's winter days are often mild enough for most outdoor activities. The Sandias tempt you with challenging mountain adventures; the Rio Grande and its cottonwood forest, the bosque, provide settings for additional outdoors pursuits.

BALLOONING

If you've never been ballooning, you may picture a bumpy ride, where changes in altitude produce the queasy feeling you get in a tiny propeller plane, but the experience is far calmer than that. The balloons are flown by licensed pilots (don't call them operators) who deftly turn propane-fueled flames on and off, climbing and descending to find winds blowing the way they want to go—there's no real steering involved, which makes the pilots' control that much more admirable. Pilots generally land balloons where the wind dictates, so chase vehicles pick you up and return you to your departure point. Even without door-to-door service, many visitors rank a balloon ride over the Rio Grande Valley as their most memorable experience.

Several reliable companies around Albuquerque offer tours. A ride costs about $150 to $200 per person.

Rainbow Ryders. One of the best balloon tours is with Rainbow Ryders, an official ride concession for the Albuquerque International Balloon Fiesta. As part of the fun, you get to help inflate and pack away the balloon. In case you missed breakfast prior to your flight, a Continental breakfast and glass of Champagne await your return. ✉ *5601 Eagle Rock Ave. NE* ☎ *505/823–1111, 800/725–2477* ⊕ *www.rainbowryders.com.*

BICYCLING

With the creation of many lanes, trails, and dedicated bike paths (by 2013 an impressive 400 miles of designated bikeways were in place), Albuquerque's city leaders are recognized for their bike-friendly efforts—a serious challenge given the committed car culture of its residents.

Albuquerque Bicycle Map. The city's public works department produces the detailed Albuquerque Bicycle Map, which can be obtained free at most bike shops or viewed on their website. ✉ *Albuquerque* ☎ *505/768–2680* ⊕ *www.cabq.gov/bike.*

★ Fodor's Choice **Paseo del Bosque Trail.** The Paseo del Bosque Trail, which follows along the Rio Grande Valley and runs flat for most of its 16-mile run, is one of the loveliest rides (or walks) in town. ⊠ *Albuquerque* ⊕ *www. cabq.gov/parksandrecreation/open-space/lands/ paseo-del-bosque-trail.*

RENTALS

Bike rental shops have clustered in the Paseo del Bosque Trail area, though rentals can also be found closer to the mountains as well.

The Bike Smith. In their location near the Paseo del Bosque Trail, the accommodating proprietors at The Bike Smith can sell you a new bike or fix you up with a rental (and any accessories needed) from an excellent selection of well-maintained mountain, road, and commuter bikes ($35–50/day). ⊠ *Rio Grande Plaza Center, 901 Rio Grande Blvd. NW, Suite D124, Old Town* ☎ *505/242–9253* ⊕ *the-bikesmithllc.com.*

Routes Bicycle Tours & Rentals. Tours—by bike and snowshoe—dominate the bike-trails-convenient Routes shop, but straight rentals are also available, by the hour or day. They include, on the bike side, cruisers, mountain bikes, kids bikes, and tandems ($15/hour to $50/day). ⊠ *404 San Felipe St. NW, Old Town* ☎ *505/933–5667* ⊕ *www. routesrentals.com.*

BIRD-WATCHING

The Rio Grande Valley, one of the continent's major flyways, attracts many migratory bird species.

★ Fodor'sChoice **Open Space Visitor Center.** Sandhill cranes make their winter home here, or stop for a snack en route to the Bosque del Apache, just south, in Socorro. Albuquerque is right in their flyway, and the Open Space center, which is replete with trails heading down to the shores of the Rio Grande, provides a most hospitable setting for them. The outdoor viewing station is complemented inside the visitor center with changing art exhibits and well-informed guides. ⊠ *500 Coors Blvd. NW, West Side* ☎ *505/897–8831* ⊕ *www. cabq.gov/openspace.*

Rio Grande Nature Center State Park. Good bird-viewing locales include the Rio Grande Nature Center State Park. ⊠ *2901 Candelaria Rd. NW, North Valley* ☎ *505/344–7240* ⊕ *www.rgnc.org.*

GOLF

Some of the best courses in the region—and there are some outstanding ones—are just outside town. The two **University of New Mexico** courses (⊕ *www.unmgolf.com*) and the four operated by the City of Albuquerque have their charms, and the rates are reasonable. Each course has a clubhouse and pro shop, where clubs and other equipment can be rented. Weekday play is first-come, first-served, but reservations are taken for weekends.

Golf Management Office. Contact the Golf Management Office for details on the four city-run courses. ✉ *Albuquerque* ☎ *505/888–8115* ⊕ *www.cabq.gov/golf.*

Los Altos Golf Course. The 18-hole Los Altos Golf Course, a city-run course and one of the region's most popular facilities, serves beginning to intermediate players. There's also a short, par-3, 9-hole executive course. ✉ *9717 Copper Ave. NE, Northeast Heights* ☎ *505/298–1897* ⊕ *www.cabq.gov/golf* ☞ *$25–$31.50; $7 for pull cart* ⚲ *18 holes, 5895–6180 yards, par 71–74.*

HIKING

In the foothills in Albuquerque's Northeast Heights, you'll find great hiking in Cibola National Forest (⊕ *www.fs.usda.gov/cibola*), which can be accessed from Tramway Boulevard Northeast, about 4 miles east of Interstate 25 or 2 miles north of Paseo del Norte. Just follow the road into the hillside, and you'll find several parking areas (there's a daily parking fee of $3). This is where you'll find the trailhead for the steep and challenging La Luz Trail (⊕ *www.laluztrail.com*), which rises for some 9 miles (an elevation gain of more than 3,000 feet) to the top of Sandia Crest. You can take the Sandia Peak Aerial Tram *(see Northeast Heights section in Exploring Albuquerque, above)* to the top and then hike down the trail, or vice versa (keep in mind that it can take up to six hours to hike up the trail, and four to five hours to hike down). Spectacular views of Albuquerque and many miles of desert and mountain beyond that are had from the trail. You can also enjoy a hike here without going the whole way—if your energy and time are limited, just hike a mile or two and back. Or enjoy one of the shorter trails that emanate from the Elena Gallegos Picnic Area (⊕ *www.cabq.gov/openspace*), just a few miles south along Tramway. No matter how far you hike, however, pack plenty of water.

9

For lovely but even less rugged terrain, the Aldo Leopold Forest and trails at the Open Space Visitor Center on the West Side will be of interest.

KAYAKING

Quiet Waters Paddling Adventures. The Rio at sunset (or in the early hours during balloon time—or just about any time) is best seen from a kayak or canoe and this reliable outfit offers rentals as well as guided and self-guided tours to help you do just that. After a 15-mile drive north from Downtown to the small historic town of Bernalillo, you are set for a serene float down the calm, cottonwood-lined waters of the middle Rio Grande. ✉ *105D Pleasant View Dr., Bernalillo* ☎ *505/771–1234* ⊕ *www.quietwaterspaddling.com.*

TAOS

Updated
by Andrew
Collins

TAOS CASTS A LINGERING SPELL. Set on an undulating mesa at the base of the Sangre de Cristo Mountains, it's a place of piercing light and spectacular views, where the desert palette changes almost hourly as the sun moves across the sky. Adobe buildings—some of them centuries old—lie nestled amid pine trees and scrub, some in the shadow of majestic Wheeler Peak, the state's highest point, at just over 13,000 feet. The smell of piñon-wood smoke rises from the valley from early autumn through late spring; during the warmer months, the air smells of fragrant sage.

The earliest residents, members of the Taos-Tiwa tribe, have inhabited this breathtaking valley for more than a millennium; about 2,000 of their descendants still live and maintain a traditional way of life at Taos Pueblo, a 95,000-acre reserve 4 miles northeast of Taos Plaza. Spanish settlers arrived in the 1500s, bringing both farming and Catholicism to the area; their influence remains most pronounced in the diminutive village of Ranchos de Taos, 4 miles south of town, where the massive adobe walls and *camposanto* (graveyard) of San Francisco de Asís Church have been attracting photographers for generations.

In the early 20th century, another population—artists—discovered Taos and began making the pilgrimage here to write, paint, and take photographs. The early adopters of this movement, painters Bert Phillips and Ernest Blumenschein, stopped here in 1898 quite by chance to repair a wagon wheel while en route from Denver to Mexico in 1898. Enthralled with the earthy beauty of the region, they abandoned their intended plan, settled near the plaza, and in 1915 formed the Taos Society of Artists. In later years, many illustrious artists—including Georgia O'Keeffe, Ansel Adams, and D. H. Lawrence—frequented the area, helping cement a vaunted arts tradition that thrives to this day. The steadily emerging bohemian spirit has continued to attract hippies, counterculturalists, New Agers, gays and lesbians, and free spirits. Downtown, along with some outlying villages to the south and north, such as Ranchos de Taos and Arroyo Seco, now support a rich abundance of galleries and design-driven shops. Whereas Santa Fe, Aspen, Scottsdale, and other gallery hubs in the West tend toward pricey work, much of it by artists living elsewhere, Taos remains very much an ardent hub of local arts and crafts production and sales. A half dozen excellent museums here also document the town's esteemed artistic history.

TOP REASONS TO GO

Small-town sophistication:
For a tiny, remote community, Taos supports a richly urbane culinary scene, a fantastic bounty of galleries and design shops, and plenty of stylish B&Bs and inns.

Indigenous and artistic roots: The Taos Pueblo and its inhabitants have lived in this region for centuries and continue to play a vital role the community. And few U.S. towns this size have a better crop of first-rate art museums, which document the history of one of the West's most prolific arts colonies.

Desert solitaire: Few panoramas in the Southwest can compare with that of the 13,000-foot Sangre de Cristo Mountains soaring over the adobe homes of Taos, and beyond that, the endless high-desert mesa that extends for miles to the west.

World-class ski slopes:
Just a 30-minute drive north of town, Taos Ski Valley has long been one of the top winter-sports resorts in the West and has recently added a luxury hotel and a number of new facilities.

About 5,800 people live year-round within Taos town limits, but another 28,000 reside in the surrounding county, much of which is unincorporated, and quite a few others live here seasonally. This means that in summer and, to a lesser extent, during the winter ski season, the town can feel much larger and busier than you might expect, with a considerable supply of shops, restaurants, and accommodations. Still, overall, the valley and soaring mountains of Taos enjoy relative isolation, low population-density, and magnificent scenery, parts of which you can access by visiting Rio Grande del Norte National Monument, one of the park service's newest properties—it was designated in 2013. These elements combine to make Taos an ideal retreat for those aiming to escape, slow down, and embrace a distinct regional blend of art, cuisine, outdoor recreation, and natural beauty.

10

ORIENTATION AND PLANNING

GETTING ORIENTED

Taos is small and resolutely rustic, but for the prosaic stretch of chain motels and strip malls that greet you as you approach from the south. Persevere to the central plaza, and you'll find several pedestrian-friendly blocks of galleries, shops, restaurants, and art museums. Easygoing Taoseños are a welcoming lot, and if you ever lose your orientation you'll find locals happy to point you where you need to go. It's difficult to reach Taos without a car, and you'll need one to reach those attractions and businesses outside the village center (the Rio Grande Gorge, Millicent Rogers Museum, and the area's best skiing and hiking). The narrow, historic streets near the plaza can be choked with traffic in the peak summer and winter seasons, especially on weekends—ask locals about the several shortcuts for avoiding traffic jams, and try walking when exploring the blocks around the plaza.

TAOS NEIGHBORHOODS

Plaza and Vicinity. More than four centuries after it was laid out, the Taos Plaza and adjacent streets remain the community's hub of commercial and social activity. Dozens of independent shops and galleries, along with several notable restaurants, hotels, and museums, thrive here. The plaza itself is a bit overrun with mediocre souvenir shops, but you only need to walk a block in any direction—especially north and east—to find better offerings.

South Side. The first Spanish settlers were agrarian, and many families continue to till the fertile land south of Taos, an area anchored by tiny Ranchos de Taos, which is home to iconic San Francisco de Asís Church, memorialized by Georgia O'Keeffe and photographer Ansel Adams. The main approach road into Taos from the south, NM 68, is lined with gas stations, convenience stores, and chain motels.

Taos Pueblo. The Pueblo is the ancient beating heart of the entire valley, the historic and architectural basis for everything that Taos has become. A small, unmemorable casino aside, this area a short drive northeast of the plaza has been spared commercial development and remains a neighborhood of modest homes and farms. The Pueblo itself is the sole draw for visitors and worth a visit.

El Prado. As you drive north from Taos toward Arroyo Seco and points north or west, you'll first take the main thoroughfare, Paseo del Pueblo Norte (U.S. 64) through the small village of El Prado, a mostly agrarian area that's notable for having several of the area's best restaurants, bed-and-breakfasts, and shops.

West Side. Taos is hemmed in by the Sangre de Cristo Mountains on the east, but to the west, extending from downtown clear across the precipitously deep Rio Grande Gorge (and the famous bridge that crosses it), the landscape is dominated by sweeping, high-desert scrub and wide-open spaces. The west side is mostly residential and makes for a scenic shortcut around the sometimes traffic-clogged plaza (from Ranchos de Taos, just follow NM 240 to Blueberry Hill Road to complete this bypass).

Arroyo Seco. Set on a high mesa north of Taos, this funky, hip village and arts center is an ideal spot to browse galleries, grab a meal at one of a handful of excellent restaurants, or simply pause to admire the dramatic views before driving on to the Enchanted Circle or Taos Ski Valley.

TAOS PLANNER

WHEN TO GO

With more than 300 days of sunshine annually, Taos typically yields good—if sometimes chilly—weather year-round. The summer high season brings warm days (upper 80s) and cool nights (low 50s), as well as frequent afternoon thunderstorms. A packed arts and festival schedule in summer means hotels and B&Bs sometimes book well in advance, lodging rates are high, restaurants are jammed, and traffic anywhere near the plaza can slow to a standstill. Spring and fall are stunning and favor mild days and cool nights, fewer visitors, and reasonable hotel prices. In winter, especially during big years for snowfall, skiers arrive en masse but tend to stay close to the slopes and only venture into town for an occasional meal or shopping raid.

10

GETTING HERE AND AROUND

AIR TRAVEL

Albuquerque International Sunport, about 130 miles away and a 2½-hour drive, is the nearest major airport to Taos. The small Santa Fe Municipal Airport, a 90-minute drive, also has daily service from Dallas, Denver, Los Angeles, and Phoenix. Alternatively, as Taos is one of the gateway towns to New Mexico if coming from Colorado, some visitors fly into Denver (five hours north) or Colorado Springs (four hours). Taos Municipal Airport, 12 miles west of town, serves only charters and private planes.

Airports Albuquerque International Sunport (*ABQ*). ✉ *220 Sunport Blvd. SE, Albuquerque* ☎ *505/244–7700* ⊕ *https://abqsunport. com.* **Santa Fe Municipal Airport** (*SAF*). ✉ *121 Aviation Dr, Santa Fe* ☎ *505/955-2900* ⊕ *www.santafenm.gov/airport.*

TRANSFERS

From Santa Fe, your best bet is renting a car. Taos Express provides bus service between Taos and Santa Fe, including a stop at Santa Fe's train station, from which you can catch the New Mexico Rail Runner train to Albuquerque (and then a free bus to the airport). The fare is just $10 round-trip, but service is offered only on weekends (one Friday evening run, and two Saturday and Sunday runs, one in the morning, one in the evening). Twin Hearts Express has shuttle service four times daily between Taos and Albuquerque Sunport ($95 round-trip), but they don't stop in Santa Fe. Additionally, during the ski season (late fall–early spring), Taos Ski Valley operates a daily shuttle between the airports in Albuquerque ($85 round-trip) and Santa Fe ($65 round-trip) and the ski valley; once at the ski valley, you have to take a taxi ($35 one-way) or the local Chili Line Shuttle bus ($2 round-trip) into Taos. Unless you're coming to Taos just for skiing, this is a pretty cumbersome and expensive option.

CAR TRAVEL

A car is your most practical means both for reaching and getting around Taos. The main route from Santa Fe is via U.S. 285 north to NM 68 north, also known as the Low Road, which winds between the Rio Grande and red-rock cliffs before rising to a spectacular view of the mesa and river gorge. You can also take the spectacular and vertiginous High Road to Taos, which takes longer but offers a wonderfully scenic ride—many visitors come to Taos via the Low Road, which is more dramatic when driven south to north, and then return to Santa Fe via the High Road, which has better views as you drive south. From Denver, it's a five-hour drive south via Interstate 25, U.S. 160 west (at Walsenburg), and CO 159 to NM 522—the stretch from Walsenburg into Taos is quite scenic.

TAXI TRAVEL

Taxi service in Taos is sparse, but Taos Cab serves the area. Rates are about $5–$7 within town, $20–$25 to Arroyo Seco, and $35 to Taos Ski Valley, plus $1 per each additional person.

VISITOR INFORMATION

Taos Ski Valley Chamber of Commerce. ⊠ *122 Sutton Pl., Taos Ski Valley* ☎ *575/776–1413, 800/517–9816* ⊕ *www.taoss-kivalley.com.*

Taos Visitor Center. ⊠ *1139 Paseo del Pueblo Sur* ☎ *505/758–3873, 800/587–9007* ⊕ *www.taos.org.*

PLANNING YOUR TIME

Whether you've got an afternoon or a week in the area, begin by strolling around Taos Plaza and along Bent Street, taking in the galleries, Native American crafts shops, and eclectic clothing stores, plus nearby museums, including the Harwood, Kit Carson Home, and Taos Art Museum. A few of the must-see attractions in the area are a bit farther afield, and you need at least two days and ideally three or four to take in everything. Among the top outlying attractions, it's possible to visit Taos Pueblo, the magnificent Millicent Rogers Museum, the village of Arroyo Seco, and the Rio Grande Gorge Bridge all in one day—you can connect them to make one loop to the north and west of the city. If you're headed south, stop at La Hacienda de los Martínez to gain an appreciation of early Spanish life in Taos and then to Ranchos de Taos to see the stunning San Francisco de Asís Church. If you approach Taos from the south, as most visitors do, you could also visit both these attractions on your way into town, assuming you arrive by early afternoon.

EXPLORING

For a town its size, Taos contains an impressive collection of fine art museums and other historic sites of note. Most of these are in the center of town and within an easy walk of Taos Plaza, but you'll need a car to visit the Millicent Rogers Museum, Rancho de Taos, and a few other notable sites.

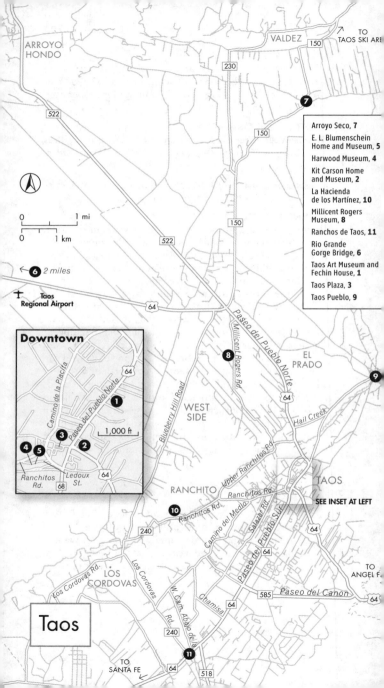

ARROYO
HONDO

VALDEZ

TO
TAOS SKI ARE

150

230

522

150

150

522

Arroyo Seco, **7**

E. L. Blumenschein
Home and Museum, **5**

Harwood Museum, **4**

Kit Carson Home
and Museum, **2**

La Hacienda
de los Martínez, **10**

Millicent Rogers
Museum, **8**

Ranchos de Taos, **11**

Rio Grande
Gorge Bridge, **6**

Taos Art Museum and
Fechin House, **1**

Taos Plaza, **3**

Taos Pueblo, **9**

0   1 mi

0   1 km

← **6** 2 miles

✈ Taos
Regional Airport

64

Downtown

64

Camino de la Placita

Paseo del Pueblo Norte

1

3

2

1,000 ft

4

5

Ranchitos
Rd.

Ledoux
St.

68

64

8

WEST
SIDE

Blueberry Hill Road

Millicent Rogers Rd.

Paseo del Pueblo Norte

EL
PRADO

9

64

Hail Creek

RANCHITO

Upper Ranchitos Rd.

Ranchitos Rd.

Ranchitos Rd.

10

240

Camino del Medio

Salazar Rd.

Paseo del Pueblo Sur

TAOS

SEE INSET AT LEFT

64

TO
ANGEL F.

Los Cordovas Rd.

LOS
CORDOVAS

Los Cordovas

W. Cam. Abalo de la

Ranchitos Rd.

Chamisa

64

585

Paseo del Canon

64

Taos

240

11

TO
SANTA FE

64

518

PLAZA AND VICINITY

TOP ATTRACTIONS

★ ~~Fodor's~~Choice **Harwood Museum.** The Pueblo Revival former home of Burritt Elihu "Burt" Harwood, a dedicated painter who studied in France before moving to Taos in 1916, is adjacent to a museum dedicated to the works of local artists. Traditional Hispanic northern New Mexican artists, early art-colony painters, post–World War II modernists, and contemporary artists such as Larry Bell, Agnes Martin, Ken Price, and Earl Stroh are represented. Mabel Dodge Luhan, a major arts patron, bequeathed many of the 19th- and early-20th-century works in the Harwood's collection, including *retablos* (painted wood representations of Catholic saints) and *bultos* (three-dimensional carvings of the saints). In the Hispanic Traditions Gallery upstairs are 19th-century tinwork, furniture, and sculpture. Downstairs, among early-20th-century art-colony holdings, look for E. Martin Hennings's *Chamisa in Bloom,* which captures the Taos landscape particularly beautifully. A tour of the ground-floor galleries shows that Taos painters of the era, notably Oscar Berninghaus, Ernest Blumenschein, Victor Higgins, Walter Ufer, Marsden Hartley, and John Marin, were fascinated by the land and the people linked to it. ✉ *238 Ledoux St., Plaza and Vicinity* ☎ *575/758–9826* ⊕ *www.harwoodmuseum.org* ⌚ *$10* ⊙ *Nov.–Mar., closed Mon. and Tues.*

★ ~~Fodor's~~Choice **Taos Art Museum and Fechin House.** The interior of this extraordinary adobe house, built between 1927 and 1933 by Russian émigré and artist Nicolai Fechin, is a marvel of carved Russian-style woodwork and furniture. Fechin constructed it to showcase his daringly colorful paintings. The house now contains the Taos Art Museum, which showcases a rotating collection of some 600 paintings by more than 50 Taos artists, including founders of the original Taos Society of Artists, among them Joseph Sharp, Ernest Blumenschein, Bert Phillips, E. I. Couse, and Oscar Berninghaus. ✉ *227 Paseo del Pueblo Norte, Plaza and Vicinity* ☎ *575/758–2690* ⊕ *www.taosartmuseum.org* ⌚ *$10* ⊙ *Closed Mon.*

WORTH NOTING

E. L. Blumenschein Home and Museum. For an introduction to the history of the Taos art scene, start with Ernest L. Blumenschein's residence, which provides a glimpse into the cosmopolitan lives led by the members of the Taos Society

10

of Artists, of which Blumenschein was a founding member. One of the rooms in the adobe-style structure dates from 1797. On display are the art, antiques, and other personal possessions of Blumenschein and his wife, Mary Greene Blumenschein, who also painted, as did their daughter Helen. Several of Ernest Blumenschein's vivid oil paintings hang in his former studio, and works by other early Taos artists are also on display. ⌧ *222 Ledoux St., Plaza and Vicinity* ☎ *575/758–0505* ⊕ *www.taoshistoricmuseums. org* ⬚*$8* ⊘ *Closed Wed. and Thurs.*

FAMILY **Kit Carson Home and Museum.** Kit Carson bought this low-slung 12-room adobe home in 1843 for his wife, Josefa Jaramillo, the daughter of a powerful, politically influential Spanish family. Three of the museum's rooms are furnished, as they were when the Carson family lived here. The rest of the museum is devoted to gun and mountain-man exhibits, such as rugged leather clothing and Kit's own Spencer carbine rifle with its beaded leather carrying case, and early Taos antiques, artifacts, and manuscripts. ⌧ *113 Kit Carson Rd., Plaza and Vicinity* ☎ *575/758–4945* ⊕ *www. kitcarsonmuseum.org* ⬚ *$7.*

Taos Plaza. The first European explorers of the Taos Valley came here with Captain Hernando de Alvarado, a member of Francisco Vásquez de Coronado's expedition of 1540. Basque explorer Don Juan de Oñate arrived in Taos in July 1598 and established a mission and trading arrangements with residents of Taos Pueblo. The settlement developed into two plazas: the plaza at the heart of the town became a thriving business district for the early colony, and a walled residential plaza was constructed a few hundred yards behind. It remains active today, home to a throng of shlocky gift shops, plus a few more noteworthy galleries and boutiques. On the southeastern corner of Taos Plaza is the Hotel La Fonda de Taos. Nine infamous erotic paintings by D. H. Lawrence that were naughty in his day but are quite tame by present standards can be viewed in a small gallery in the hotel. ⌧ *Plaza and Vicinity.*

SOUTH SIDE

WORTH NOTING
La Hacienda de los Martínez. Spare and fortlike, this adobe structure built between 1804 and 1827 on the bank of the Rio Pueblo served as a community refuge during Comanche and Apache raids. Its thick walls, which have few windows,

surround two central courtyards. Don Antonio Severino Martínez was a farmer and trader; the hacienda was the final stop along El Camino Real (the Royal Road), the trade route the Spanish established between Mexico City and New Mexico. The restored period rooms here contain textiles, foods, and crafts of the early 19th century. There's a working blacksmith's shop, usually open to visitors on Saturday, and weavers create beautiful textiles on reconstructed period looms. ✉ *708 Hacienda Rd., off Ranchitos Rd. (NM 240), South Side* ☎ *575/758–1000* ⊕ *www.taoshistoricmuseums.org* ✆ *$8.*

Ranchos de Taos. A few minutes' drive south of the center of Taos, this village still retains some of its rural atmosphere despite the road traffic passing through. Huddled around its famous adobe church and dusty plaza are cheerful, remodeled shops and galleries standing shoulder to shoulder with crumbling adobe shells. This ranching, farming, and budding small-business community was an early home to Taos Native Americans before being settled by Spaniards in 1716. A few of the ancient adobe dwellings contain shops, galleries, and restaurants. ✉ *South Side.*

TAOS PUEBLO

★ Fodor'sChoice **Taos Pueblo.** For nearly 1,000 years the mud-
FAMILY and-straw adobe walls of Taos Pueblo have sheltered Tiwa-speaking Native Americans. A United Nations World Heritage Site, this is the largest collection of multistory pueblo dwellings in the United States. The pueblo's main buildings, Hlauuma (north house) and Hlaukwima (south house), are separated by a creek. These structures are believed to be of a similar age, probably built between 1000 and 1450. The dwellings have common walls but no connecting doorways—the Tiwas gained access only from the top, via ladders that were retrieved after entering. Small buildings and corrals are scattered about.

10

The pueblo today appears much as it did when the first Spanish explorers arrived in New Mexico in 1540. The adobe walls glistening with mica caused the conquistadors to believe they had discovered one of the fabled Seven Cities of Gold. The outside surfaces are continuously maintained by replastering with thin layers of mud, and the interior walls are frequently coated with thin washes of white clay. Some walls are several feet thick in places. The roofs of each of the five-story structures are supported by large timbers, or vigas, hauled down from the mountain forests. Pine or aspen *latillas* (smaller pieces of wood) are placed side by side between the vigas; the entire roof is then packed with dirt.

Even after 400 years of Spanish and Anglo presence in Taos, inside the pueblo the traditional Native American way of life has endured. Tribal custom allows no electricity or running water in Hlauuma and Hlaukwima, where varying numbers (roughly 150) of Taos Native Americans live full-time. About 1,900 others live in conventional homes on the pueblo's 95,000 acres. The crystal-clear Rio Pueblo de Taos, originating high above in the mountains at the sacred Blue Lake, is the primary source of water for drinking and irrigating. Bread is still baked in *hornos* (outdoor domed ovens). Artisans of the Taos Pueblo produce and sell (tax-free) traditionally handcrafted wares, such as mica-flecked pottery and silver jewelry. Great hunters, the Taos Native Americans are also known for their work with animal skins and their excellent moccasins, boots, and drums.

Although the population is predominantly Catholic, the people of Taos Pueblo, like most Pueblo Native Americans, also maintain their native religious traditions. At Christmas and other sacred holidays, for instance, immediately after mass, dancers dressed in seasonal sacred garb proceed down the aisle of St. Jerome Chapel, drums beating and rattles shaking, to begin other religious rites.

The pueblo **Church of San Geronimo,** or St. Jerome, the patron saint of Taos Pueblo, was completed in 1850 to replace the one destroyed by the U.S. Army in 1847 during the Mexican War. With its smooth symmetry, stepped portal, and twin bell towers, the church is a popular subject for photographers and artists.

The public is invited to certain ceremonial dances held throughout the year (a full list of these is posted on the pueblo website's Events page): highlights include the Feast of Santa Cruz (May 3); Taos Pueblo Pow Wow (mid-July); Santiago and Santa Ana Feast Days (July 25 and 26); San Geronimo Days (September 29 and 30); Procession of the Virgin Mary (December 24); and Deer Dance or Matachines Dance (December 25). While you're at the pueblo, respect all rules and customs, which are posted prominently. There are some restrictions, which are posted, on personal photography. ⊠ *120 Veterans Hwy., off Paseo del Pueblo Norte,*

Taos Pueblo ⊹ Turn right just north of Kachina Lodge Hotel
☎ 575/758–1028 ⊕ *www.taospueblo.com* ✉ *$16.*

WEST SIDE

TOP ATTRACTIONS

★ Fodor's Choice **Millicent Rogers Museum.** More than 7,000 pieces of spectacular Native American and Hispanic art, many of them from the private collection of the late Standard Oil heiress Millicent Rogers, are on display here. Among the pieces are baskets, blankets, rugs, kachina dolls, carvings, tinwork, paintings, rare religious artifacts, and, most significantly, jewelry (Rogers, a fashion icon in her day, was one of the first Americans to appreciate the turquoise-and-silver artistry of Native American jewelers). Other important works include the pottery and ceramics of Maria Martinez and other potters from San Ildefonso Pueblo (north of Santa Fe). Docents conduct guided tours by appointment, and the museum hosts lectures, films, workshops, and demonstrations. The two-room gift shop has exceptional jewelry, rugs, books, and pottery. ⊠ *1504 Millicent Rogers Rd., off Paseo del Pueblo Norte, just south of junction with NM 150* ☎ *575/758–2462* ⊕ *www.millicentrogers.org* ✉ *$10* ⊙ *Nov.–Mar., closed Mon.*

FAMILY **Rio Grande Gorge Bridge.** It's a dizzying experience to see the Rio Grande 650 feet underfoot, where it flows at the bottom of an immense, steep rock canyon. In summer the reddish rocks dotted with green scrub contrast brilliantly with the blue sky, where you might see a hawk lazily floating in circles. The bridge is the second-highest suspension bridge in the country. Hold on to your camera and eyeglasses when looking down. Many days just after daybreak, hot-air balloons fly above and even inside the gorge. There's a campground with picnic shelters and basic restrooms on the west side of the bridge. ⊠ *U.S. 64, 8 miles west of junction with NM 522 and NM 150, West Side.*

10

ARROYO SECO

★ Fodor's Choice **Arroyo Seco.** Established in 1834 by local Spanish farmers and ranchers, this charming village of about 1,700 has today become a secluded, artsy escape from the sometimes daunting summer crowds and commercialism of the Taos Plaza—famous residents include actress Julia Roberts and former U.S. Defense Secretary Donald Rumsfeld, who own ranches adjacent to one another. You reach the tiny commercial district along NM 150, about 5 miles north of the intersection with U.S. 64 and NM 522 (it's about 9 miles north of the plaza). The drive is part of the joy of visiting, as NM 150 rises steadily above the Taos Valley, offering panoramic views of the Sangre de Cristos—you pass through Arroyo Seco en route to the Taos Ski Valley.

Arroyo Seco is without any formal attractions or museums, and that's partly its charm. The main reasons for making the trip here are to behold the dramatic scenery, grab a bite at one of the handful of excellent restaurants (ice cream from **Taos Cow Cafe** and tamales from **Abe's Cantina** are both revered by locals), and browse the several galleries and boutiques, whose wares tend to be a little more idiosyncratic but no less accomplished than those sold in Taos proper. ⊠ *Arroyo Seco* ⊕ *www.visitseco.com.*

WHERE TO EAT

For a relatively small, remote town, Taos has a sophisticated and eclectic dining scene. It's a fine destination for authentic New Mexican fare, but you'll also find several upscale spots serving creative regional fare utilizing mostly local ingredients, a smattering of excellent Asian and Middle Eastern spots, and several very good cafés and coffeehouses perfect for a light but bountiful breakfast or lunch.

WHAT IT COSTS				
	$	**$$**	**$$$**	**$$$$**
Restaurants	under $18	$18–$24	$25–$30	over $30

Prices in the restaurant reviews are the average cost of a main course at dinner or, if dinner is not served, at lunch.

Restaurant reviews have been shortened. For full information, visit Fodors.com.

PLAZA AND VICINITY

★ Fodor'sChoice ✕ **Byzantium.** *Eclectic.* Off a grassy courtyard
$$$ near the Blumenschein and Harwood museums, this enchanting locals' favorite defies its traditional-looking adobe exterior to present an eclectic menu with American, Asian, Mediterranean, and Middle Eastern influences. You might start with mussels steamed in a clay pot with white wine, butter, roasted garlic, and the addictively good house-baked bread, before moving on to shrimp poached in a

Where to Eat in Taos

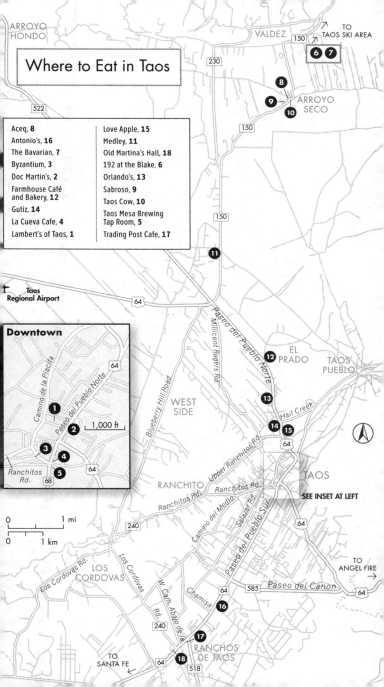

ARROYO HONDO

VALDEZ

TO TAOS SKI AREA

150

6 7

230

8

9 ARROYO SECO

10

522

150

Aceq, **8**	Love Apple, **15**
Antonio's, **16**	Medley, **11**
The Bavarian, **7**	Old Martina's Hall, **18**
Byzantium, **3**	192 at the Blake, **6**
Doc Martin's, **2**	Orlando's, **13**
Farmhouse Café and Bakery, **12**	Sabroso, **9**
Gutiz, **14**	Taos Cow, **10**
La Cueva Cafe, **4**	Taos Mesa Brewing Tap Room, **5**
Lambert's of Taos, **1**	Trading Post Cafe, **17**

150

11

Taos Regional Airport

64

Paseo del Pueblo Norte

Millicent Rogers Rd.

12 EL PRADO

TAOS PUEBLO

Downtown

Camino de la Placita

64

Paseo del Pueblo Norte

1

2 1,000 ft

3

4

5

64

68

Ranchitos Rd.

13

Hail Creek

14 **15**

64

Blueberry Hill Road

WEST SIDE

Upper Ranchitos Rd.

TAOS

SEE INSET AT LEFT

RANCHITO

Ranchitos Rd.

Ranchitos Rd.

Camino del Medio

Salazar Rd.

Paseo del Pueblo Sur

0   1 mi
0   1 km

240

LOS CORDOVAS

Los Cordovas Rd.

Los Cordovas Rd.

W. Cam Abajo de la Rd.

Chamisa

64

585

Paseo del Canon

64

TO ANGEL FIRE

240

16

TO SANTA FE

17

18

RANCHOS DE TAOS

64

518

Thai green curry sauce. **Known for:** well-curated wine and craft-beer list; house-baked bread with marmalade; Thai shrimp curry. [$] *Average main: $28* ✉ *112 Camino La Placita* ☎ *575/751–0805* ⊗ *Closed Tues. and Wed. No lunch.*

$$$ ✕ **Doc Martin's.** *Southwestern.* The old-world restaurant of the Historic Taos Inn takes its name from the building's original owner, a local physician who saw patients in the rooms that are now the dining areas. The creative menu hews toward innovative takes on comforting classics, with an emphasis on sustainable ingredients—a favorite is the relleno platter comprising a pair of blue corn–beer battered Anaheim chiles, green chile, pumpkin seeds, and goat cheese cream. **Known for:** chiles rellenos; beef short ribs with a red-wine reduction; among the best margaritas in town. [$] *Average main: $26* ✉ *Historic Taos Inn, 125 Paseo del Pueblo Norte, Plaza and Vicinity* ☎ *575/758–1977* 🌐 *www.taosinn.com.*

$ ✕ **La Cueva Cafe.** *Mexican.* This casual Mexico–meets–New Mexico eatery in an 1850s building is run by Mexico-born couple Juana and Horacio Zarazua, who have built a devoted following working previously in some of the best restaurants in town. Their specialty is regional Mexican food, including ceviche, chipotle shrimp tacos, and several other seafood dishes, plus chile rellenos, chicken mole enchiladas, and some familiar New Mexico–style standbys. **Known for:** tortilla soup; chicken mole enchiladas; regional Mexican seafood dishes. [$] *Average main: $11* ✉ *135 Paseo del Pueblo Sur, Plaza and Vicinity* ☎ *575/758–7001* 🌐 *www.lacuevacafe.com.*

★ Fodor's Choice ✕ **Lambert's of Taos.** *Contemporary.* Superb
$$$ service, creative cuisine, and an utterly romantic setting inside a historic adobe house a short walk north of the plaza define this Taos landmark that's been a go-to for special meals since the mid-'90s (it was previously located a few blocks away). The rich fare here fuses regional and Mediterranean recipes and ingredients and includes such standouts as red-beet risotto with chèvre and watercress, and braised Colorado lamb shank with black eye pea–root veggie ragout, au jus, and turmeric raita. **Known for:** $6 happy hour with some great appetizer deals; refined service; the "bowl of bliss" dessert of sautéed apples, spice cake, toffee sauce, and vanilla ice cream. [$] *Average main: $29* ✉ *123 Bent St., Plaza and Vicinity* ☎ *575/758–1009* 🌐 *www.lambertsoftaos.com.*

$ ✕ **Taos Mesa Brewing Tap Room.** *Pizza.* You don't have to be a craft-beer fan to enjoy this convivial taproom a five-minute walk south of the plaza, although it is one of two outposts of revered Taos Mesa Brewing (the other is in Taos Ski Valley), and it's a terrific place to sample a crisp Take A Knee IPA or a ruby-red Amarillo Rojo red ale. Pizza lovers also appreciate this spot, which serves delicious, generously topped pies—the inferno, with chorizo, chiles, taleggio and mozzarella cheese, and hot honey has a devoted following. **Known for:** live rock and pop music on many evenings; the spicy "inferno" pizza; hop-forward locally brewed beers. [$] *Average main: $10* ✉ *210 Paseo del Pueblo Sur, Plaza and Vicinity* ☎ *575/758–1900* 🌐 *www.taosmesabrewing.com.*

SOUTH SIDE

$ 🍴 **Antonio's.** *Mexican.* Chef Antonio Matus has been delighting discerning diners in the Taos area for many years with his authentic, boldly flavorful and beautifully plated regional Mexican cuisine. In this intimate art-filled restaurant with a slate courtyard, Matus focuses more on regional Mexican than New Mexican fare. **Known for:** red-chile pork posole; chile en nogada; tres leches (three milks) cake. [$] *Average main: $15* ✉ *1379 Paseo del Pueblo Sur, South Side* ☎ *575/758–2599* 🌐 *www.antoniosthetasteofmexico.com* 🕒 *Closed Sun.*

$$ 🍴 **Old Martina's Hall.** *American.* This enchanting South-meets-Southwestern-style restaurant across the road from the famed San Francisco de Asís Church is in a restored Pueblo Revival building with thick adobe walls and sturdy viga-and-latilla ceilings—it was run as a rowdy dance hall for generations by the town's iconic Martinez family (former resident and late actor Dennis Hopper used to party here). It's no less convivial today, as both an inviting spot for cocktails and happy hour snacks as for dining, in one of the beautiful salons with modern spherical chandeliers and local artwork. **Known for:** happy hour snacks and cocktails; eclectic menu with Southern influences; striking architecture and historic vibe. [$] *Average main: $19* ✉ *4140 NM 68, South Side* ☎ *575/758–3003* 🌐 *www.oldmartinashall.com* 🕒 *Closed Sun.*

$$ 🍴 **Trading Post Cafe.** *Italian.* This casual restaurant serving mostly modern Italian fare with regional accents has long ranked among the top culinary spots in town. Intelligent and attentive service along with well-presented contemporary Southwestern art make any meal a pleasure. **Known for:** house-made pastas; Chef Rene's meatballs; excellent wine list. [$] *Average main: $21* ✉ *4179 Paseo del Pueblo*

Sur, South Side ☎ *575/758–5089* 🌐 *www.tradingpostcafe.com* ⏲ *Closed Mon. No dinner Sun.*

EL PRADO

★ $ FodorsChoice 🍴 **Farmhouse Café and Bakery.** *American.* The best seats at this rambling restaurant in a scenic complex that also contains Overland Sheepskin Company and Red Arrow Emporium home furnishings are on the long covered patio, which is surrounded by gardens and wind sculptures and offers sweeping views of mountains. The flavorful breakfasts and lunches here use ingredients sourced from more than 20 area farms and ranches, and the bakery turns out decadent made-from-scratch carrot cake, scones, cinnamon rolls, and other treats, many of them gluten-free. **Known for:** house-baked pies, cakes, and scones; huevos rancheros; veggie, local bison, and organic beef burgers. [$] *Average main: $10* ✉ *1405 Paseo del Pueblo Norte, El Prado* ☎ *575/758–5683* 🌐 *www.farmhousetaos.com* ⏲ *No dinner.*

★ $ FodorsChoice 🍴 **Gutiz.** *Eclectic.* This ambitious and consistently terrific favorite for lunch and breakfast (served all day) blends French, Spanish, and South American culinary influences. Best bets in the morning include caramelized French toast made with thick homemade bread and seasonal fruit, and a scrambled egg tower with Manchego cheese. **Known for:** French toast; steamed clams and mussels; charming patio with mountain views. [$] *Average main: $12* ✉ *812B Paseo del Pueblo Norte, El Prado* ☎ *575/758–1226* 🌐 *www.gutiztaos.com* ⏲ *Closed Mon. No dinner.*

★ $$ FodorsChoice 🍴 **Love Apple.** *Contemporary.* It's easy to drive by the small adobe former chapel that houses this delightful farm-to-table restaurant a short drive north of Taos Plaza, just beyond the driveway for Hacienda del Sol B&B, but slow down—you don't want to miss the culinary magic of Chef Andrea Meyer, who uses organic, mostly local ingredients in the preparation of simple yet sophisticated creations like homemade sweet-corn tamales with red-chile mole, a fried egg, and crème fraîche, and tacos (using homemade tortillas) filled with grilled antelope, potato-Gruyère gratin, and parsley gremolata. The price is right, too—just remember it's cash only, and there are 13 tables. **Known for:** boldly flavored, locally sourced cuisine; romantic setting inside former chapel; cash only. [$] *Average main: $19* ✉ *803 Paseo del Pueblo Norte, El Prado* ☎ *575/751–0050* 🌐 *www.theloveapple.net* 💳 *No credit cards* ⏲ *Closed Mon. No lunch.*

$$ ✕ **Medley.** *Modern American.* Set in a rustic-chic roadhouse on the scenic road between El Prado and Arroyo Seco that adjoins one of the area's best wineshops (it often hosts wine tastings), Medley strikes a happy balance between gastro-pub and special-night-out restaurant. You could make a meal of a few shareable small plates—tuna tartare tostadas, mac-and-cheese with roasted Hatch chiles, crispy-chicken sliders with sriracha mayo—or dive into one of the more substantial entrée offerings, such as mango-tamari-glazed salmon or a 10-ounce porterhouse steak with brussels sprouts hash and house-made apple-bacon jam. **Known for:** cheese and charcuterie plates; grilled whole ruby trout with salsa verde and preserved lemon; extensive, well-chosen wine selection. Ⓢ *Average main: $23* ✉ *100 NM 150 (Taos Ski Valley Rd.), El Prado* ☎ *575/776–5656* ⊕ *www.medleytaos.com* ⊙ *Closed Mon.*

★ **Fodor's**Choice ✕ **Orlando's.** *Southwestern.* This family-run local
$ favorite is likely to be crowded during peak hours, while guests wait patiently to devour perfectly seasoned favorites such as *carne adovada* (red chile–marinated pork), blue-corn enchiladas, and scrumptious shrimp burritos. You can eat in the cozy dining room, outside on the umbrella-shaded front patio, or call ahead for takeout if you'd rather avoid the crowds. **Known for:** pork tamales; carne adovada; potent margaritas. Ⓢ *Average main: $11* ✉ *1114 Don Juan Valdez La., off Paseo del Pueblo Norte, El Prado* ☎ *575/751–1450.*

ARROYO SECO

★ **Fodor's**Choice ✕ **Aceq.** *Modern American.* Head to this cozy
$$ bistro tucked behind some galleries in Arroyo Seco's charming little business district for super, reasonably priced farm-to-table food with a decidedly global bent, plus one of the most interesting craft-beer lists in the state. There are just a few tables in the simple dining room with chunky wood tables and a small bar, plus some outdoor tables on a quiet patio—reservations are a good idea, especially on weekends. **Known for:** red-chile bison tacos; superb beer and wine lists; house-made pasta with a daily-changing preparation. Ⓢ *Average main: $19* ✉ *480 NM 150 (Taos Ski Valley Rd.), Arroyo Seco* ☎ *575/776–0900* ⊕ *www.aceqrestaurant.com* ⊙ *No lunch.*

$$$ ✕ **Sabroso.** *Modern American.* Sophisticated, innovative cuisine and outstanding wines are served in this 150-year-old adobe hacienda, where you can also relax in lounge chairs near the bar, or on a delightful patio surrounded

10

by plum trees. The Mediterranean-influenced contemporary American menu changes regularly, but an evening's entrée might be lemon-thyme-honey-glazed game hen with-grilled asparagus and potatoes dauphinoise. **Known for:** fireplace-warmed dining room; gorgeous patio; excellent and popular happy hour. $ *Average main: $29* ✉ *470 NM 150 (Taos Ski Valley Rd.), Arroyo Seco* ☎ *575/776–3333* 🌐 *www.sabrosotaos.com* ⏲ *Closed Tues. No lunch.*

★ $ FAMILY Fodor's Choice ✕ **Taos Cow.** *Café.* Locals, hikers, skiers headed up to Taos Ski Valley, and visitors to funky Arroyo Seco flock to this cozy storefront café operated by the famed Taos Cow ice-cream company. Offering a nice selection of made-to-order sandwiches and other savory bites, this isn't merely a place to sample amazing homemade ice cream (including such innovative flavors as pistachio–white chocolate, lavender, and Chocolate Rio Grande—chocolate ice cream packed with dark-chocolate chunks and pecans). **Known for:** ice cream in distinctive flavors; bagel sandwiches; turkey-and-Brie sandwiches. $ *Average main: $8* ✉ *485 NM 150 (Taos Ski Valley Rd.), Arroyo Seco* ☎ *575/776–5640* 🌐 *www.taoscow.com* ⏲ *No dinner.*

TAOS SKI VALLEY

★ $$$ Fodor's Choice ✕ **The Bavarian.** *German.* The restaurant inside the romantic, magically situated alpine lodge, which also offers Taos Ski Valley's most luxurious accommodations, serves outstanding contemporary Bavarian-inspired cuisine, such as baked artichokes and Gruyère, and braised local lamb shank with mashed potatoes and red wine–roasted garlic-thyme jus. Lunch is more casual and less expensive, with burgers and salads available. **Known for:** soft-baked pretzels with mustard; distinctive Bavarian Alps ambience; imported German beers. $ *Average main: $26* ✉ *100 Kachina Rd., Taos Ski Valley* ☎ *575/776–8020* 🌐 *www.skitaos.com/things-to-do/bavarian* ⏲ *Closed for a few weeks in spring and fall and Tues. and Wed. in summer; call to confirm hrs outside ski season.*

$$ ✕ **192 at the Blake.** *Modern American.* This modern-rustic spot inside the swank new Blake hotel is warmed by a roaring fireplace and draws skiers and hikers with its terrific selection of craft beers and cocktails, plus an extensive menu of tasty bar snacks and a few more substantial—but still shareable—items, like a sliced-thin beef rib eye with ancho-chile demiglace and oven-roasted trout. Top draws among the smaller plates include wild boar stew, truffle fries, sautéed mussels in a lime–coconut–red chile broth,

flatbread pizzas, and wild boar stew. **Known for:** wild boar stew; creatively topped flatbread pizzas; apres-ski cocktails and hobnobbing. [$] *Average main: $20* ✉ *107 Sutton Pl., Taos Ski Valley* ☎ 🌐 *www.skitaos.com/things-to-do/192.*

WHERE TO STAY

The hotels and motels along NM 68 (Paseo del Pueblo), most of them on the south side of town, suit every need and budget; rates vary little between big-name chains and smaller establishments—Hampton Inn is one of the best maintained of the chains. Make advance reservations and expect higher rates during ski season (usually from late December to early April, and especially for lodgings on the north side of town, closer to the ski area) and in the summer. The Taos Ski Valley has a number of condo and rental units, but there's little reason to stay up here unless you're in town expressly for skiing or perhaps hiking in summer—it's too far from Taos proper to be a convenient base for exploring the rest of the area. The area's many B&Bs offer some of the best values, when you factor in typically hearty full breakfasts, personal service, and, often, roomy casitas with private entrances.

WHAT IT COSTS

	$	$$	$$$	$$$$
Hotels	under $110	$110–$180	$181–$260	over $260

Prices are for two people in a standard double room in high season, excluding 12%–13% tax.

Hotel reviews have been shortened. For full information, visit Fodors.com.

PLAZA AND VICINITY

$$$ ★ **El Monte Sagrado.** *Resort.* This posh, eco-minded, and decidedly quirky boutique resort—part of New Mexico's stylish Heritage Hotels & Resorts brand—has some of the swankiest rooms in town as well as a fabulous spa. **Pros:** eco-friendly; imaginative decor; terrific spa. **Cons:** unusual decor isn't to everybody's taste; service doesn't always measure up to premium rates; there's a $25 resort fee. [$] *Rooms from: $190* ✉ *317 Kit Carson Rd., Plaza and Vicinity* ☎ *575/758–3502, 855/846–8267* 🌐 *www.elmonte-sagrado.com* 🛏 *84 rooms* 🍴 *No meals.*

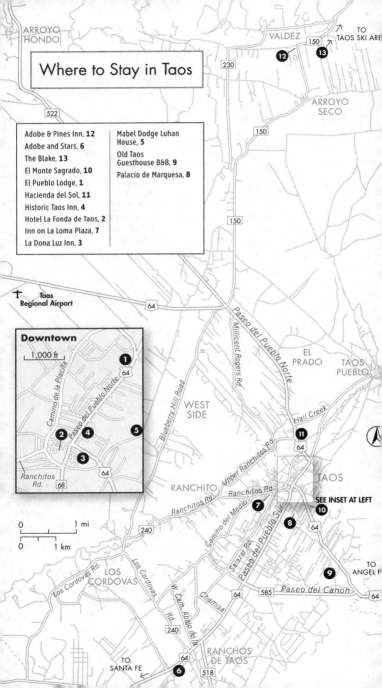

Where to Stay in Taos

Adobe & Pines Inn, **12**
Adobe and Stars, **6**
The Blake, **13**
El Monte Sagrado, **10**
El Pueblo Lodge, **1**
Hacienda del Sol, **11**
Historic Taos Inn, **4**
Hotel La Fonda de Taos, **2**
Inn on La Loma Plaza, **7**
La Dona Luz Inn, **3**

Mabel Dodge Luhan House, **5**
Old Taos Guesthouse B&B, **9**
Palacio de Marquesa, **8**

Downtown

1,000 ft

0   1 mi
0   1 km

★ Fodor's Choice 🏨 **El Pueblo Lodge.** *Hotel.* Among the budget-oriented properties in town, this well-maintained adobe-style hotel with a fun retro sign out front and the vibe of an old-school motel is a real gem. **Pros:** terrific value; short walk north of the plaza; complimentary charcoal and utensils to use on barbecue. **Cons:** nothing fancy (but still bright decor and clean rooms). [$] *Rooms from: $124* ✉ *412 Paseo del Pueblo Norte, Plaza and Vicinity* ☎ *575/758–8700, 800/433–9612* 🌐 *www.elpueblolodge.com* 🛏 *50 rooms* 🍴 *Breakfast.*

$$

$$ 🏨 **Historic Taos Inn.** *B&B/Inn.* A 10-minute walk north of Taos Plaza, this celebrated property is a local landmark, with some devotees having been regulars here for decades. **Pros:** a short walk from the plaza; colorfully furnished rooms, exudes character and history; the coziest rooms are a bargain. **Cons:** noise from street traffic and the bar; some rooms are very small. [$] *Rooms from: $125* ✉ *125 Paseo del Pueblo Norte, Plaza and Vicinity* ☎ *575/758–2233, 844/276–8598* 🌐 *www.taosinn.com* 🛏 *44 rooms* 🍴 *No meals.*

$$$ 🏨 **Inn on La Loma Plaza.** *B&B/Inn.* Surrounded by thick walls, this early-1800s Pueblo Revival building—and the surrounding gardens—capture the spirit and style of Spanish-colonial Taos. **Pros:** towering trees and lush gardens; a short walk from plaza; extremely comfy rooms and beds. **Cons:** lots of stairs; on a busy street; one of the pricier small properties in town. [$] *Rooms from: $205* ✉ *315 Ranchitos Rd., Plaza and Vicinity* ☎ *575/758–1717, 800/530–3040* 🌐 *www.vacationtaos.com* 🛏 *5 rooms, 1 suite, 2 studios* 🍴 *Breakfast.*

$ 🏨 **La Dona Luz Inn.** *B&B/Inn.* Paul "Paco" Castillo, who hails from a long line of local Taos artists and curio-shop owners, runs this festive and friendly B&B just a block off of Kit Carson Road and a few minutes' stroll from the plaza. **Pros:** affordable rooms; a short walk from the plaza; fun, local artwork throughout. **Cons:** in a busy and slightly noisy area (especially in summer). [$] *Rooms from: $109* ✉ *114C Kit Carson Rd., Plaza and Vicinity* ☎ *575/758–9000* 🌐 *www.stayintaos.com* 🛏 *7 rooms* 🍴 *Breakfast.*

$$ 🏨 **La Fonda de Taos.** *Hotel.* This handsomely updated and elegant historic property (there's been a hotel on this location since 1820) is ideal if you wish to be in the heart of the action—it's directly on the plaza. **Pros:** great central location; the building has a great history. **Cons:** less than ideal if you're seeking peace and quiet; some rooms are quite small; not suitable for young kids. [$] *Rooms from:*

$149 ⊠ 108 S. Plaza, Plaza and Vicinity ☎ 575/758–2211 ⊕ www.lafondataos.com ⌁ 25 rooms ◉ No meals.

$$ 🖾 **Mabel Dodge Luhan House.** B&B/Inn. Quirky and off-beat—much like Taos—this National Historic Landmark was once home to the heiress who drew illustrious writers and artists—including D.H. Lawrence, Willa Cather, Georgia O'Keeffe, Ansel Adams, Martha Graham, and Carl Jung—to Taos. **Pros:** historically relevant; rural setting, yet just blocks from the plaza; smallest rooms are very reasonably priced. **Cons:** lots of stairs and uneven paths. Ⓢ Rooms from: $116 ⊠ 240 Morada La. ☎ 575/751–9686, 800/846–2235 ⊕ www.mabeldodgeluhan.com ⌁ 21 rooms ◉ Breakfast.

★ Fodor'sChoice 🖾 **Palacio de Marquesa.** B&B/Inn. Tile hearths,
$$$ French doors, and traditional viga ceilings grace this sophisticated inn whose rooms stand out from the pack for their clean, uncluttered looks, posh linens, and decor inspired by female artists of local acclaim, from modernist Agnes Martin to transplanted British aristocrat Dorothy Brett. **Pros:** tranquil and secluded setting; sophisticated, contemporary rooms with lots of luxury touches; walking distance from plaza. **Cons:** A little pricey. Ⓢ Rooms from: $207 ⊠ 405 Cordoba Rd., Plaza and Vicinity ☎ 575/758–4777, 855/846–8267 ⊕ www.marquesataos. com ⌁ 8 rooms ◉ No meals.

SOUTH SIDE

$$ 🖾 **Adobe & Pines Inn.** B&B/Inn. Native American and Mexican artifacts decorate the main house of this B&B, which has expansive mountain views. **Pros:** quiet rural location; closest accommodation to historic Ranchos de Taos; beautiful gardens. **Cons:** a bit of a drive south of plaza; least expensive rooms are a bit small. Ⓢ Rooms from: $115 ⊠ 4107 NM 68, South Side ☎ 575/751–0947, 855/828–7872 ⊕ www.adobepines.com ⌁ 8 rooms ◉ Breakfast.

★ Fodor'sChoice 🖾 **Old Taos Guesthouse B&B.** B&B/Inn. Once a
$$ ramshackle 180-year-old adobe hacienda, this homey B&B
FAMILY on 7½ verdant acres has been brought beautifully back to life and is fully outfitted with the owners' hand-carved doors and furniture, Western artifacts, and antiques—all rooms have private entrances, and some have fireplaces. **Pros:** beautifully appointed; private entrance to each room; serene setting. **Cons:** small bathrooms; some rooms are dark; a short drive from town. Ⓢ Rooms from: $149 ⊠ 1028 Witt Rd., South Side ☎ 575/758–5448 ⊕ www.oldtaos.com ⌁ 9 rooms ◉ Breakfast.

EL PRADO

★ Fodor'sChoice 🏨 **Hacienda del Sol.** *B&B/Inn.* Art patron Mabel
$$ Dodge Luhan bought this house about a mile north of Taos Plaza in the 1920s and lived here with her husband, Tony Luhan, while building their main house. **Pros:** cozy public rooms; private setting; some excellent restaurants within walking distance. **Cons:** traffic noise; some rooms are less private than others. [$] *Rooms from: $160* ✉ *109 Mabel Dodge La., El Prado* ☎ *575/758–0287, 866/333–4459* 🌐 *www.taoshaciendadelsol.com* ⇨ *12 rooms* 🍴 *Breakfast.*

ARROYO SECO

$$ 🏨 **Adobe and Stars.** *B&B/Inn.* This light-filled adobe-style contemporary inn was built in 1996 on a plateau in Arroyo Seco with panoramic views in all directions—it's directly in the shadows of the Sangre de Cristos, a quick drive to the ski valley. **Pros:** big windows in the rooms let in lots of light; short drive or leisurely stroll from shops and eateries; dramatic setting with stunning views. **Cons:** a 20-minute drive from the plaza; no TVs in rooms. [$] *Rooms from: $129* ✉ *584 NM 150, 1 mile north of Arroyo Seco village center* ☎ *575/776–2776, 800/211–7076* 🌐 *www.taosadobe.com* ⇨ *8 rooms* 🍴 *Breakfast.*

TAOS SKI VALLEY

★ Fodor'sChoice 🏨 **The Blake.** *Resort.* Part of a continuing effort
$$$$ on the part of Taos Ski Valley's new ownership to up its game, this luxury boutique hotel opened just steps from the resort's lifts in late 2016 and has quickly developed a reputation as the swankiest accommodation in the Taos region. **Pros:** steps from the ski area's Lifts 1 and 5; huge rooms, and suites have well-stocked kitchenettes; one of the best spas in the Taos area. **Cons:** a 30-minute drive from Taos; very quiet in these parts during spring and fall low season. [$] *Rooms from: $306* ✉ *107 Sutton Pl., Taos Ski Valley* ☎ *575/776–5335, 888/569–1756* 🌐 *www.skitaos.com/theblake* ⇨ *80 rooms* 🍴 *No meals.*

NIGHTLIFE AND PERFORMING ARTS

Evening entertainment is modest in Taos, but a few cool and distinctive nightspots keep things interesting for night owls. In addition to the bars listed here, note that a few restaurants in town are fun for bar options, too, including Old Martina's Hall in Ranchos de Taos, Medley in El

Prado, Sabroso in Arroyo Seco, and 192 at the Blake in Taos Ski Valley.

NIGHTLIFE

★ Fodor'sChoice **Adobe Bar.** This local meet-and-greet spot, often dubbed "Taos's living room," books talented acts, from solo guitarists to small folk groups and, two or three nights a week, jazz musicians. It's a favorite spot for happy hour—there's a great menu of appetizers and cocktails, and the patio is a lovely hangout on warm evenings. ⊠ *Taos Inn, 125 Paseo del Pueblo Norte* ☎ *575/758–2233* ⊕ *www.taosinn. com/adobe-bar.*

Alley Cantina. Housed in the oldest structure in downtown Taos, this friendly spot has jazz, folk, and blues—as well as shuffleboard, pool, and board games for those not moved to dance. It's also one of the few places in town for a late-night bite. ⊠ *121 Teresina La.* ☎ *575/758–2121* ⊕ *www. alleycantina.com.*

★ Fodor'sChoice **KTAOS Solar Bar.** A fun place to cap off a day of exploring Arroyo Seco or playing outside in Taos Ski Valley, this bar and restaurant is part of the KTAOS Solar Center, home to the world-celebrated and solar-powered KTAOS (101.9 FM) radio station. It's a first-rate live-music venue that brings in all types of great rock, blues, folk, and indie bands. You can dine and drink in the festive bar or out on a sprawling green lawn with stunning views of the Sangre de Cristos. On Fridays, family-friendly movies are shown for free on a giant screen. ⊠ *9 NM 150, just east of junction with U.S. 64, El Prado* ☎ *575/758–5826* ⊕ *ktao. com/SolarCenter/stationbar.*

★ Fodor'sChoice **Parcht Bottleshop + Bites.** Although it's on Taos Plaza, this intimate, softly lighted wine bar can be a little tricky to find—it's down a short hallway beneath its sister operation, the much larger Gorge Bar and Grill, and it's also home to a first-rate beer-and-wine shop. Persevere, however, as the build-your-own meat and cheeseboards and other tasty snacks are superb, as is the selection of craft beer and vino. Save room for a house-made peanut butter cup. ⊠ *103 E. Plaza, Plaza and Vicinity* ☎⊕ *www.parcht.com.*

★ Fodor'sChoice **Taos Mesa Brewing.** It's worth the 15-minute drive northwest of Taos Plaza to reach this fabulously bizarre-looking pub and microbrewery near the airport, just a few miles east of the Rio Grande Gorge Bridge. In a high-ceilinged, eco-friendly building with soaring windows, sample exceptionally well-crafted Scottish Ale, Black Widow Porter, and Kolsch 45. Live music and entertainment is presented on indoor and outdoor stages—the latter has amazing mountain and mesa views. Tasty tapas and bar snacks are served, too. You can also sip the same beers and eat outstanding pizza at the Taos Mesa Brewing Tap Room, near the plaza, and there's another branch up at Taos Ski Valley. ✉ *20 ABC Mesa Rd., West Side* ☎ *575/758–1900* ⊕ *www.taosmesabrewing.com.*

PERFORMING ARTS

Long a beacon for visual artists, Taos has also become a magnet for touring musicians, especially in summer, when performers and audiences are drawn to the heady high-desert atmosphere. Festivals celebrate the visual arts, music, poetry, and film.

MUSIC

★ **Fodor's** Choice **Taos Chamber Music Group.** Since 1993, this esteemed group of musicians has performed traditional—Bach, Beethoven, Brahms—and contemporary chamber concerts. Performances are held at the Harwood Museum of Art during about eight weekends from September through late May. ☎ *575/770–1167* ⊕ *www.taoschambermusicgroup.org.*

Taos School of Music Program and Festival. From mid-June to early August the Taos School of Music fills the evenings with the sounds of chamber music at the Taos School of Music Program and Festival. Running strong since 1963, this is America's oldest chamber music summer program and possibly the largest assembly of top string quartets in the country. Concerts are presented a couple of times a week from mid-June through early August, at the Taos Community Auditorium and at Hotel St. Bernard at Taos Ski Valley. Tickets cost $25. The events at Taos Ski Valley are free. ✉ *Taos* ☎ *575/776–2388* ⊕ *www.taosschoolofmusic.com.*

10

SHOPPING

Retail options on Taos Plaza consist mostly of T-shirt emporiums and souvenir shops that are easily bypassed, though a few stores carry quality Native American artifacts and jewelry. The more distinctive galleries and boutiques begin barely a block north on Bent Street, including the John

Dunn House Shops, and extend just east on Kit Carson Road (U.S. 64). You'll find another notable cluster of galleries and shops, along with a few good restaurants, up north in Arroyo Seco.

ART GALLERIES

★ **Fodor's**Choice **David Anthony Fine Art.** Showing some of the top contemporary artists—both representative and abstract—as well as beautifully designed cabinets and other furniture known for their decorative tin and steel doors, DAFA also hosts occasional musical performances in its airy gallery a short walk east of the plaza. Art highlights include contemporary glass sculptures by Jennifer Hecker and Leon Applebaum, portrait photography by William Coupon, and paintings of kachinas by John Farnsworth. ⊠ *132 Kit Carson Rd.* ☏ *575/758–7113* ⊕ *www.davidanthonyfineart.com.*

Ed Sandoval Gallery. This colorful art space shows the work of artist Ed Sandoval, who is known for his trademark *Viejito* (Old Man) images and swirling, vibrantly colored landscapes. ⊠ *102-B Paseo del Pueblo Norte* ☏ *575/751–3502, 888/751–3502* ⊕ *www.edsandovalgallery.com.*

Inger Jirby Gallery. This popular gallery displays Jirby's whimsical, brightly colored landscape paintings. Be sure to stroll through the lovely sculpture garden. ⊠ *207 Ledoux St.* ☏ *575/758–7333* ⊕ *www.jirby.com.*

Michael McCormick & Sons Gallery. This esteemed gallery is home to the sensual, stylized female portraits of Miguel Martinez and the iconic portraits of Malcolm Furlow. The gallery also has an extensive collection of Rembrandt etchings. ⊠ *106-C Paseo del Pueblo Norte* ☏ *575/758–1372* ⊕ *www.mccormickgallery.com.*

★ **Fodor's**Choice **Robert L. Parsons Fine Art.** This is one of the best sources of early Taos art-colony paintings, antiques, and authentic antique Navajo blankets. Inside you'll find originals by such luminaries as Ernest Blumenschein, Bert Geer Phillips, Oscar Berninghaus, Joseph Bakos, and Nicolai Fechin. ⊠ *131 Bent St.* ☏ *575/751–0159, 800/613–5091* ⊕ *www.parsonsart.com.*

★ **Fodor's**Choice **Total Arts Gallery.** If you have time for just one contemporary gallery, make a point of stopping in this building displaying works by some of the area's most celebrated artists, including Barbara Zaring, David Hettinger, Doug Dawson, and Melinda Littlejohn. Themes vary greatly from abstract paintings and sculptures to more traditional landscapes and regional works. ⊠ *122-A Kit Carson Rd.* ☎ *575/758–4667* ⊕ *www.totalartsgallery.com.*

BOOKS

Brodsky Bookshop. This venerable shop specializes in new and used books—contemporary literature, Southwestern classics, and children's titles. Amiable proprietor Rick Smith can help you sort among the hundreds of titles. ⊠ *226-A Paseo del Pueblo Norte* ☎ *575/758–9468.*

CLOTHING

Andean Softwear. Andean Softwear, which was begun at the ski valley in 1984 but has a second location close to the plaza, carries warm, sturdy, but beautifully designed clothing and textiles, as well as jewelry. Much of the wares here come from Peru, Bolivia, and Ecuador, as the name of the store implies, but you'll also find imports from Bali, Mexico, Turkey, and plenty of other far-flung locales with distinct arts traditions. Note the deliciously soft alpaca sweaters from Peru. ⊠ *116 Sutton Pl., Taos Ski Valley* ☎ *575/776–2508* ⊕ *www.andeansoftware.com.*

Artemisia. Look to this boutique for its wide selection of one-of-a-kind wearable art by local artist Annette Randell. Many of her creations incorporate Native American designs. The store also carries jewelry, bags, and accessories by several local artists. ⊠ *117 Bent St.* ☎ *575/737–9800* ⊕ *www.artemisiataos.com.*

★ Fodor'sChoice **Overland Sheepskin Company.** This spacious store carries high-quality sheepskin coats, hats, mittens, and slippers, many with Taos beadwork. This is the original location of what has become a network of about a dozen stores, mostly in the West, and the setting—in the shadows of the Sangre de Cristos, amid a complex of several other shops along with a great little café for breakfast and lunch—is itself a reason for a visit. ⊠ *Overland Ranch, 1405 Paseo del Pueblo Norte, El Prado* ☎ *575/758–8820, 888/754–8352* ⊕ *www.overland.com.*

10

COLLECTIBLES AND GIFTS

★ Fodor'sChoice **Arroyo Seco Mercantile.** Packed to the rafters with a varied assortment of 1930s linens, handmade quilts, candles, organic soaps, vintage cookware, hand-thrown pottery, decorated crosses, and souvenirs, this colorful shop is a highlight of shopping in the charming village of Arroyo Seco. ✉ *488 NM 150, Arroyo Seco* ☎ *575/776–8806* ⊕ *www.secomerc.com.*

Coyote Moon. Coyote Moon has a great selection of south-of-the-border folk art, painted crosses, jewelry, and Day of the Dead figurines, some featuring American rock stars. ✉ *120-C Bent St., Plaza and Vicinity* ☎ *575/758–4437.*

Moxie. The motto of this colorful gift gallery is "fair trade & handmade," and it stocks a fantastic array of housewares and decorative items as well as men's and women's clothing. Check out the soft alpaca blankets, batik shirts, African Zulu baskets, and whimsical ornaments. ✉ *216-B Paseo del Pueblo Norte* ☎ *575/758–1256* ⊕ *www.taosmoxie.com.*

Taos Drums. This is the factory outlet for the Taos Drum Factory. The store, 5 miles south of Taos Plaza (look for the large tepee), stocks handmade pueblo log drums, leather lamp shades, and wrought-iron and Southwestern furniture. ✉ *3956 NM 68, South Side* ☎ *575/758–9844, 800/424–3786* ⊕ *www.taosdrums.com.*

HOME FURNISHINGS

Casa Cristal Pottery. Casa Cristal Pottery, 2½ miles north of the Taos Plaza, has a huge stock of stoneware, serapes, clay pots, Native American ironwood carvings, fountains, sweaters, ponchos, clay fireplaces, Mexican blankets, tiles, piñatas, and blue glassware from Guadalajara. ✉ *1306 Paseo del Pueblo Norte, El Prado* ☎ *575/758–1530.*

Country Furnishings of Taos. Set inside a rambling, picturesque adobe house, Country Furnishings of Taos sells folk art from northern New Mexico, handmade furniture, metal-work lamps and beds, and colorful accessories. ✉ *534 Paseo del Pueblo Norte* ☎ *575/758–4633* ⊕ *www.cftaos.com.*

★ Fodor'sChoice **Starr Interiors.** Starr Interiors has a striking collection of Zapotec Indian rugs and hangings, plus colorfully painted Oaxacan animals and masks and other folk art and furnishings. ✉ *117 Paseo del Pueblo Norte, Plaza and Vicinity* ☎ *575/758–3065* ⊕ *www.starr-interiors.com.*

Taos Blue. Taos Blue carries jewelry, pottery, and contemporary works (masks, rattles, sculpture) by dozens of talented Native Americans, as well as Spanish Colonial–style santos. ✉ *101-A Bent St., Plaza and Vicinity* ☎ *575/758–3561* ⊕ *www.taosblue.com.*

Taos Tin Works. This colorful gallery and studio in El Prado sells handcrafted tinwork, such as wall sconces, mirrors, lamps, and table ornaments by Marion Moore. ✉ *1204-D Paseo del Pueblo Norte, El Prado* ☎ *575/758–9724* ⊕ *www. taostinworks.com.*

NATIVE AMERICAN ARTS AND CRAFTS

Buffalo Dancer. This shop on the plaza buys, sells, and trades Native American arts and crafts, including pottery, belts, kachina dolls, hides, and silver-coin jewelry. ✉ *103-A E. Plaza* ☎ *575/758–8718* ⊕ *www.buffalodancer.com.*

SPORTING GOODS

★ **Fodor'sChoice Cottam's Ski & Outdoor.** This is your one-stop for hiking and backpacking gear, maps, fishing licenses and supplies, and ski and snowboard equipment and rentals, along with related clothing and accessories. There are also branches near the ski lifts at Taos Ski Valley and Angel Fire, and near the ski area in Santa Fe. ✉ *207-A Paseo del Pueblo Sur* ☎ *575/758–2822* ⊕ *www.cottamsskishops.com.*

SPORTS AND THE OUTDOORS

Whether you plan to cycle around town, jog along country lanes, or play a few rounds of golf, keep in mind that the altitude in Taos is higher than 7,000 feet. It's best to keep physical exertion to a minimum until your body becomes acclimated to the altitude—a full day to a few days, depending on your constitution.

10

BICYCLING

Taos-area roads are steep and hilly, and none have marked bicycle lanes, so be careful while cycling. The West Rim Trail offers a fairly flat but view-studded 9-mile ride that follows the Rio Grande Canyon's west rim from the Rio Grande Gorge Bridge to near the Taos Junction Bridge.

Gearing Up Bicycle Shop. You can rent or buy bikes and equipment at this full-service bike shop. Staff can provide advice on the best routes and upcoming group rides. ✉ *616 Paseo del Pueblo Sur* ☎ *575/751–0365* ⊕ *www.gearingup-bikes.com.*

GOLF

Taos Country Club. Views from the course at the Taos Country Club are some of the most dazzling in northern New Mexico. The layout is stunning and quite hilly, and water hazards are few. ✉ *54 Golf Course Dr., Carville Bourg* ☎ *575/758–7300* ⊕ *www.taoscountryclub.com* 🖾 *$43–$75* ⚑ *18 holes, 7302 yards, par 72* ☞ *Facilities: driving range, putting green, golf carts, pull carts, rental clubs, lessons, pro shop, restaurant, bar.*

HIKING

★ Fodor'sChoice **Wheeler Peak.** Part of a designated wilderness area of Carson National Forest, this iconic mountain summit—New Mexico's highest, at 13,161 feet—can only be reached by a rigorous hike or horseback ride. The most popular and accessible trail to the peak is the Williams Lake Trail, which is about 8 miles round-trip and begins in Taos Ski Valley just east of the Bavarian lodge and restaurant. Only experienced hikers should tackle this strenuous trail all the way to the top, as the 4,000-foot elevation gain is taxing, and the final mile or so to the peak is a steep scramble over loose scree. However, for a moderately challenging and still very rewarding hike, you take the trail to the halfway point, overlooking the shores of rippling Williams Lake. Numerous other rewarding hikes of varying degrees of ease and length climb up the many slopes that rise from the village of Taos Ski Valley—check with rangers or consult the Carson National Forest website for details. Dress warmly even in summer, take plenty of water and food, and pay attention to *all* warnings and instructions distributed by rangers. ✉ *Parking area for trailhead is along Kachina Rd. by the Bavarian lodge, Taos Ski Valley* ☎ *575/758–6200* ⊕ *www.fs.usda.gov/main/carson/home.*

LLAMA TREKKING

FAMILY **Wild Earth Llama Adventures.** Specializing in one of the more offbeat outdoor recreational activities in the area, this company offers a variety of llama treks, from one-day tours to excursions lasting several days in the Sangre de Cristo Mountains. Llamas are used as pack animals on these trips. Day hikes start at $125 and include gourmet lunches. Longer trips feature comfy overnight camping and delicious meals. ⊠ *Taos* ☎ *575/586–0174, 800/758–5262* ⊕ *www.llamaadventures.com.*

RIVER RAFTING

★ Fodor'sChoice The Taos Box, at the bottom of the steep-walled canyon far below the Rio Grande Gorge Bridge, is the granddaddy of thrilling white water in New Mexico and is best attempted by experts only—or on a guided trip—but the river also offers more placid sections such as through the Orilla Verde Recreation Area (one of the two main parcels of newly christened Rio Grande del Norte National Monument), just south of Taos in the village of Pilar (here you'll also find a small shop and café called the Pilar Yacht Club, which caters heavily to rafters and fishing enthusiasts), and the Rio Grande Gorge Visitor Center, a font of information on outdoor recreation in the region. Spring runoff is the busy season, from late March through June, but rafting companies conduct tours from early March to as late as November. Shorter two-hour options usually cover the fairly tame section of the river.

Big River Raft Trips. In business since 1983, this respected outfitter offers dinner float trips as well as half- and full-day rapids runs (with picnic lunches included). ⊠ *Pilar* ☎ *575/758–9711, 800/748–3746* ⊕ *www.bigriverrafts.com.*

Los Rios River Runners. The experienced guides here will take you to your choice of spots—the Rio Chama, the Lower Gorge, or the thrilling Taos Box. ⊠ *Taos* ☎ *575/776–8854* ⊕ *www.losriosriverrunners.com.*

Rio Grande Gorge Visitor Center. The Bureau of Land Management operates this visitor center in Pilar and can provide lists of registered river guides, information about running the river on your own, and plenty of other guidance on hiking and exploring the area. This is one of two visitor centers that make up the new Rio Grande del Norte National Monument (the other is north of Taos, at the Wild Rivers Recreation Area). ⊠ *2873 NM 68, near junction with NM 570, Pilar* ☎ *575/751–4899* ⊕ *www.blm.gov/visit/rgdnnm.*

10

SKIING

★ Fodor'sChoice **Taos Ski Valley.** With 113 runs—just more half of them for experts—and an average of more than 320 inches of annual snowfall, Taos Ski Valley ranks among the country's most respected, and challenging, resorts. In 2014, new owners came in and immediately began a long-awaited refurbishment and expansion of the resort, which has included new lifts and terrain and the opening in 2016 of a luxury hotel, The Blake. The slopes, which cover a 2,600-foot vertical gain of lift-served terrain and another 700 feet of hike-in skiing, tend to be narrow and demanding (note the ridge chutes, Al's Run, Inferno), but about a quarter of them (e.g., Honeysuckle) are for intermediate skiers, and another quarter (e.g., Bambi, Porcupine) are for beginners. Taos Ski Valley is justly famous for its outstanding ski school, which underwent an $8-million upgrade and expansion in 2017—it's one of the best in the country. ✉ *End of NM 150, 20 miles north of Plaza, Taos Ski Valley* ☎ *575/776–2291, 800/776–1111* ⊕ *www. skitaos.com* 🎫 *Lift tickets $105.*

TRAVEL SMART
SANTA FE

GETTING HERE AND AROUND

A car is the best way to take in Santa Fe and the surrounding region. City buses and taxis are available in Santa Fe, Albuquerque, and Taos, as are Lyft and Uber, but buses are not very convenient for visitors, and the costs of taxis and ride-sharing services can quickly exceed that of a rental car, especially if you're staying outside the city centers. You can get around Santa Fe's Plaza area as well as some Taos and Albuquerque neighborhoods on foot, but a car is essential for roaming farther afield and visiting many of north-central New Mexico's most prominent attractions and scenic byways.

▌ AIR TRAVEL

Most visitors to the area fly into Albuquerque, home of the region's main airport, but Santa Fe also has a charmingly small and handily located airport with daily nonstop service to a few key hubs. From Albuquerque, ground transportation is available to both Santa Fe (65 miles away) and Taos (130 miles), although most visitors rent a car.

Albuquerque's airport is served by all major U.S. airlines and has direct flights from most major West Coast and Midwest cities and a few cities on the East Coast (JFK in New York City on JetBlue, Atlanta on Delta, and Orlando and Baltimore-Washington on Southwest). Santa Fe Municipal Airport has direct flights on American Airlines from Dallas and Phoenix and United Airlines from Denver. Flights into Santa Fe tend to cost a bit more than those to Albuquerque, but the convenience can be well worth the extra expense. If you're venturing north from Santa Fe up to Taos, you might also consider flying into Denver, which is an hour or two farther than Albuquerque (the drive is stunning) but offers a huge selection of direct domestic and international flights.

Flying time between Albuquerque and Dallas is 1 hour and 45 minutes; Los Angeles, 2 hours; Chicago, 2 hours and 45 minutes; New York, 4 to 4½ hours (direct, which is available only on JetBlue; factor in another hour if connecting).

▌**TIP**→ **Long layovers don't have to be only about sitting around or shopping. These days they can be about burning off vacation calories. Check out ⊕ www.airportgyms.com for lists of health clubs that are in or near many U.S. and Canadian airports.**

Airport Information Albuquerque International Sunport. ☏ 505/244–7700 ⊕ www.abqsunport.com. **Denver International Airport.** ☏ 303/342–2000 ⊕ www.flydenver.com. **Santa Fe Municipal Airport (SAF).** ☏ 505/955–2900 ⊕ www.santafenm.gov/airport.

GROUND TRANSPORTATION

From the terminal at Albuquerque's airport, Sandia Shuttle provides scheduled van service to hotels, bed-and-breakfasts, and several other locations around Santa Fe; the cost per person is $33 each way. RoadRunneR Shuttle & Charter offers airport shuttle van service as well as private rides from both the Albuquerque and Santa Fe airports to throughout Santa Fe and the surrounding area (including Albuquerque, Los Alamos, and Española)—for a price, you can charter a shuttle to just about any town in the state. From Albuquerque, RoadRunneR charges $33 each way to most Santa Fe hotels and $44 each way to most Santa Fe residences and other businesses. From Santa Fe Airport, the cost is $16 each way to most addresses in town.

Shuttle Contacts RoadRunneR Shuttle & Charter. ☎ 505/424–3367 ⊕ www.rideroadrunner.com. **Sandia Shuttle Express.** ☎ 505/474–5696, 888/775–5696 ⊕ www.sandiashuttle.com.

▌ BUS TRAVEL

There's no intercity bus service to Santa Fe, but you can get to Albuquerque from a number of cities throughout the Southwest and Rocky Mountain regions, and then catch a Rail Runner *(see below)* commuter train from Albuquerque's bus station to Santa Fe. This strategy really only makes sense if you're unable or unwilling to drive or fly; bus travel in this part of the world is relatively economical but quite time-consuming.

Bus Information Greyhound. ☎ 800/231–2222 ⊕ www.greyhound.com.

▌ CAR TRAVEL

A car is a basic necessity in New Mexico, as even the few cities are challenging to get around solely using public transportation. Distances are considerable, but you can make excellent time on long stretches of interstate and other four-lane highways with speed limits of up to 75 mph. If you wander off major thoroughfares, slow down. Speed limits here generally are only 55 mph, and for good reason. Many such roadways have no shoulders; on many twisting and turning mountain roads speed limits dip to 25 mph. For the most part, the scenery on rural highways makes the drive a form of sightseeing in itself.

Interstate 25 runs north from the state line at El Paso through Albuquerque and Santa Fe, then angles northeast into Colorado and up to Denver. Interstate 40 crosses the state from Arizona to Texas, intersecting with Interstate 25 in Albuquerque, from which it's an hour's drive to Santa Fe. Although it's a long drive from big cities like Los Angeles, Dallas, and Chicago, plenty of visitors drive considerable distances to visit Santa Fe, which makes a great stop on a multiday road trip around the Four Corners region, or across the Southwest.

U.S. and state highways connect Santa Fe, Albuquerque, and Taos with a number of key towns elsewhere in New Mexico and in neighboring states. Many of these highways, including large stretches of U.S. 285 and U.S. 550, have four lanes and high speed limits. You can make nearly as good time on these roads as you can on interstates. Throughout the region, you're likely to encounter some unpaved surface streets. Santa Fe has a higher percentage of dirt roads than any other state capital in the nation.

Morning and evening rush-hour traffic is light in Santa Fe. It can get a bit heavy in Albuquerque. Keep in mind that there are only a couple of main routes from Santa Fe to Albuquerque, so if you encounter an accident or some other obstacle, you can expect significant delays. It's a big reason to leave early and give yourself extra time when driving to Albuquerque to catch a plane.

Parking is plentiful and either free or inexpensive in Santa Fe, Albuquerque, and Taos. During the busy summer weekends, however, parking in Santa Fe's most popular neighborhoods—the Plaza, Canyon Road, and the Railyard District—can be a bit more challenging. There are pay lots both Downtown and in the Railyard District.

Here are some common distances and approximate travel times between Santa Fe and several popular destinations, assuming no lengthy stops and averaging the 65 to 75 mph speed limits: Albuquerque is 65 miles and about an hour; Taos is 70 miles and 90 minutes; Denver is 400 miles and 6 hours;

Phoenix is 480 miles and 7 to 8 hours; Las Vegas is 630 miles and 9 to 10 hours; Dallas is 650 miles and 10 to 11 hours, and Los Angeles is 850 miles and 12 to 14 hours.

GASOLINE

Once you leave Santa Fe or other larger communities in the region, there's a lot of high, dry, lonesome country in New Mexico—it's possible to go 50 or 60 miles in some of the less-populated areas between gas stations. **For a safe trip, keep your gas tank full.** Self-service gas stations are the norm in New Mexico. The cost of unleaded gas in New Mexico is close to the U.S. average, but it's usually a bit higher in small out-of-the-way communities, and significantly cheaper on some Indian reservations—on the drive between Santa Fe and Albuquerque, the gas stations just off Interstate 25 at Santo Domingo Pueblo (exit 259), San Felipe Pueblo (exit 252), and Sandia Pueblo (234) all have very low-priced gas.

RENTAL CARS

All the major car-rental agencies are represented at Albuquerque's airport, and several of them have branches at Santa Fe airport (Avis and Hertz) or in Downtown Santa Fe (Avis, Budget, Enterprise, Hertz).

Rates at the airports in Albuquerque and Santa Fe can vary greatly depending on the season (the highest rates are usually in summer) but typically begin at around $30 a day and $180 a week for an economy car with air-conditioning, automatic transmission, and unlimited mileage.

If you want to explore the backcountry, consider renting an SUV, which will cost you about $40 to $60 per day and $200 to $400 per week, depending on the size of the SUV and the time of year. You can save money by renting at a non-airport location, as you then are able to avoid the hefty (roughly) 10% in extra taxes charged at airports.

ROAD CONDITIONS

Arroyos (dry washes or gullies) are bridged on major roads, but lesser roads often dip down through them. These can be a hazard during the rainy season, late June to early September. Even if it looks shallow, don't try to cross an arroyo filled with water. Wait a little while, and it will drain off almost as quickly as it filled. If you stall in a flooded arroyo, get out of the car and onto high ground if possible. In the backcountry, never drive (or walk) in a dry arroyo bed if the sky is dark anywhere in the vicinity. A sudden thunderstorm 15 miles away can send a raging flash flood down a wash in a matter of minutes.

Unless they are well graded and graveled, avoid unpaved roads in New Mexico when they are wet. The soil contains a lot of caliche, or clay, which gets slick when mixed with water. During winter storms roads may be shut down entirely; check with the State Highway Department for road conditions.

At certain times in fall, winter, and spring, New Mexico winds can be vicious for large vehicles like RVs. Driving conditions can be particularly treacherous in passages through foothills or mountains where wind gusts and ice are concentrated.

New Mexico has a high incidence of drunk driving and uninsured motorists. Factor in the state's high speed limits, many winding and steep roads, and eye-popping scenery, and you can see how important it is to drive as alertly and defensively as possible.

Contact New Mexico Department of Transportation Road Advisory Hotline. ☎ *800/432–4269* ⊕ *www. nmroads.com.*

ROADSIDE EMERGENCIES

In the event of a roadside emergency, call 911.

▮ **TRAIN TRAVEL**

Amtrak's *Southwest Chief,* from Chicago to Los Angeles via Kansas City, stops in Las Vegas, Lamy (near Santa Fe), and Albuquerque.

The *New Mexico Rail Runner Express* runs numerous times on weekdays from early morning until late evening, and less often on weekends. Tickets cost $2 to $10 one-way, depending on the distance traveled; day passes are available (and will save you money on round-trip journeys).

Contacts Amtrak. ☎ *800/872-7245* ⊕ *www.amtrak.com.* **New Mexico Rail Runner Express.** ☎ *866/795-7245* ⊕ *www.riometro.org.*

▮ GETTING AROUND SANTA FE

BUS TRAVEL

The city's bus system, Santa Fe Trails, covers 10 major routes through town and is useful for getting from the Plaza to some of the outlying attractions. Route M is most useful for visitors, as it runs from Downtown to the museums on Old Santa Fe Trail south of town, and Route 2 is handy if you're staying at one of the motels out on Cerrillos Road and need to get into town (if time is a factor for your visit, a car is a much more practical way to get around). Individual rides cost $1, and a daily pass costs $2. Buses run from early morning to mid-evening about every 30 minutes on weekdays, every hour on weekends.

Bus Contacts Santa Fe Trails. ☎ 505/955–2001 ⊕ santafenm.gov/transit.

GUIDED TOURS

Enchanted Journeys de Santa Fe. Owned by a former hotel concierge, this reliable tour company offers guided half- and full-day adventures for up to four passengers to Chimayó, Georgia O'Keeffe country, Taos, wineries, and other top draws around the area. They can also work with you to create custom trips and to provide airport transportation. ☎ 505/310–3883 ⊕ www.enchantedjourneysdesantafe.com.

Food Tour New Mexico. Savor some of the tastiest posole, blue-corn enchiladas, margaritas, craft beers, and sweets on lunch and dinner excursions in Santa Fe and Albuquerque, which make four to five stops at locally revered hot spots. ☎ 505/465–9474 ⊕ www.foodtournewmexico.com.

Great Southwest Adventures. This reliable group-oriented company conducts guided tours in 7- to 35-passenger van and bus excursions to Bandelier, Pecos National Historic Park, Tent Rocks National Monument, Taos (via the "Low Road" through the Gorge), O'Keeffe country, and elsewhere in the region. The company can also arrange single- and multiday custom trips throughout the region for groups of any size. ☎ 505/455–2700 ⊕ www.swadventures.com.

Historic Walks of Santa Fe. Get to know the fascinating stories behind many of Santa Fe's most storied landmarks on these engaging strolls through Downtown and along Canyon Road. Other walks focus on ghosts, galleries, shopping, and food, and Bandelier, Chimayó, and Taos excursions are also offered. ☎ 505/986–8388 ⊕ www.historicwalksofsantafe.com.

Santa Fe Tour Guides Association. To find an experienced local to lead you on a personal tour, visit the website of this member-based organization of about 30 reliable and vetted independent tour guides, many of whom specialize in specific topics, from art history to hiking. ☎ ⊕ www.santafetourguides.org.

ESSENTIALS

▪ ACCOMMODATIONS

Although New Mexico itself has relatively affordable hotel prices, even in Albuquerque, tourist-driven Santa Fe (and to a slightly lesser extent Taos) can be fairly pricey, especially during high season, from spring through fall, with rates particularly dear during major Santa Fe festivals (such as the Indian and Spanish markets). Generally, you'll pay the most at hotels within walking distance of the Plaza and in some of the scenic and mountainous areas north and east of the city; B&Bs usually cost a bit less, and you can find some especially reasonable deals on Airbnb, which has extensive listings throughout the region. The least expensive Santa Fe accommodations are south and west of town, particularly along drab and traffic-clogged Cerrillos Road, on the south side of town. Rates in Albuquerque, just an hour away, can be half as expensive (sometimes even less), except during busy festivals, particularly the Balloon Fiesta in early October.

Check to make sure there's not a major event planned for the time you're headed to the area, and book well ahead if so.

If you book through an online travel agent (Expedia, Orbitz, etc.), discounter, or wholesaler, confirm your reservation with the hotel before leaving home—just to be sure everything was processed correctly.

Be sure you understand the hotel's cancellation policy. Some places allow you to cancel without any kind of penalty—even if you pre-paid to secure a discounted rate—if you cancel at least 24 hours in advance. Others require you to cancel a week in advance or penalize you the cost of one night. Small inns and B&Bs are most likely to require you to cancel far in advance. Most hotels allow children under a certain age to stay in their parents' room at no extra charge, but others charge for them as extra adults; find out the cutoff age for discounts.

APARTMENT AND HOUSE RENTALS

Santa Fe (and Taos as well) is popular for short- and long-term vacation rentals. *See the book's individual chapters for rental agency listings in these locations.*

BED AND BREAKFASTS

B&Bs in these parts run the gamut from rooms in locals' homes to grandly restored adobe or Victorian homes. Rates in Santa Fe and Taos can be high, but there are several properties that offer excellent value for very comparable prices; they're a little lower in Albuquerque and rival those of chain motels in the outlying areas.

See the book's individual chapters for names of local reservation agencies.

HOME EXCHANGES

With a direct home exchange you stay in someone else's home while they stay in yours. Some outfits also deal with vacation homes, so you're not actually staying in someone's full-time residence, just their vacant weekend place.

Exchange Clubs Home Exchange. com. ☎ 888/609–4660 ⊕ www. homeexchange.com. **HomeLink International.** ☎ 800/638–3841 ⊕ www.homelink.org. **Intervac U.S.** ☎ 866/884–7567 ⊕ www.inter-vac-homeexchange.com.

HOSTELS

Hostels offer bare-bones lodging at low, low prices—often in shared dorm rooms with shared baths—to people of all ages, though the primary market is young travelers, especially students. Most hostels serve breakfast; dinner and/or shared cooking facilities may also be available. In some hostels you aren't allowed to be in your room during the day, and there may be a curfew at night. Nevertheless, hostels provide a sense of community, with public rooms where travelers often gather to share stories. Many hostels are affiliated with Hostelling International (HI), an umbrella group of hostel associations with some 4,000 member properties in more than 80 countries. Other hostels are completely independent and may be nothing more than a really cheap hotel.

Membership in any HI association, open to travelers of all ages, allows you to stay in HI-affiliated hostels at member rates. One-year membership is about $30 for adults; hostels charge about $10 to $30 per night. Members have priority if the hostel is full; they're also eligible for discounts around the world, even on rail and bus travel in some countries.

Albuquerque, Cedar Crest (on the Turquoise Trail, near Albuquerque), Santa Fe, and Taos each have hostels, but none are HI members.

Information Hostelling International—USA. ⊕ www.hihostels.com.

▌ EATING OUT

New Mexico is justly famous for its distinctive cuisine, which utilizes ingredients and recipes common to Mexico, the Rockies, the Southwest, and the West's Native American communities. Most longtime residents like their chile sauces and salsas with some fire—throughout north-central New Mexico chile is sometimes celebrated for its ability to set off smoke alarms. Most restaurants offer a choice of red or green chile with one type typically being milder than the other (ask your server, as this can vary considerably). If you want both kinds with your meal, when your server asks you if you'd like "red or green," reply "Christmas." If you're not used to spicy foods, you may find even the average chile served with chips to be quite a lot hotter than back home—so proceed with caution or ask for chile sauces on the side. Excellent barbecue and steaks also thrive throughout northern New Mexico, with other specialties being local game (especially elk and bison) and trout. Santa

Fe, Albuquerque, and Taos also abound with sophisticated restaurants specializing in farm-to-table contemporary fare, often with Mediterranean, Asian, and other global influences. It's also fairly easy to find extensive lists of interesting domestic and foreign wines, craft beers, and artisan cocktails in this part of the state. The restaurants we list are the cream of the crop in each price category.

MEALS AND MEALTIMES

In cities like Santa Fe and Albuquerque, you'll find at least a few restaurants that serve food (sometimes from a bar menu) late, until 10 or 11, and sometimes a bit later on weekends. In smaller communities, including Taos, many kitchens stop serving around 8 pm. It's prudent to call first and confirm closing hours if you're looking forward to a leisurely or late dinner.

Unless otherwise noted, the restaurants listed *in this guide* are open daily for lunch and dinner.

PAYING

Credit cards are widely accepted at restaurants in major towns and cities and even most smaller communities, but in the latter places, you may occasionally encounter smaller, independent restaurants that are cash only. Many smaller establishments take MasterCard and Visa but not Discover and American Express.

For guidelines on tipping see Tipping below.

RESERVATIONS AND DRESS

In Santa Fe and Taos, it's a good idea to make a reservation if you can, especially at top restaurants during busy times. We only mention policies specifically when reservations are essential (there's no other way you'll ever get a table) or when they are not accepted. For the hottest restaurants in Santa Fe, especially in summer, book as far ahead as you can, and reconfirm as soon as you arrive. It's exceedingly unlikely you'll find a restaurant anywhere in New Mexico where men are expected to wear jackets or ties, but at upscale restaurants in Santa Fe, and to a lesser extent in Taos and Albuquerque, you may notice that the majority of diners dress in smartly casual attire—slacks, closed-toe shoes, dress shirts.

Online reservation services make it easy to book a table before you even leave home. You can use Open Table to reserve meals at many restaurants in Santa Fe, Albuquerque, and Taos.

Contacts OpenTable. ⊕ *www. opentable.com.*

▌ HOURS OF OPERATION

Although hours differ little in New Mexico from other parts of the United States, some businesses do keep shorter hours here than in more densely populated parts of the country. Within the state, businesses in Santa Fe, Albuquerque, and Taos do tend to keep later hours than in rural areas. Hours of individual banks, post offices, and many other shops and services can vary greatly, so it's always wise to phone ahead before visiting.

Most major museums and attractions are open daily or six days a week (with Monday or Tuesday being the most likely day of closing). Hours are often shorter on Saturday and especially Sunday, and a handful of museums in the region stay open late one night a week, usually Friday. It's always a good idea to call ahead if you're planning to go out of your way to visit a museum, shop, or attraction in a smaller town.

In Santa Fe and Albuquerque, you can find some convenience stores and drugstores open 24 hours, and quite a few supermarkets open until 10 or 11 at night. Bars and nightclubs stay open until 1 or 2 am.

▌ MONEY

In New Mexico, Santa Fe is by far the priciest city: meals, gasoline, and accommodations all cost significantly more in the state's capital. Overall travel costs in Santa Fe, including dining and lodging, typically run 30% to 50% higher than in Albuquerque and other communities in the state. Taos, too, can be a little expensive because it's such a popular tourist destination, but you have more choices for economizing there than in Santa Fe. As the state's largest metropolitan area, Albuquerque has a full range of price choices, and even high-end hotels and restaurants are quite a lot less expensive than in Santa Fe.

CREDIT CARDS

It's a good idea to inform your credit-card company before you travel, especially if you're going abroad and don't travel internationally very often. Otherwise, the credit-card company might put a hold on your card owing to unusual activity—not a good thing halfway through your trip. Record all your credit-card numbers—as well as the phone numbers to call if your cards are lost or stolen—in a safe place, so you're prepared should something go wrong. Both MasterCard and Visa have general numbers you can call (collect if you're abroad) if your card is lost, but you're better off calling the number of your issuing bank, since MasterCard and Visa usually just transfer you to your bank; your bank's number is usually printed on your card.

Reporting Lost Cards American Express. ☎ 800/992–3404 in U.S., 336/393–1111 collect from abroad ⊕ www.americanexpress.com. **Discover.** ☎ 800/347–2683 in U.S., 801/902–3100 collect from abroad ⊕ www.discovercard.com. **MasterCard.** ☎ 800/622–7747 in U.S., 636/722–7111 collect from abroad ⊕ www.mastercard.com. **Visa.** ☎ 800/847–2911 in U.S., 303/967–1096 collect from abroad ⊕ www.visa.com.

▌ PACKING

Typical of the Southwest and southern Rockies, temperatures can vary considerably in north-central New Mexico from sunup to sundown. Generally, you should pack for warm days and chilly nights from late spring through early fall, and for genuinely cold days and freezing nights in winter if you're headed to Taos and Santa Fe (Albuquerque runs about 10 to 15 degrees warmer). Because temperatures vary greatly even within this relatively compact area, it's important to check local weather conditions before you leave home and pack accordingly. In April for instance, you may need to pack for nighttime lows in the 20s and daytime highs in the 60s in Taos, but daytime highs in the low 80s and nighttime lows in the 40s in Albuquerque. Any time of year pack at least a few warm outfits, gloves, a hat and a jacket; in winter pack very warm clothes—coats, parkas, and whatever else your body's thermostat and your ultimate destination dictate. Sweaters and jackets are also needed in summer at higher elevations, because though days are warm, nights can dip well below 50°F. And bring comfortable shoes; you're likely to be doing a lot of walking.

Bring skin moisturizer; even people who rarely need this elsewhere in the country can suffer from dry and itchy skin in New Mexico. Sunscreen is a necessity. And bring sunglasses to protect your eyes from the glare of lakes or ski slopes, not to mention the brightness present everywhere. High altitude can cause headaches and dizziness, so at a minimum drink at least half your body weight in ounces in water (150-pound person = 75 ounces of water), and eat plenty of juicy fruit. When planning even a short day trip, espe-cially if there's hiking or exercise involved, always pack a bottle or two of water—it's very easy to become dehydrated in New Mexico. Check with your doctor about medication to alleviate symptoms.

▌ RESOURCES

ONLINE TRAVEL TOOLS

Check out the New Mexico Tourism site (⊕ *www.state.nm.us*) for information tips on visiting and even living in the Land of Enchantment. Monthly *New Mexico Magazine* (⊕ *www.nmmagazine.com*) is a long-running publication with regular stories on culture and travel throughout the state. An excellent source of information on the state's recreation pursuits is the New Mexico Outdoor Sports Guide (⊕ *www.nmosg.com*). Check the site of the New Mexico Film Office (⊕ *www.nmfilm.com*) for a list of movies shot in New Mexico as well as links to downloadable clips of upcoming made–in–New Mexico movies. Visit ⊕ *www.farmersmarketsnm.org* for information on the dozens of great farmers' markets around the state, ⊕ *www.nmwine.com* for tours and details related to the region's fast-growing wine-making industry, and ⊕ *www.nmbeer.org* for details on north-central New Mexico's dozens of craft breweries.

Safety Transportation Security Administration (*TSA*). ⊕ *www.tsa.gov.*

▮ TAXES

Sales taxes vary by municipality in New Mexico; it's 8.3% in Santa Fe, 8.5% in Taos, and 7.5% in Albuquerque. If you're on a budget and plan on renting a car and/or staying in hotels, be sure to ask for the exact amount of your lodgers and rental car taxes, as they can be quite steep and can make a big dent in a tight budget.

▮ TIME

New Mexico observes Mountain Standard Time, switching over with most of the rest of the country to daylight saving time in the spring through fall. In New Mexico, you'll be two hours behind New York and one hour ahead of Arizona (except during daylight saving time, which Arizona does not observe) and California.

▮ TIPPING

The customary tipping rate for taxi drivers is 15% to 20%, with a minimum of $2; bellhops are usually given $2 per bag in luxury hotels, $1 per bag elsewhere. Hotel maids should be tipped $2 per day of your stay. A doorman who hails or helps you into a cab can be tipped $1 to $2. You should also tip your hotel concierge for services rendered; the size of the tip depends on the difficulty of your request, as well as the quality of the concierge's work. For an ordinary dinner reservation or tour arrangements, $3 to $5 should do; if the concierge scores seats at a popular restaurant or show or performs unusual services (getting your laptop repaired, finding a good pet-sitter, etc.), $10 or more is appropriate.

Waiters should be tipped 15% to 20%, though at higher-end restaurants, a solid 20% is more the norm. Many restaurants add a gratuity to the bill for parties of six or more. Ask what the percentage is if the menu or bill doesn't state it. Tip $1 per drink you order at the bar, though if at an upscale establishment, those $15 martinis might warrant a $2 tip.

▮ VISITOR INFORMATION

The New Mexico Department of Tourism can provide general information on the state, but you'll find more specific and useful information by consulting the local tourism offices and convention and visitors bureaus in Santa Fe as well as in other cities and towns throughout north-central New Mexico. Note that in addition to the main location below, Tourism Santa Fe has additional visitor information centers on the Plaza at Plaza Galeria (⊠ *66 E. San Francisco St.*), which is open daily, and in the Railyard District (⊠ *410 S. Guadalupe St.*), which is open Monday–Saturday.

Contacts Indian Pueblo Cultural Center. ☎ *505/843–7270, 866/855–7902* ⊕ *www.indianpueblo.org.* **New Mexico Tourism Department Visitor Center.** ⊠ *Lamy Bldg., 491 Old Santa Fe Trail, Old Santa Fe Trail and South Capitol* ☎ *505/827–7336* ⊕ *www.newmexico.org.* **Tourism Santa Fe.** ⊠ *Santa Fe Community Convention Center, 201 W. Marcy St., The Plaza* ☎ *505/955–6200, 800/777–2489* ⊕ *www.santafe.org.*

INDEX

Z

PHOTO CREDITS

NOTES

NOTES

Fodor's InFocus SANTA FE 2018

Editorial: Douglas Stallings, *Editorial Director*; Margaret Kelly, Jacinta O'Halloran, *Senior Editors*; Kayla Becker, Alexis Kelly, Amanda Sadlowski, *Editors*; Teddy Minford, *Content Editor*; Rachael Roth, *Content Manager*

Design: Tina Malaney, *Design and Production Director;* Jessica Gonzalez, *Production Designer*

Photography: Jennifer Arnow, *Senior Photo Editor*

Maps: Rebecca Baer, *Senior Map Editor*; Mark Stroud (Moon Street Cartography), *Cartographer*

Production: Jennifer DePrima, *Editorial Production Manager*; Carrie Parker, *Senior Production Editor*; Elyse Rozelle, *Production Editor*

Business & Operations: Chuck Hoover, *Chief Marketing Officer*; Joy Lai, *Vice President and General Manager*; Stephen Horowitz, *Director of Business Development and Revenue Operations;* Tara McCrillis, *Director of Publishing Operations;* Eliza D. Aceves, *Content Operations Manager and Strategist*

Public Relations and Marketing: Joe Ewaskiw, *Manager;* Esther Su, *Marketing Manager*

Writers: Lynne Arany, Andrew Collins

Editor: Rebecca Baer

Production Editor: Elyse Rozelle

2nd Edition

ISBN 978-1-64097-086-1

ISSN 2333–7958

SPECIAL SALES

This book is available at special discounts for bulk purchases for sales promotions or premiums. For more information, e-mail SpecialMarkets@fodors.com.

PRINTED IN THE UNITED STATES OF AMERICA

10 9 8 7 6 5 4 3 2 1

ABOUT OUR WRITERS

First lured to New Mexico for its rich cultural heritage and an archaeology career, Lynne Arany was soon firmly in thrall to this stunning state and its Mexico neighbor. A frequent contributor to *Fodor's New Mexico* and *Fodor's New York City* guides and other travel series, among them *Access: New York City* and *Born to Shop*, she is the co-author of *Little Museums* and *The Reel List*, as well as consulting editor for the acclaimed *New Mexico: A Guide for the Eyes*. She has also written for the *New York Times* and *New Mexico* magazine. Interests and digressions center on traditional arts and vernacular architecture—whether in Budapest, Glasgow, Tamazulapan, or the Faroe Islands. And while her once-stalwart gold Corvair has long been retired, she always delights in the wonders to be found along New Mexico's byways.

Former Fodor's staff editor Andrew Collins is based in Mexico City, but resided in New Mexico for many years and still visits often (usually stuffing his suitcase with fresh green chiles and local IPA). A longtime contributor to this guide, he also contributed to dozens of other Fodor's guidebooks, including *Pacific Northwest* and *National Parks of the West*. He's a frequent contributor to *New Mexico Magazine*, produces the site LoveWinsUSA.com, and writes for a number of both LGBTQ and mainstream magazines and websites. He also teaches travel writing and food writing for New York City's Gotham Writers' Workshop.

EUGENE FODOR

Hungarian-born Eugene Fodor (1905–91) began his travel career as an interpreter on a French cruise ship. The experience inspired him to write *On the Continent* (1936), the first guidebook to receive annual updates and discuss a country's way of life as well as its sights. Fodor later joined the U.S. Army and worked for the OSS in World War II. After the war, he kept up his intelligence work while expanding his guidebook series. During the Cold War, many guides were written by fellow agents who understood the value of insider information. Today's guides continue Fodor's legacy by providing travelers with timely coverage, insider tips, and cultural context.